Cognitive Readiness in Project Teams

Reducing Project Complexity and Increasing Success in Project Management

Cognitive Readiness in Project Teams

Reducing Project Complexity and Increasing Success in Project Management

Edited by
Carl Belack
Daniele Di Filippo
Ivano Di Filippo

Routledge
Taylor & Francis Group

A PRODUCTIVITY PRESS BOOK

First edition published in 2019
by Routledge/Productivity Press
52 Vanderbilt Avenue, 11th Floor New York, NY 10017
2 Park Square, Milton Park, Abingdon, Oxon OX14 4RN, UK

First issued in paperback 2021

Printed on acid-free paper

ISBN-13: 978-1-138-59231-5 (hbk)
ISBN-13: 978-1-03-209376-5 (pbk)
ISBN-13: 978-0-429-49005-7 (eBook)

Library of Congress Cataloging-in-Publication Data

Names: Belack, Carl, editor. | Di Filippo, Daniele, editor. | Di Filippo, Ivano, editor.
Title: Cognitive readiness in project teams : reducing project complexity and increasing success in project management / Carl Belack, Daniele Di Filippo, and Ivano Di Filippo.
Description: New York, NY : Routledge, 2019. | .
Identifiers: LCCN 2018044806 (print) | LCCN 2018045461 (ebook) | ISBN 9780429490057 (e-Book) | ISBN 9781138592315 (hardback : alk. paper)
Subjects: LCSH: Project management. | Teams in the workplace--Psychological aspects.
Classification: LCC HD69.P75 (ebook) | LCC HD69.P75 B436 2019 (print) | DDC 658.4/022--dc23
LC record available at https://lccn.loc.gov/2018044806

**Visit the Taylor & Francis Web site at
http://www.taylorandfrancis.com**

Contents

Foreword

The discipline of portfolio, program, and project management (PPPM) has matured significantly during the past sixty years, as witnessed by the application of PPPM strategies, processes, methods, information systems, and tools within essentially all areas of human endeavor in every corner of the world, plus the formation and worldwide growth of PPPM-related professional associations and standard practices.

However, in spite of the concurrent advances in robotics and artificial intelligence, the planning and execution of complex portfolios, programs, and projects still depends on *people* with many skills to come together in teams to conceive, plan, schedule, and execute the many tasks that must be accomplished to approve, expend the time, money, and resources, control and execute the work, and thereby achieve the goals of each project, program, and portfolio. Of course, the powerful information systems, methods, and tools that are in use today by executives and project managers enable the people who are the members of the project teams to do the right thing in the right way at exactly the right time with a high probability of success—unless unforeseen changes have occurred! Project teams must have and apply sufficient *cognitive readiness* to be able to recognize changes as they occur and quickly modify their plans and schedules to overcome or minimize the impact of those changes.

Today, the PPPM best practices and approved standards recognize the importance of the so-called soft skills (which are actually very hard to develop) of leadership, teambuilding, and people management. While we often spend large amounts of time and money to plan and schedule a project prior to its approval, insufficient time and money are typically allocated and used to identify the critical team members of a new complex project and build them into a high-performance team by developing their individual and team cognitive readiness.

The purpose of this book is to increase awareness, understanding, and practical application of cognitive readiness in executives, program and project managers, project stakeholders, and most importantly in project teams. The editors have carefully selected authors who are established authorities in the fields of cognitive psychology and cognitive neuroscience, and who have demonstrated good understanding of the difficulties surrounding effective complex program and project management.

"The various project management standards refer to a number of processes for managing people in projects, including allocating them as resources, ways of leading them, communicating, resolving conflicts, and building teamwork among them. However, little attention has been paid to the *human behavior* aspects of people in project management. The field of cognitive psychology coupled with cognitive neuroscience now enables us to apply this knowledge of human thinking and behavior in practical ways to continually improve the 'soft' or people skills of project and program managers, their team members, and their project and program stakeholders."*

The awareness and understanding of the key aspects of cognitive readiness in complex project teams, together with the project benefits that team cognitive readiness can generate—that this book presents—will be of great value to every executive, stakeholder, program and project manager, and project team member who wishes to achieve the success of every project to which they are assigned.

Russell D. Archibald

I'm honoured to have been asked to offer a foreword to this intriguing, profound, and potentially significant work.

It is a particular pleasure as a European Commissioner to congratulate an excellent network of international experts and researchers. Their work brings together the apparently arid professional challenges of project management and the apparently obscure mind sciences. In the century when we may hope to crack the issues of artificial intelligence, we owe it to humanity to press on with a sound understanding of our own brains!

---

* Archibald, R., Di Filippo, I., Di Filippo, D. and Archibald, S. November 2013. Unlocking a project team's high-performance potential. *PM World Journal*, II (Issue XI).

My hope is that the tools and lessons of this work, amply demonstrated in one field of professional need, will be an exemplar for the extension of similar endeavours in other professional fields.

For two reasons:

■ If Europe can hold its lead in the application of cognitive learning to professional excellence, we may maintain an edge in our navigation of the ongoing digital revolution.
■ If we maximise our "cognitive professional excellence," our society will be very well placed to enjoy the augmented strengths that artificial intelligence can bring, without having to fear that it spells the end of human mastery of our world.

I am sure that you the reader will be fascinated by the humanistic and positive vision that emerges from these pages.

Mariya Gabriel

Preface

Overall Purpose

The purpose of this book is to present new and important brain-based competencies for project managers and executives of complex projects. The authors, who include professionals from the fields of complex project management and neuroscience, discuss cognitive readiness as a natural part of an innovative approach to project management. The focus on cognitive readiness, a newly recognized and fundamental set of leadership competencies, has neuroscience as a foundation with mindfulness, cognitive intelligence, emotional intelligence, and social intelligence as its pillars and is intended to help produce the next generation of project managers and project team members.

Cognitive readiness allows the project manager and the team to be aware of the set of advanced cognitive competencies (Augmented cognition as we will see in Chapter 6) of each other and provide for a fuller integration of those competencies earlier in the project.

This book highlights various aspects of human interaction from the perspective of cognitive readiness throughout an expanded project life cycle.* This expanded life cycle offers a wider perspective of the project manager's role in managing a complex project, both technically and

---

* Archibald, R., Di Filippo, I., and Di Filippo, D. December 2012. The six-phase comprehensive project life cycle model including the project incubation/feasibility phase and the post-project evaluation phase. *PM World Journal*, 1 (Issue V). (www.pmworldjournal.net). A holistic systems perspective of projects and programs is required today to achieve the full benefits of systems thinking in project management. To achieve this perspective, the need to establish a Comprehensive Project Life Cycle definition and to promote its application on all important projects is first presented. This Comprehensive Project Life Cycle Model recognizes that there is always a Project Incubation/Feasibility Phase prior to the currently existing Project Starting Phase of most project management (PM) standards, and also recognizes that there must be an additional Post-Project Evaluation Phase after the standard Project Close-Out Phase.

cognitively, as detailed by Dr. Harold Kerzner.* In its *Navigating Complexity: A Practice Guide* (PMI 2014),† the Project Management Institute groups issues around project complexity into three categories—human behavior, systems behavior, and ambiguity.‡ The editors of our book view cognitive readiness as an essential framework for managing and minimizing the effects of complexity that stem from both human behavior and ambiguity. Additionally, cognitive readiness would enable a project team to more easily absorb systems behavior through a greater understanding of one another's individual and combined capabilities for handling those behaviors. As such, cognitive readiness should be recognized as a primary set of leadership competencies both for self-management and for successfully developing and managing high-performing teams in a complex project environment.

To prepare this book, experts from around the globe, from multiple disciplines (please see the Acknowledgement section), have contributed chapters on the topics of thinking, learning, and cognitive styles (styles will be dealt with in a successive volume). Distinguished project management professionals, scientists, and researchers have contributed to help define the book's table of contents and to provide substantive information as to how cognitive readiness fits into the domain of project management. The current status of the contents is shown in the table that appears above. The table of contents was finalized during the second quarter of 2017. The book project is viewed as an "open" initiative with a diverse range of perspectives from editors, authors, contributing experts, and peer reviewers. The main goal of this book is to raise awareness among the international business community, general organizations, project managers, and executives, as to the benefits of cognitive readiness and its importance in a global business environment, the impact of which requires supplemental leadership competencies in order to maximize the probability of project success. Rather than being an academic treatise, it is written in a style that can be more easily absorbed by project managers, project teams, and those in organizational project management offices—those who are most immediately affected and benefited by its detail and recommendations. In reading the contents, both the project managers

---

* Kerzner, H. 2015. *Project Management 2.0: Leveraging Tools, Distributed Collaboration, and Metrics for Project Success.* (John Wiley & Sons, Hoboken, NJ), p. 116.

† Project Management Institute. 2014. *Navigating Complexity: A Practice Guide.* (PMI, Inc., Newtown Square), p. 11.

‡ https://colorsinprojects.ro/wp-content/uploads/2015/10/Recomand%C4%83m_White-paper-Simona-Bonghez.pdf

and the executives will find the principles explained in these chapters of immediate practical use.

Overall Objective

The objective of this book is to present the most recent theories and research on cognitive readiness in a way that represents diverse perspectives that include its application to real situations. This presentation is to promote cognitive readiness' inclusion in a common body of project management knowledge that can be readily accepted by practitioners. As far as the authors can ascertain, the book is an original attempt to raise interest in cognitive readiness by the project management community.[*]

While the primary audiences of the book are project managers and executives, the authors do not exclude use in the related fields of organizational behavior and business education.

According to a first call to action the authors have reported in one of their previous research reports,[†] they see several audiences for this work on cognitive readiness, so that the book will be of interest to several other audiences, including project team members, corporate and organizational management, academia, trainers, researchers, business schools, and graduate students.

One of the hypotheses presented in the text is that high-performing teams can and should be developed with a working understanding of cognitive readiness and its related fields, such as multiple intelligences and mindfulness. Further, the text presents how a project team can improve its behavioral efficiency, raising an advanced cognitive competence (or augmented cognition competence). As mentioned earlier, cognitive readiness will thus provide a critical new dimension of project management soft skills. Finally, the book will address methods and tools to enable organizations to measure and enhance cognitive readiness.

---

[*] It should be noted that the United States Armed Forces has already conducted research on cognitive readiness. Some other authors have provided seminal works on the subject. With this endeavor we hope to be the first to introduce cognitive readiness into the project management profession, inspiring our audience to customize cognitive readiness to their needs.

[†] http://pmworldjournal.net/wp-content/uploads/2013/11/pmwj16-nov2013-archibald-di-filippo-unlocking-high-performance-FeaturedPaper-FINAL1.pdf page 37.

Our Work's Influence on Project Management Stakeholders

Cognitive competence or capabilities contribute to the holistic competence philosophy of project management. In particular, the International Project Management Association and the Project Management Institute have already begun research into the basic tenets of this book, which are included in "The Eye of Competence" (IPMA) and "The Talent Triangle" (PMI). As stated by the International Project Management Association, "The eye of competence represents the integration of all the elements of project management as seen through the eyes of the project manager when evaluating a specific situation."* After processing the information received, the competent and responsible project manager takes appropriate action. The project manager's awareness of his inner intelligences such as emotional, social, or cognitive; the outer representation of his cognitive styles; and the inner or intelligences status of the project or program management team members and the stakeholders, as well as the outer as represented by the environment. This awareness may help the project or program to take steps to be effective in the development of a resilient and high-performing team.

For its part, the Project Management Institute, in the *Pulse of the Profession* has developed a talent triangle that cites three critical types of project management skills—technical skills, strategic and business skills, and leadership skills. In the Institute's opinion, competence or capabilities in leadership skills accounts for 81 percent of a project manager's probable success with technical being 9 percent, strategic and business being 9 percent, and other skills 1 percent. Moreover, the same research found that the lack of focus on talent development contributes to the poor performance of programs and projects. Competencies or capabilities that were previously successful, while still necessary, may not be sufficient for today's project managers and teams in the face of increasing project complexity and uncertainty.

Additionally, the *Project Management Institute's Pulse of the Profession In-Depth Report: Navigating Complexity*[†] highlights and explains the importance of this talent triangle in illustrating the skill sets of the next generation of project managers. While technical skills are core to project and program management, the report states, the Project Management

---

* https://www.ipma.world/individuals/standard/ (as shown on November 5, 2018)
† PMI's Pulse of the Profession In-Depth Report: Navigating Complexity. September 2, 2013. Copyright 2013 Project Management Institute, Inc. PMI.org/Pulse.

Institute's research tells readers that technical skill sets are not enough in today's increasingly complex and competitive global marketplace. The report states that companies are seeking to add skills in leadership and business intelligence—competencies or capabilities that can support longer-range strategic objectives by contributing to the bottom line. The ideal skill set— the talent triangle—is a combination of technical, leadership, and strategic and business management expertise. What this means to project and program talent—what this means to the audience—is a focus on developing the additional skills one needs to meet the evolving demands on the organization.

The authors contend that cognitive readiness serves as a framework for human interaction and decision-making that underlie project work to become effective and to enhance the teamwork experience.

Cognitive Readiness Facilitates Second Order Project Management

The methods, tools, processes, and best practices for today's professional project managers are based on standards first developed during the 1960s by the United States' Department of Defense and National Aeronautics and Space Administration. The primary focus was on the "hard" skills, which most project managers are familiar with today—work breakdown structures, estimating, assigning resources, arrow diagramming method, scheduling, and tracking methods. Over time, these methods and tools were refined to include quality control processes, and advanced scheduling methods of the critical path method, critical chain, and tracking techniques, such as earned value management. Professional organizations, such as the Project Management Institute, the International Project Management Association, and the Association for Project Management, developed standards around these areas of hard skills. "Soft" skills, including managing stakeholders, communications, human resources, and others were only an afterthought. As standards began to be revised, the increased importance of soft skills was noted and practices were developed. This development, however, was based on project management practices of reductionist thinking and Newtonian or Cartesian causality. However, research and the integration of disciplines have significantly changed the study of management generally and project management specifically in the last half-century. The acceleration of technological change and the resulting globalization of the workforce, transportation, and communications have changed the way business is conducted today. Globalization and the acceleration of technological change have also increased the complexity of the business or organizational environment, and the complexity of the management of the attendant projects.

In a 2010 project management journal, Manfred Saynisch posited that this more complex business environment necessitates the need for a new framework for project management—one that not only includes the traditional project management approach, but also a complementary approach that includes soft and hard skills reframed for a complex world rather than a reductionist one.* This complementary approach addresses evolution and chaos theory, complex systems theory, as well as psychological, social, and pedagogical sciences.†

It is the authors' belief that cognitive readiness is the underlying foundation for these important soft skills to which Saynisch refers, the mastery of which will increasingly determine the future success of managing projects and organizations in our complex global business environment. As such, cognitive readiness should be considered a critical success factor in implementing second order project management.

---

* Saynisch, M. December 2010. Mastering complexity and changes in project, economy, and society via project management second order (PM-2). *Project Management Journal—PMJ*, 31 (Nr. 5), (John Wiley/PMI) pp. 4–20.
† *ibid.*, Figure 2, p. 6.

Acknowledgments

The research that initiated the journey of cognitive readiness, mindfulness, and their role within the field of project and program management was begun by researchers: Russell D. Archibald, Daniele Di Filippo, Ivano Di Filippo, and eventually Shane Archibald. Over time, many minds and voices have joined the first three researchers to support this book. Unfortunately, we will not be able to provide an exhaustive list due to memory or space. However, one should know that those voices and minds came from many research fields and backgrounds, including academia, neuroscience, project management, and the many areas within project management, including training and consulting. The group of contributors and others who have offered their input have inspired one another, provided one another new strength to continue the research, provided the keys to internal motivation, and of course, provided the essential text upon which this book was built.

A special note of appreciation must be given to our supportive publisher, Taylor & Francis, in particular to Kristine Mednansky, who represents Taylor & Francis. With her grace, empathy, and patience, this text was able to become reality.

Russell D. Archibald, globally-recognized author, consultant, and lecturer on project management, the Honorary Chairman of the program of which this book is a major part, has never waivered in providing the project the crucial support both technical and personal.

One would also be remiss if one did not recognize the official reviewers: Dr. David Frame, Academic Dean at the University of Management and Technology; Dr. Christophe Bredillet, Director of the School of Management at Université du Québec à Trois-Rivières; and David Pells, Managing Editor at PM World Inc. As well as, Rebecca Winston, internationally acknowledged executive with experience in running highly technical organizations with global reach, who, besides being a contributing author, has served as a technical editor to review our examples of project and program management.

Along the way, the work contained in the text had many key supporters, including Pier Luigi Guida, Editor-In-Chief at *Il Project Manager*, a magazine, who assisted one of the researchers to publish the first thought article, Di Filippo's 2011 "The Critical Buffering Theory,"* which began this journey and gave further contributions to the project. Another such publisher was David Pells, Editor-in-Chief of *PM World Journal*, for publishing the first three research articles of this project:

■ R. Archibald, D. Di Filippo and I. Di Filippo "The Six Phase Comprehensive Project Life cycle Model"† *PM World Journal*, December 2012.
■ R. Archibald, S. Archibald, D. Di Filippo and I. Di Filippo. "Unlocking a Project Team's High-Performance Potential Using Cognitive Readiness"‡ *PM World Journal*, November 2013.
■ R. Archibald, S. Archibald, D. Di Filippo and I. Di Filippo. "Linking the Comprehensive Six-Phases Project Life Cycle Model and Project Team Cognitive Readiness with the Total Cost Management Framework,"§ *PM World Journal*, December 2014.

The concepts contained in this text benefited from professional friends who have allowed the contributors to this book and the prior research papers to introduce those concepts to a wider audience at various congresses. Gianluca Di Castri, past President and now Vice Chair in Italian, Association for Total Cost Management, is one such friend who introduced the project at the World Congress International Cost Engineering Council, October 2014, through a paper presented by Russell D. Archibald: "Linking the Comprehensive Six-Phases Project Life Cycle Model and Project Team Cognitive Readiness with the Total Cost Management Framework." Massimo Pica, former Italian Army General and now Board Member at the Italian Association for Total Cost Management, who graciously took the brochure project and placed it on The North Atlantic Treaty Organization tables and

---

* https://www.francoangeli.it/riviste/Scheda_Rivista.aspx?IDArticolo=43784&Tipo=Articolo%20 PDF&lingua=it&idRivista=162
† https://pmworldjournal.net/wp-content/uploads/2012/12/PMWJ5-Dec2012-ARCHIBALD-DI-FILIPPO-Featured-Paper1.pdf (as shown on November 5, 2018)
‡ https://pmworldjournal.net/wp-content/uploads/2013/11/pmwj16-nov2013-archibald-di-filippo-unlocking-high-performance-FeaturedPaper-FINAL1.pdf (as shown on November 5, 2018)
§ https://pmworldjournal.net/wp-content/uploads/2014/12/pmwj29-dec2014-Archibalds-DiFilippos-Linking-ICEC-paper-second-edition.pdf (as shown on November 5, 2018)

spread the word about what the project was investigating. Of course, not to be forgotten is Eugenio Rambaldi, President of Associazione Italiana Responsabili ed Esperti di Gestione Progetto, who provided his high support to the project through his professional contribution.

Gregory Balestrero, former Chief Executive Officer of the Project Management Institute, Inc., offered his professional support to the project and moral sustainment. His sustainment took a personal turn for Ivano Di Filippo, conveying to him a thought of inestimable value: *"It will not be an easy road to bring all of this to success. It will be frustrating at times, but you will succeed. Keep your expectations low, but your vision high…when people say no, it is only one stop in your journey. In a way, keep focused on changing the mind of one key executive in the world….and in time others will change. Make your vision a reality by creating a work that people can hold in their hand, like a book or a smaller monograph and then people can think more clearly about It."* (2015).

Globally recognized expert on project, program, and portfolio management, Harold Kerzner, gave from the beginning of this research project, his sustainment, crucial in the first phases of a project that began as a dream. For Richard Boyatzis, Distinguished University Professor, and a Professor in the Departments of Organizational Behavior, Psychology, and Cognitive Science at Case Western Reserve University, who in addition to being a contributor to this book, gave continuous, genuine support. He is a person that every person should encounter once in his or her life.

One must also acknowledge the strong support that the project and book has received from the two leading project management associations in the world: Mark Langley, Chief Executive Officer of the Project Management Institute, Inc., who sent Ricardo Triana as a speaker to the October 2017 Round Table in Rome; and, Reinhard Wagner, former International Project Management Association, World President and current Chairman of the Council, who sent Martin Sedlmayer, World Vice President, as a speaker to the October 2017 Round Table in Rome. Reinhard Wagner must also be recognized for his continued support of the research project during six research years.

Invaluable support and continued sustainment has also been received from: Stacy Goff, former president of International Project Management Association, United States of America; Tom Taylor and Miles Shepherd, both currently Vice Presidents for the Association of Project Management in the United Kingdom; Enrico Mastrofini, Istituto Italiano di Project Management President; Graziano Trasarti, Istituto Italiano di

Project Management, Vice President; Massimo Pirozzi, Istituto Italiano di Project Management, Secretary; Federico Minelle, Istituto Italiano di Project Management, scientific committee; and the Executive Council formed by Biagio Tramontana, Maurizio Monassi, and Vito Introna of Istituto Italiano di Project Management, as well as all the members of Istituto Italiano di Project Management Board of Directors* for having organized the second Round Table during the Project Management Expo 2017,[†] including a special thank you to Claudia Spagnuolo, Project Manager of Project Management Expo 2017.

A text on subjects such as those covered in this book must rely on the intellectual contributions of universities and their staff. Therefore, special appreciation goes to Marco Sampietro, Associate Professor of Practice of Leadership, Organization and Human Resources at SDA[‡] Bocconi School of Management, where he is faculty member at the Master of Business Administration and at the Global Executive Master of Business Administration and Program Director of the Project Management and Team Leadership executive education courses; Antonio Bassi, lecturer at Professional University School of Italian, Switzerland and member of the project team for the definition of the International Organization for Standardization standards, International Organization for Standardization 21500, and International Organization for Standardization; Maria Elena Nenni, professor at LUISS[§] Business School; Massimo Egidi, past LUISS Guido Carli (this institution is best known by its acronym) Rector and current Councilor President at LUISS Guido Carli; and Fabrizio Gerli, Associate Professor of Business Organization and Human Resources Management at Ca' Foscari University of Venice, who in addition to being a contributor to this book, has given continuous genuine support. With his high technical competencies and his outstanding emotional and social competence, he has successfully managed several crucial organizational and relationship situations for the realization of the book.

The European Commission has also been a strong and constant supporter of this book; in particular, these members should be recognized: Robert Madelin, Chairman and Chief Strategist at the consultancy network FIPRA International, who served from 2004–2016 at the European Commission as Senior Adviser for Innovation to President Juncker, as Director General

---

* https://www.isipm.org/chi-siamo/gli-organi-istituzionali/consiglio-direttivo
† https://www.pmexpo.it/2017/programma/r010tr
‡ This institution is best known by its acronym
§ This institution is best known by its acronym

for Communications Networks, Content, and Technology, and as Director General for Health and Consumer Policy; and Mariya Gabriel, Commissioner, Digital Economy and Society in European Commission, who welcomed the project and especially this book with a great endorsement by writing the foreword for this book.

Special appreciation goes to the Center for Healthy Minds directed by Richard Davidson for giving a number of excellent responses to questions. Also, special appreciation should be expressed to Cheryl Bolstad, past Principal Scientist at Touchstone Evaluation Inc. and now Principal Systems Research and Analysis Engineer at Sandia National Laboratories; Rebecca Grier, past research staff member at the Institute for Defense Analyses; Mica Endsley, past chief scientist in the United States Air Force and now President at Situation Awareness Technologies, Inc; and Sae Schatz, Director at Advanced Distributed Learning Initiative, for their contributions when speaking about their mutual experiences regarding cognitive readiness.

In addition to the foregoing, no list of individuals to be acknowledged would be complete without naming the following contributors: Federico Fioravanti, Gennaro Di Napoli, Roberto Mori, Alessandro Cagliesi, Stanislaw Gasik, Wayne Abba, Joel Carboni, Jorge Eliecer Tarazona, Darci Prado, Carla Messikomer, Janice Thomas, Erik Mansson, Lindsay Benjamin, Guy Shtub, Lindsey Kugel, Kathleen B. Hass, Ann Herrmann-Nehdi, Jo Keeler, Matthew Lieberman, Bob Prieto, Jean-Pierre Debourse, Wayne Abba, Franco Caron, Shakir Zuberi, and Murray Woolf.

Finally, Ivano Di Filippo, one of the book's editors, must recognize Maurizio Anshu Ferro, Zen monk and main spiritual guide of SHOBOGENDO Zen Center in Milano, for being his spiritual guide throughout this long journey.

We wish to thank our families for their loving support.

About the Editors and Contributors

Russell D. Archibald, PhD (Honorary) in Strategy, Programme, and Project Management, MSc Mechanical Engineering, PMI Fellow, and member No. 6, Honorary Fellow APM/IPMA. Co-author with Shane Archibald of *Leading and Managing Innovation: What Every Executive Team Must Know about Project, Program, and Portfolio Management*, second edition 2015, CRC Press. Russ has held engineering and executive positions in aerospace, petroleum, telecommunications, and automotive manufacturing in the United States, France, Mexico, and Venezuela. Since 1982, he has been a consultant to companies, agencies, and development banks in sixteen countries on four continents, and has taught project management principles and practices to thousands of managers and specialists around the world.

http://russarchibald.com

Carl Belack has been a practitioner, consultant, writer, and educator in the field of project and program management for the past 40 years. His experience spans diverse industries including defense acquisition, construction, manufacturing, hardware and software development, finance, and professional services. During the last six years, he has turned his attention to exploring the contributions of human behavior and uncertainty to the complexity of project and program environments. He is co-author of both *Managing Complex Projects* (with Dr. Harold Kerzner) and PMI's *Navigating Complexity: A Practice Guide*. He is also the principal consultant and owner of Carl Belack Consulting and an Adjunct Professor of Project Management at Boston University. Carl has a BS degree from the U.S. Military Academy at West Point and MA, MIA, and MPhil degrees from Columbia University.

https://www.linkedin.com/in/carl-belack-714413/

Sara Bonesso, is Associate Professor of Business Organization and Human Resources Management at the Ca' Foscari University of Venice and Vice-director of the Ca' Foscari Competency Centre. Her research interests lie in the fields of organizational behavior and human resources management. Her recent research investigates the development of emotional and social competencies, the impact of behavioral competencies on entrepreneurial intent, innovation, employability, and career development.

https://www.linkedin.com/in/sara-bonesso-5597b333/

Richard Eleftherios Boyatzis, Distinguished University Professor, Professor in departments of Organizational Behavior, Psychology, and Cognitive Science at Case Western Reserve University, Adjunct Professor at ESADE.* He was ranked #9 Most Influential International Thinker by HR Magazine in 2012 and 2014. His Massive Open Online Courses Inspiring Leadership Through Emotional Intelligence has over 750,000 enrolled from 215 countries. Having authored more than 200 articles, his books include *The Competent Manager, Primal Leadership* with Daniel Goleman and Annie McKee, and *Resonant Leadership*, with Annie McKee.

https://www.linkedin.com/in/richard-boyatzis-401822a/

---

* This institution is best known by its acronym.

Laura Cortellazzo, is a Ph.D. candidate in Management Science Department at Ca' Foscari University of Venice and ESADE Business School in Barcelona. She conducts research activities in the fields of human resource management and organizational behavior, focusing especially on the assessment and development of behavioral competencies. She is active in teaching activities in higher education.

https://www.linkedin.com/in/laura-cortellazzo-171a1065/

Daniele Di Filippo, Information Technology Engineer, obtained a bachelor's degree in software engineering in 2012 and in 2014 he earned a master's degree in software engineering. Through his participation in business engineering courses he has acquired computer engineering and business engineering competencies. He was part of the logistics management at User Modeling, Adaptation, and Personalization 2013 International Conference, Roma Tre University. Now he has been working in IT and Strategy Consulting, focusing on ICT Quality Governance and Interoperability, working with the International Public Administration. Since 2011, he has participated, as program manager, of an international project management research and innovation aimed to highlight the importance of cognitive readiness in complex projects.

https://www.linkedin.com/in/daniele-di-filippo-1512007b/

Ivano Di Filippo, Managing Director for Project Management Research and Innovation within the Board of Directors in Istituto Italiano di Project Management is a certified Project Manager with Istituto Italiano di Project Management and International Neuroscientific Researcher for Project Management Research & Innovation. He studied medicine at the La Sapienza University of Rome and has worked for ten years as a professional IT and web programmer. He is a scholar of oriental disciplines and has been studying and practicing Zen for over thirty years. Since 2011, he has been taking part, as program director, of an international project management research and innovation team aimed to take cognitive readiness in complex projects.

https://www.linkedin.com/in/ivano-di-filippo-69054335/

Mariya Gabriel, European Commissioner—Digital Economy and Society. Related departments: Communications Networks, Content and Technology—Informatics. Related topics: Digital single market ICT Research & Innovation.

https://ec.europa.eu/commission/ commissioners/2014-2019/gabriel_en

Fabrizio Gerli, is Associate Professor of Business Organization and Human Resources Management at the Ca' Foscari University of Venice. He is also one of the founders and the Director of the Ca' Foscari Competency Centre. His research interests embrace human resources management, organizational design, and organizational behavior and investigation of the fields of management education, emotional and social competencies, emerging jobs, entrepreneurship, career development, inter-firm and inter-industry competency modeling, and lean manufacturing.

https://www.linkedin.com/in/fabriziogerli/

Daniel Goleman, best known for his worldwide bestseller *Emotional Intelligence*, is most recently co-author of *Altered Traits: Science Reveals How Meditation Changes Your Mind, Brain and Body.* A frequent speaker to businesses of all kinds and sizes, Goleman has worked with leaders around the globe, examining the way social and emotional competencies impact the bottom-line. Goleman's articles in the *Harvard Business Review* are among the most frequented requested reprints of all time.

His article there, "The Focused Leader," won the 2013 HBR McKinsey Award for best article of the year. Goleman has been ranked among the 25 most influential business leaders by several business publications, including *TIME* and *The Wall Street Journal.*

https://www.linkedin.com/in/danielgoleman/

Dave Gunner heads up Hewlett Packard Enterprise's Global Project and Programme Management Academy and its global project management profession whose main focus is to continually improve and optimize its project and programme management capability of 10,000+ practitioners. Dave Gunner Possesses a vast and in-depth knowledge of Project and Programme Management disciplines, including innovative approaches on how to manage complexity. He has proven programme and project management delivery experience spanning over twenty years; with a record of successful results involving large and complex IT systems integration programmes and projects. He has been responsible for the creation and implementation of a programme to assess the development needs of the project management community, based on putting knowledge into practice.

https://www.linkedin.com/in/dave-gunner-complexity/

George Pitagorsky, Chief Information Officer, Executive Director, and Enterprise Architect at New York City Department of Education—Office of School Support Services. He is a master facilitator, coach, meditation teacher, and consultant with more than forty years' experience in working with individuals interested in applying wisdom teachings in daily life, and in organizations, managing change and performance improvement with a special focus on project engagement and service management. He is the author of *The Zen Approach to Project Management: Working from Your Center to Manage Expectations and Performance, Managing Conflict in Projects: Applying Mindfulness and Analysis, Managing Expectations:*

A Mindful Approach to Achieving Success and many courses, articles, and papers.

https://www.linkedin.com/in/georgepitagorsky/

Dan Radecki, is a Executive Director and Global Team Leader of Research and Development, scientist and leader. In addition, as a recognized expert and speaker on leadership development, he has been able to leverage his experience to create high-performing teams within his organizations. His current focus lies in translation of preclinical data into successful clinical programs and marketed therapies, by providing operational, medical, scientific, and leadership support to global project teams.

https://www.linkedin.com/in/dan-radecki-3932939/

Rebecca (Delehant) Winston, is an internationally recognized expert in project management, Fellow in the Project Management Institute, Inc., subject matter expert and Chair for the United States Committee for the Technical Committee-258, project, programme, and portfolio management for the International Organizational of Standards. Ms. Winston is the President and Owner of Winston Strategic Management Consulting working for public and private organizations in the areas of project management and strategic planning. She is currently volunteering the Project Management Institute Educational Foundation Board of Directors and the National Academies of Science, Engineering, and Medicine in the United States.

https://www.linkedin.com/in/rwinston/

Chapter 1

Complexity and Complex Projects

Carl Belack, Daniele Di Filippo, and Ivano Di Filippo

Contents

Introduction

Complex systems surround everyone, in all they do, in all they experience, and in who they are. Human beings contain complex systems: the sympathetic and parasympathetic nervous systems; the circulatory system; the digestive system; the endocrine system. As such, each human being is a system that contains other systems, a *system of systems*. Nature is full of these individual systems and of systems of systems and is itself an immense system of systems in which human beings merely play a small part. Note, no universal definition of complex systems exists. But in general, complex systems consist of multiple, diverse, autonomous, yet interdependent and intra-dependent parts or sub-systems.

So why is there so much talk and focus of late among business leaders about complexity? And why is there growing interest about project and program complexity and how it affects project and program managers and the projects, programs, and other work that they manage? This chapter will first contain a discussion of complexity by taking a high-level look at complexity science, what it is, and how and when it emerged. This review will include a discussion of what a complex system is: what are its characteristics, and how is it different from a simple or complicated system? The discussion will then provide an examination of how complexity theory is applied to projects and programs, as well as project and program management. What are some of the characteristics of complex projects and programs? What models or frameworks are being used to help project and program managers understand complexity? Finally, the chapter will be closed with a review of some of the primary causes of complexity.

Complexity and Complex Systems

Complexity science began in the late 1960s as an outgrowth of cybernetics, systems theory, and dynamic systems (also referred to as dynamical systems) theory (Figure 1.1). Complexity science is the study of complex systems, and it ultimately led to the development of complexity theory. Despite having been the subject of much research and discussion by experts across many professions, there is no accepted definition of what complexity actually is. One of the most respected research foundations on complexity is the Santa Fe Institute (www.santafe.edu). In its online course, *Introduction to Complexity,* its instructor at the time, Melanie Mitchell, noted that, rather than having a single definition, each profession seems to be defining complexity as it relates to its specific domain. To emphasize the point during the course, Mitchell interviewed experts from several professions (including mathematics, computer science, and biology) and asked them to define complexity. In her book, *Complexity: A Guided Tour,* Mitchell covers a broad range of topics associated with complexity including dynamics, chaos, prediction, information, computation, evolution, and networking (Mitchell, 2009). And while there is certainly no unanimity among these experts on the definition of complexity, there are certainly discernable similarities across professions and industries when describing specific characteristics of complex systems. In her book, Mitchell cites three common properties

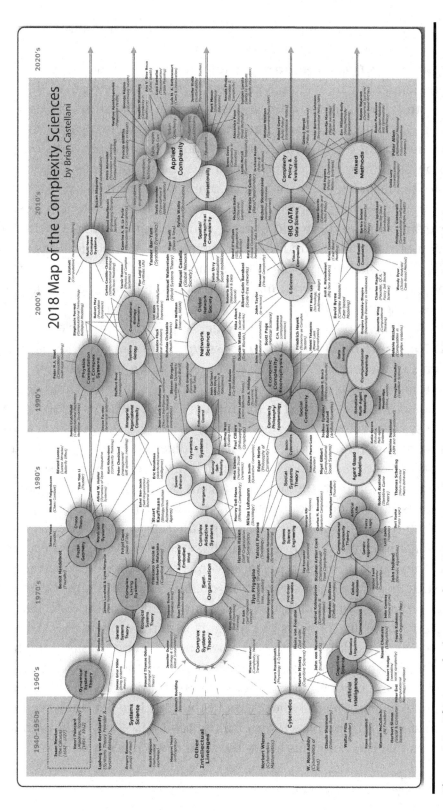

Figure 1.1 The complexity map. http://www.art-sciencefactory.com/complexity-map_feb09.html (accessed on April 23, 2018.)

of complex systems: (1) complex collective behavior; (2) signaling and information processing; and (3) adaptive behavior.*

Complex collective behavior generally refers to the interaction of many independent or individual components in a large network with no central control. For example, one can visualize the interactions of eusocial beings (e.g., ants, bees, meerkats, humans) and the social networks they create. In the age of developed technology, human social networks occur on both physical (face-to-face) and virtual (via the web) planes. One can also relate this network behavior to the complex system that a project or program represents with its networks of human resources and activities. Another example from the world of project and program management is the networking of stakeholders and the management of communications among stakeholders or stakeholder groups. For some complex projects or programs, it may be useful to use network maps of these interactions. Such maps may illustrate how and when the interconnections exist and the expected activation of stakeholders during the project or program life cycles.

Signaling and information processing occurs among the internal components of the system, detecting and processesing information it receives from outside of the system. For example, each of the internal systems noted above contained in the human body generates information that those systems pass on to components *within* each system, such as the stomach signaling the intestines that partially digested food is on the way, and *among* the systems, such as the stomach or the circulatory system to the brain and the brain to the nervous system. Additionally, the human body receives information from external sources, such as the aroma of food or the light from a television screen striking the retina, and subsequently processes that information. Anyone who has been involved in projects or programs can think of many types of information exchanged within the project, such as estimates, status reports, quality test results, and other such information that would be classified as signals or information. One particular type of signal on many projects or programs is a trigger metric for risk, wherein a date is established prior to when the project or program manager believes the risk may be realized to begin to initiate the mitigation strategy. This trigger metric is based upon a set of assumptions that the project or program management team believes about the risk. It is not unlike the body telling the stomach to prepare to receive the food based upon the signals or assumptions that the body has about the food to be received.

---

* Mitchell, M. *Complexity: A Guided Tour.* (Oxford Press, New York), pp. 12–13.

Adaptability enables the system to regulate itself by making changes to improve its probability of survival or success. The process of evolution is a clear example of adaptation. When a nation feels threatened by another nation, it may make changes to its systems of defense in order to protect its citizens and enhance their survival. If a project is running behind schedule, the project manager may seek additional or different resources to bring it back on schedule. The program manager may modify the integrated schedule of the work to be done in the projects, programs, and other work to be done within the program.

After considering those common properties, and despite the lack of a commonly agreed-to definition of a complex system, Mitchell suggests two possible working definitions:

■ "A system in which large networks of components with no central control and simple rules of operation give rise to complex collective behavior, sophisticated information processing, and adaptation via learning or evolution."
■ "A system that exhibits non-trivial emergent and self-organizing behaviors."*

The second definition introduces two new properties of complex systems: emergence and self-organization. These two properties represent characteristics that for the purposes of this text begin to more fully describe one of the primary differences between a simple or complicated system and a complex system—predictability. Simple and complicated systems follow Newtonian and Cartesian logic; in other words, they are reductionist and linear, and therefore their outcomes, with varying levels of work required to do so, should be relatively predictable. Complex systems tend to be dynamic, chaotic, and have far less predictable outcomes, governed by quantum mechanics rather than Newtonian rules. This unpredictability may be said to arise from additional characteristics that are associated with the world of quantum mechanics— systems that are neither reductionist nor linear but exhibit both emergence and self-organization. What exactly do these characteristics imply?

Non-Reductionist

Reductionist systems indicate that the whole system can be broken down into the component parts. An automobile, while a complicated piece of

---

* Mitchell, *op. cit.,* p. 12.

machinery, can be broken down into its major components, subcomponents, and eventually into individual parts. The work required to assemble that automobile can be broken down using a work breakdown structure. Activities of a simple or complicated project or program can ultimately be defined in a similar way by using a work breakdown structure. Normally these work breakdown structures should be developed in the planning process for an entire project, with high-level planning packages used as a place holder for later-stage phases when using rolling-wave planning. *This breakdown process may not be the case with a complex project.* A work breakdown structure may be used to get the project or program started, and possibly to complete some of the initial higher-level work, but at some point or points during the project, the way forward may not be so clear as to allow the use of the work breakdown structure. Multiple parallel efforts may be needed to search for a path forward, and once one is found or created a continuation of the original work breakdown structure may again be used to the extent possible until another ambiguous point is reached. In other words, it may be a non-continuous process with multiple iterations and attempts to fit the pieces together into a logical and reasonable work breakdown structure.

Non-Linear

Linear systems move from stage to stage in a progressive series of steps that can be graphically represented by a straight line. For instance, if one plots the length of a series of paperclips against the number of paperclips, one would end up with a linear graph. In earned value metrics, the S-curve of a planned project budget over time is generally linear. Of course, the S-curve is derived from the planned spending over time of the work, material, and other items taken into consideration of a defined work breakdown structure. Since, as was noted previously, a complex project experiences starts and stops, linearity in scheduling and budgeting are difficult to achieve.

The phenomenon of *emergence* involves the spontaneous arising of a "greater" entity with different properties from simpler entities. There are many examples of emergence throughout the natural world, science, economics, religion, and other areas. Most people know that when a molecule of oxygen gas is combined with two molecules of hydrogen gas a liquid, water, is formed. Water is the emergent phenomenon of this process. The human concept of the "mind" has emerged from the workings of the

brain, although some argue that the two are the same (Mischel, 2016).*
Swarming behavior, exhibited by many biological species, such as birds, fish,
insects, and antelope herds is an emergent, self-organizing property of large
groups. A project or program team of diverse individuals coming together
and eventually working as one high-performing team is an example of
emergence in a project setting.

Swarming was just noted as one example of *self-organization* among
large groups of biological entities. Self-organization involves the spontaneous
development of some form of order arising from a system that was initially
disordered. Tornadoes and hurricanes are examples of ordered weather
systems that arise from disordered weather. A market economy is a self-
organizing system. Project stakeholders on large projects tend to organize
themselves into groups with similar interests to promote those interests in
order to influence project or program outcomes. This self-organizing of
stakeholders on projects and programs can change over time as the focus
of the scope of work changes or as there are changes in the objectives of
the project or program, but the action of organizing into groups of similar
interests to promote those similar interests to influence the project or
program outcomes remains the same.

Many readers may recognize some of these as characteristics of
environments in which they work and manage projects or programs.
However, they may realize that it is not difficult to distinguish simple work
efforts from more difficult or complex work efforts. But how is one to
distinguish between a difficult or complicated work effort and one that is
a complex effort? In his course Understanding Complexity, Professor Scott
Page of the University of Michigan, suggests using a landscape analogy to
appreciate this distinction (Page, 2009). The analogies he uses are Mount
Fuji, a rugged landscape, and a dancing landscape. In thinking about these
landscapes, the readers should put themselves somewhere on the lower level
of the landscapes and define success as when they can reach the highest
point on the landscape. For example, using the previously stated analogies:

▪ Mount Fuji is the simplest to navigate of the three scenarios. The
surrounding area is relatively flat and it is fairly easy to see where the
peak is and determine how to reach it from any point on the landscape.
Reaching the peak is just a matter of applying the right effort.

---

* http://longnow.org/seminars/02016/may/02/marshmallow-test-mastering-self-control/, accessed
August 30, 2017.

- ▪ Rugged landscape (Page uses the Appalachian mountain range as an example, but other similar landscapes may be used) is used to represent a complicated environment. It has many local peaks but only one geographically highest peak. One may find oneself in a valley within sight of a local peak, and upon reaching the top of the peak find that there are other higher peaks that have to be climbed. However, because the landscape is stable and does not change, the highest peak can eventually be determined and reached.
- ▪ A dancing landscape is one that is unstable, one that changes frequently. Imagine a landscape in which earthquakes occur on a regular basis. Once a peak has been scaled the climber may find that she is no longer on a peak but in a valley due to the change in the landscape. This environment is complex—change is the rule rather than the exception.

Project and program managers, particularly those experienced in managing complex projects or programs, will also be familiar with projects or programs that operate in landscapes similar to those in the foregoing descriptions. With all of this general information about complexity and complex systems in mind, the chapter will now be turned exclusively to examining current thought and theory about project and program complexity.

Complexity in Projects

Complexity in projects has developed commensurate with complexity in business. Business complexity has significantly increased in the last twenty years as the technological revolution has enabled rapid, worldwide communications, supply chain globalization, social networks, artificial intelligence, and robotics. This increased complexity has become a major concern at organizational C-levels over the past ten years, as executives try to explore ways to adapt their organizations or make their organizations more adaptable to this challenging environment. Similar concerns affect those individuals who are involved in the project and program management processes today. The processes, methods, and tools that have been developed for a simpler business environment tend to fail to fully meet the management needs of today's complex projects, or they seem to be a barrier to success. In order to meet that gap, various approaches to project and program complexity have evolved over the last ten to fifteen years. The more notable approaches are discussed in the following paragraphs.

Quite naturally, the first areas to be discussed were how to define a complex project or program or, more practically, how would an organization distinguish a project or program that was complex from one that was not. The need to make this distinction arises from an organization's requirement to assign the appropriate levels of project and program managers and team members to projects and the program components that might require higher levels of expertise and experience. The then-CEO of the International Centre for Complex Project Management (ICCPM), Stephen Hayes, noted the characteristics of complex projects as ones

- "Involving uncertainty, ambiguity, dynamic interfaces, and significant political or external influences"
- "That run over a period which exceeds the technology being used at the start of the projects"
- "In which you know what you want to produce, but you don't know how you're going to build it."*

To assist in the determination process, a number of measurement and categorization methods have been developed to help determine if a project is indeed complex. Two of the more notable ones are the Helmsman Complexity Scale and the Crawford-Ishikawa Factor Table for Evaluating Roles (CIFTER). The scale is part of the Helmsman Institute's framework for project success. It looks at three major areas: the organization, the execution team, and the degree of difficulty. Projects are examined against five criteria:[†]

- Context complexity
- People complexity
- Ambiguity
- Technical challenge
- Project management challenge

---

* Adapted from a presentation by Stephen Hayes, CEO ICCPM, at the *ICCPM Research and Innovation Conference*, Lille, France, 16 August 2010.
† https://iccpm.com/sites/default/files/kcfinder/files/Guide_to_the_Complexity_Scale_v_1.2.pdf, accessed on August 15, 2017.

The scale is constructed similar to the Richter scale, 1–10, to denote a project's complexity. The reader can view a more detailed description of the Helmsman Institute's approach at the International Centre for Complex Project Management website noted in the last endnote.

The Global Alliance for the Project Professions (GAPPS) developed an approach for categorizing project complexity with the specific purpose of helping an organization understand which projects will require project managers with higher levels of competence in order to increase the probability of successful project outcomes. This approach is the Crawford-Ishikawa Factor Table for Evaluating Roles table, previously cited in the prior paragraph. The table looks at a seven project factors and rates each from 4 (high) to 1 (low). The combined score assists the organization in categorizing project complexity. The seven factors are[*]

- Stability of overall project context
- Number of distinct disciplines, methods, or approaches used
- Magnitude of external factors (legal, social, environmental) on project performance
- Financial impact on project stakeholders
- Strategic importance of the project on the performing organization(s)
- Stakeholder agreement on product characteristics
- Number and types of interfaces among the project and other organizational entities

Another interesting approach to determining project complexity is offered in *Tools for Complex Projects* (Remington and Pollack, 2007). Its authors, Kaye Remington and Julien Pollack, suggest that there are four major areas in which complexity arises in projects: structural, technical, directional, and temporal. These four major areas can be described as follows:

- Structurally complex projects have a large number of interconnected parts that are difficult to define, difficult to schedule, difficult to track, and may have other characteristics that are difficult to measure or fit into an established process.
- Technically complex projects reflect International Centre for Complex Project Management's third characteristic—you know what you want to make but you don't know how you can make it.

---

[*] http://globalpmstandards.org/tools/complexity-rating/project-complexity/, accessed on August 15, 2017.

■ Directionally complex projects result from a lack of understanding or agreement on the direction of the project due to competing and hidden agendas, interpersonal disagreements among project team members and other stakeholders, poor interpersonal communications, or other competing, diverging, or hidden activities of any one or more requirement holder or other stakeholder.

■ Temporally complex projects represent projects in which expectations for project outcomes keep changing and, as the authors suggest, for those involved, "it feels like standing on quicksand."* Readers will be reminded of the dancing landscapes noted earlier in the previous section where landscapes were used as an analogy for different levels of complexity.

A more recent project complexity assessment tool can be found in the Project Management Institute's *Navigating Complexity: A Practice Guide.*† In this 2014 publication, a method is offered for assessing the complexity of a project. The assessment consists of forty-eight questions that might be asked about a project management team or the project or program to determine the project's degree of complexity. A sample of these questions is shown below:‡

■ Are the program or project assumptions likely to remain stable?

■ Does the program or project manager have the authority to apply internal or external resources to the program or project activities?

■ Does the program or project have the support, commitment, and priority from the organization and functional groups?

■ Have realistic expectations been set around the program or project success?

■ Is there a high level of confidence that new information generated from progressive elaboration is captured appropriately in the program or project plan?

■ Is it possible to terminate, suspend, or cancel a program or project activity when there is evidence that achievement of the desired outcome is not possible?

---

* Remington, K., and Pollack, J. 2007. *Tools for Complex Projects*. (Gower Publishing, Burlington), p. 61.
† In full disclosure, the author of this chapter was a principal co-author of the cited PMI publication.
‡ PMI. 2014. *Navigating Complexity: A Practice Guide*. (Newtown Square, PMI), pp. 33–35.

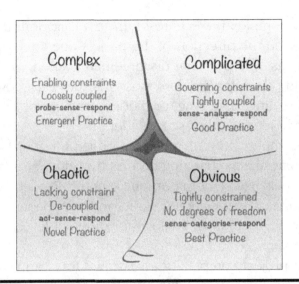

Figure 1.2 The Cynefin framework. (https://upload.wikimedia.org/wikipedia/commons/1/15/Cynefin_as_of_1st_June_2014.png, accessed on August 16, 2017.)

As the reader can see, the assessment is somewhat more detailed than those previously described; however, the questions are specific examples of the more general areas described in the earlier assessment tools. The questions in the tool should illicit discussion among the project or program management team to evaluate the project from its initiation to its closure. No one answer is weighted to say the project or program is complex. Instead, it is the weight of the combined responses and the review of those responses by the project or program management team and their senior management leadership or governing body that will ultimately make that determination and the determination of the tools, processes, and methods that should be applied.

Finally, David Snowden, the CEO and Chief Scientific Officer of Cognitive Edge, a consulting company in Leckeridge, England developed the Cynefin Framework (depicted in Figure 1.2) while he was working for IBM. It is described as a "sense-making device" to "help managers, policy-makers, and others reach decisions."* David and Mary Boone described the four contexts of the framework in the *Harvard Business Review* (Snowden and Boone, 2007). (Note: In the earlier versions of the framework, the "obvious" context is called the "simple" context.)

Each domain requires different actions. *Simple* and *complicated* contexts assume an ordered universe, where cause-and-effect

* https://en.wikipedia.org/wiki/Cynefin_framework, accessed on August 16, 2017.

relations are perceptible, and right answers can be determined based on the facts. *Complex and chaotic* contexts are unordered—there is no immediately apparent relationship between cause and effect, and the way forward is determined based on emerging patterns.*

The authors continue their description by noting that in the ordered world, fact-based management is the norm. While in the unordered world, pattern-based management shows the way forward.† The dark area in the center of the four contexts is the area of disorder in which managers will need to draw on various practices from the four contexts as appropriate. Note also the overlap between the *obvious* and *chaotic* contexts showing that even simple projects, if not managed appropriately, can become chaotic.

The Cynefin framework introduced the chaotic context into the picture. If one peruses the complexity map in Figure 1.1, it can be noted that complexity theory was, in part, an outgrowth of chaos theory. One of chaos theory's contributions was the concept of ***sensitive dependence on initial conditions***. Most readers are familiar with the term "the butterfly effect." This term was originated by the French mathematician Henri Poincaré, who made significant contributions to dynamical systems theory in 1887 when trying to solve what was known as the "three body problem" using Newton's laws to try to determine the gravitational effects three bodies have on one another. Poincaré believed that this sensitive dependence would make it very difficult for meteorologists to accurately predict long-term weather conditions. Studying this same phenomenon in 1963, Edward Lorenz discussed whether the flapping of a butterfly's wings in Brazil could influence the development of a tornado in Texas. The subsequent mathematical phenomenon he discovered was that some non-linear dynamical systems, complex systems, produce periodicity when graphed. The graphic distribution over time of such a system resembles the shape of the wings of a butterfly (Figure 1.3). In this example, the initial conditions in a weather system eventually produced havoc in a subsequent, nonetheless distant, weather system. From a project or program perspective, consider the havoc that occurs in a project or program team when senior management establishes overly optimistic budget and schedule estimates and how that ultimately affects the conduct of the project or program components. Another frequently seen impact is the addition of

---

* Snowden, D. and Boone, M. November 2007. A leader's framework for decision making. *Harvard Business Review*, (Harvard University Press, Cambridge), p. 4.
† For a more detailed description the reader is directed to the noted HBR article and the video by David Snowden on the Cognitive Edge website: http://cognitive-edge.com/.

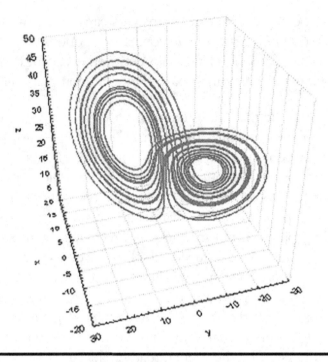

Figure 1.3   Lorenz butterfly attractor. (Kevin Dooley, Flcker.com, license at https:// creativecommons.org/licenses/by/2.0/legalcode.)

requirements under the heading of "stretch goals" for internal organization projects, which is another way to add scope without adding budget or schedule. (See Chapter 4 for a discussion of how optimistic, and frequently unattainable, project expectations arise.)

This type of effect is also indicative of yet another characteristic of a complex system—***phase transitions***—which occur when a system moves from one physical state to another. One should imagine a child at the beach with a bucket of sand. If the child slowly pours the sand in a continuous steady stream onto a flat surface the height of the sand cone will rise at a linear rate until the pile can no longer sustain the weight of the sand. At this point, the top of the pile collapses, and if the sand continues to be poured onto the pile, it will build up again until it reaches its next collapse point. This point of collapse is the phase transition point.*

---

* For readers interested in further material on this topic, it is suggested that they explore the "logistic map" used to determine growth of biological population size which uses the simple equation:

$$x_{t+1} = Rx_t(1-x_t).$$

As the value R increases, an initially stable system begins to exhibit oscillations and, eventually, period-doubling (bifurcations) leading to a chaos.

Having reviewed a number of definitions and models around complexity, complex systems, and complex projects, a definition for a complex adaptive project will now be suggested to guide readers through the remainder of the book.

A ***complex adaptive project*** is one that

■ Has a *network of components* each of which has varying influence on other connected components, and therefore exhibits *complex collective behavior*
■ *Signals and processes information*
■ Is *adaptive*
■ Is *nonlinear* and has *phase transitions*
■ Is *non-reductionist*
■ Exhibits *emergence*
■ Is *sensitive to initial conditions*
■ Has a tendency for *self-organization.*

The Human Dimension of Project Complexity

Having examined all of the foregoing material, the authors of *Navigating Complexity: A Practice Guide* categorized project complexity into three groups:*

■ Human behavior
■ Systems behavior
■ Ambiguity

The authors went on to say that almost any cause of project complexity falls into one of the three categories. Systems behavior, which has been studied for a number of decades, will not be addressed in this book. Readers are encouraged to explore this topic on their own to continue their further education on project complexity.† The primary purpose of this book is to look at the roots of project complexity that can be traced back to human behavior in general and particularly human behavior in the face of project environmental ambiguity.

---

* *op.cit.*, p. 11.
† An excellent book with which to do this is Jackson (2003), cited in the bibliography.

Kathrine Hass: *"As complexity science teaches us, human behavior is complex because humans are always reacting to their environment, and therefore human activity is impossible to predict. In addition, teams are complex adaptive systems within the larger program, the program is also a complex adaptive system operating within a complex adaptive organization; the organization is trying to succeed (by changing and adapting) within a complex adaptive global economy."*

The editors and authors of this book believe that for too long project and program management standards have focused on the "hard skills" of project management, generally considered to be those that allow the project or program manager to manage the cost, schedule, and scope. In the last two decades that trend has started to shift towards the "soft skills," such as team motivation, communication, flexibility, and leadership. In fact, the key to future project success appears to fall squarely on the shoulders of one soft skill—leadership. The Project Management Institute's Talent Triangle represents the three skill sets for the next generation of project managers— technical project management, strategic and business management, and leadership.* The report says,

> Four out of five high performers (81 percent) report that the most important acquired skills for project managers to successfully manage projects that are highly complex are leadership skills.†

It also says that 75 percent of organizations feel that leadership skills are the most important skills for project managers to have in order to be successful in managing complex projects.‡ Many lists have been composed to capture the set of leadership skills. Some of the common skills that are found in those lists include the following: active listening, public speaking, written and oral communication, motivation, team building, delegating, ability to prioritize, and conflict management.

In a ground-breaking 2010 paper (Saynisch, 2010),§ Manfred Saynisch suggests that in our increasingly complex environment, a new order of

---

* http://www.pmi.org/-/media/pmi/documents/public/pdf/learning/thought-leadership/pulse/
  navigating-complexity.pdf, p. 13, accessed on August 17, 2017.
† *ibid.*, p. 14.
‡ *ibid.*, p. 14.
§ This paper won the 2007 IPMA Research Award and the ICCPM Research Prize 2010.

project management needs to arise: one that combines current, traditional project management practices and standards, *PMBOK® Guide*, ISO 21500:2012, PRINCE2, and other standard- or practice-related texts, with new "second order project management," PM-2. The complementary PM-2 practices and standards would be based in natural and social sciences, theory of evolution, cognition theory, chaos and complex systems theories, and other related theories and studies. It is just those theories, particularly those associated with human behavior, that this book begins to examine and relate to the practice of project and program management through examples and other texts on the practice.

The cognition theory that Saynisch mentions are discussed in this book in the context of **cognitive readiness**. This book contends that cognitive readiness is a necessary requirement for project and program managers and project and program teams in order to increase the probability of successful project and program outcomes. Cognitive readiness involves understanding and maximizing human behavioral outcomes. It is defined as the mental preparation, including skills, knowledge, abilities, motivations, and personal dispositions, needed to establish and sustain outstanding individual and team performance in the complex and rapidly changing environment of project, program, and portfolio management.

The next chapter posits a cognitive readiness framework that will guide the reader through the book. It uses neuroscience as its foundation, supporting the pillars of mindfulness, cognitive intelligence, emotional intelligence, and social intelligence. It will build on those pillars by examining the importance of mindfulness, suggest ways to maximize human behavior in decision making and interpersonal relationships, and develop new competencies to increase the leadership potential of project managers, program managers, and team members.

Summary

This chapter began with an examination of complexity and complex. It was noted that there is no generally agreed-upon definition of complexity, but that a number of characteristics accurately describe the workings and phenomena associated with complex systems, such as

- Complex collective behavior
- Signaling and information processing

- Adaptability
- Non-reductionist
- Nonlinear
- Emergent
- Self-organizing

A few different perspectives of complexity in a project environment and methods that might be used to determine if a project is complex or the degree to which such complexity exists were presented. These perspectives and methods included:

- International Centre for Complex Project Management complex project characteristics
- Helmsman Complexity Table
- Crawford-Ishikawa Factor Table for Evaluating Roles complexity evaluation tool

Also presented were perspectives that both categorized and evaluated project complexity.

- Remington/Pollack's Tools for Complex Projects
- PMI's Navigating Complexity: A Practice Guide

The Cynefin framework presented a way to view the spectrum of complexity in projects in terms of the obvious, complicated, complex, and chaotic; constraints; and practices associated with each domain. It also suggested approaches for each.

Finally, in this chapter the importance that human behavior contributes to project complexity was previewed, and the concept of *cognitive readiness* was introduced, which will be the primary focus of the remainder of the book.

The next chapter posits a cognitive readiness framework that will guide the reader through the book. It uses neuroscience as its foundation for the pillars of mindfulness, cognitive intelligence, emotional intelligence, and social intelligence. The chapter information will build on those pillars by examining the importance of mindfulness and will suggest ways to maximize human behavior in decision making and interpersonal relationships to develop new competencies to increase the leadership potential of project managers and team members.

Chapter 2

The Cognitive Readiness Framework

Carl Belack, Daniele Di Filippo, and Ivano Di Filippo

Contents

Introduction

Chapter 1 introduced the concept of cognitive readiness in the context of the management of complex projects. In fact, the authors believe that it is the single-most important factor in achieving project and program success in a complex environment.

In this chapter, the history of cognitive readiness will be explored. Other items that will be addressed are the reason for cognitive readiness' importance in the complex environment faced by many project and program managers and team members in their work today; the need for project leadership, not just by the project manager but by various project team members throughout the project lifecycle; and, a model with which the reader, including project and program managers, may visualize the key concepts of cognitive readiness, which are designed to increase the effectiveness of leadership across the project team. This model will serve as a framework for the rest of the chapters and will help guide readers through the intricacies of the pillars upon which cognitive readiness rests: neuroscience, mindfulness, and cognitive, emotional, and social intelligences.

Cognitive Readiness

As noted in Chapter 1, cognitive readiness is the mental preparation, including skills, knowledge, abilities, motivations, and personal dispositions needed to establish and sustain outstanding individual and team performance in the complex and rapidly changing environment of project, program, and portfolio management.

But what exactly is cognitive readiness, as the concept has evolved to be understood and accepted? Today's current understanding of cognitive readiness appears to have originated within the United States Department of Defense. Battlefields have always been complex environments with constantly challenging and changing situations, including changing requirements, multiple battlefronts, terrain changes, weather changes, and personnel changes, to which the battle's participants need to adjust and respond. Moreover, those participants need to recognize the challenges and changes as they occur, and to exploit the evolving situation in order to prevail over their opponents. In a 2002 paper, John Morrison and J.D. Fletcher defined military cognitive readiness as "the mental preparation (including skills, knowledge, abilities, motivations, and personal dispositions) an individual needs to establish and sustain competent performance in the complex and unpredictable environment of military operations."* Note the similarity to the definition used in this book with respect to cognitive readiness in project management. The situational analysis to which cognitive readiness is to be applied requires the adjustment and response to changing environmental factors, the identification of risks, the development of risk mitigation strategies, and the adjustment of those mitigation strategies as the battle or project progresses, just to name a few parallels.

---

* Morrison, J.E., and Fletcher, J.D. 2002. *Cognitive Readiness*. IDA Paper P-3735 (Institute for Defense Analyses, Alexandria, VA), pp. I–3.

Morrison and Fletcher note the psychological nature of cognitive readiness' determinative factors. They also describe ten components that underlie the term's operability, including

- Situation awareness
- Memory
- Transfer of training
- Metacognition
- Automaticity
- Problem solving
- Decision-making
- Mental flexibility and creativity
- Leadership
- Emotion*

In later writings, Fletcher and Alexander Wind refined these components to *exclude* transfer of training, automaticity, leadership, and emotion. But they added the following additional components: pattern recognition, teamwork, communication, adaptive expertise, interpersonal skills, resilience, and critical thinking.[†]

Until the latter part of the twentieth Century, the industrial age's business environment seldom emulated the changing conditions of a battlefield. However, with the advent of the information age, that could no longer be said to be true. Today's business environment and many of the projects undertaken in its behalf clearly involve frequent change and unpredictability. As a result of the unpredictability and ambiguity of complex projects, project managers and team members should be trained for and be expected to assume cognitive responsibilities in order to react both individually and as a whole, delivering an effective response to unpredictable events. Therefore, the need for cognitively ready project teams, as well as cognitively ready organizations, has become a vital concern for serious-minded business executives. Reviewing the operability component list, one finds many of the terms that are applicable to today's project and program teams. One can argue for the addition or deletion of a specific term or two, but overall the terms are applicable. Given the need for flexibility and agility

---

* *ibid.*, ES1-3.
[†] Fletcher, J.D., and Wind, A. 2014. The evolving definition of cognitive readiness for military operations, in O'Neil, H.F. et al. (eds.). *Teaching and Measuring Cognitive Readiness* (Springer Science and Business Media, New York), p. 29. DOI 10.1007/978-1-4614-7579-8_2

in project and program management in today's organizations, one should be reviewing individuals and teams for their cognitive readiness per the organization's view of the operability definition. The organization should spend time defining the operational terms and conveying those terms to the individuals and teams performing project and program management in their organizations, as well as the senior management to whom they report.

Much can be done to prepare project and program managers and their teams to assume their cognitive responsibilities prior to a project or program start and throughout their duration in order to reach a performance standard that is at the level of excellence, which is often termed to be meeting the objectives of the customer. One cannot develop a high-performance team needed to engage a complex project's multifaceted and ever-changing demands by limiting training or mentoring to observed performance of best practices described in previous projects or even in current project or program management standards. The individuals within the teams must be introduced to, trained, and mentored in the inner world of cognition. Successful outcomes in complex projects require that project managers and team members, who are an essential and inevitable component of the project, as a complex system, perform at the highest level of their cognitive competencies. This need is not to be underestimated, as the reader will uncover in the chapters that follow, because these same competencies lead to an increasingly efficient use of both technical and project management knowledge and skills. An example of the knowledge and skills referred to in this area is the ability to handle multiple communication channels for the multiplicity of stakeholders associated with projects and programs.

Organizations typically spend a great deal of time and money to develop a project's detailed plans, establish and justify its business case, identify its funding sources, and authorize its implementation. However, frequently little time and money is expended to train, mentor, and develop the project team as part of the project startup phase in order to enable the team's efficient operation. While some project teams eventually achieve high-performance capabilities over time, substantial benefits can be lost during the interim period. The need to expend resources to enable the team's efficient operation from project startup also applies whenever there is a baseline change, especially one where new team members are introduced or existing team members are being asked to draw upon other skill sets. Additionally, project team-building methods have failed to capitalize on advances in the cognitive sciences. The purpose of this book is to clearly explain these advances and provide guidance to help organizations, executives, and project and program managers develop cognitively-ready project teams and leaders. In order to do so in a meaningful way, this chapter will present a Cognitive Readiness Framework, the components of which will form the remainder of the book. However, first we will take a brief detour to present the intersection of cognitive readiness and project leadership.

Project Leadership

A key ingredient in any complex project endeavor is leadership. The Project Management Institute's (hereinafter known as Institute) *Talent Triangle* shows leadership, defined as competency in guiding and motivating, as one of its three legs (the other two were technical management and strategic and business management). The Institute's *Pulse of the Profession In-Depth Report: Navigating Complexity* states that "75 percent of organizations rank project manager leadership as most important for the successful navigation of complexity in projects."* The same publication shows that responding organizations rated leadership skills the most important of the three legs of the triangle by an overwhelming margin (81% leadership and 9% each for technical and strategic/business management).† But what kind of skills does the Institute mean when it says leadership? Another Institute publication breaks down leadership skills as follows:

- Brainstorming
- Coaching and mentoring
- Conflict management
- Emotional intelligence
- Influencing
- Interpersonal skills
- Listening
- Negotiation
- Problem solving
- Team building‡

---

* https://www.pmi.org/-/media/pmi/documents/public/pdf/learning/thought-leadership/pulse/navigating-complexity.pdf, p. 14, accessed on March 9, 2018.
† *ibid.* p. 15.
‡ https://www.pmi.org/-/media/pmi/documents/public/pdf/certifications/talent-triangle-flyer.pdf, accessed on March 9, 2018.

The International Project Management Association describes complexity of initiatives through three groups: capability, context, and management/leadership. The context and management leadership perspectives include:

■ Strategy-related complexity
■ Organization-related complexity
■ Socio-cultural-related complexity
■ Team-related complexity
■ Innovation-related complexity
■ Autonomy-related complexity*

While the terminology appears to be different, the terms cover the same attributes and skills as they relate to cognitive readiness. Project and program management teams, along with their senior management stakeholders, need to be focused on the cognitive readiness attributes and skills from the initiation through the closure of the project or program. To facilitate this enabling process, senior management and the organizations in which they function should be continually focused on the perspective of development, training, and mentoring of these attributes and skills as projects are being initiated continually in organizations or transitioned into other projects.

As one progresses through this book one will recognize that these attributes, skills, and perspectives are directly related to cognitive readiness. However, to enhance successful outcomes amidst complexity in projects, perspectives are not only needed by project and program managers but also by many of the project and program team members as well.

In his groundbreaking book, Nick Obolensky cites the need for what he terms polyarchic leadership.† This type of leadership is in large part due to the inevitable change in future organizational structures. He reviews these changing structures starting with the functional silos that developed with the advent of Taylorism (the practice of scientific management designed to improve productivity in a labor-dominated industrial setting) through today's typical organizational structure, the cross-functional matrix. The matrix structure was developed as an increasing need for cross-functional participation was required in

---

* http://www.ipma.world/individuals/certification/complexity/, accessed on March 9, 2018.
† Obolensky, N. 2010. *Complex Adaptive Leadership: Embracing Paradox and Uncertainty.* (Gower Publishing, Surrey), pp. 5–6.

producing organizational outcomes such as projects and programs. This cross-functional matrix also shows most business or organization's reluctance to abandon completely the outdated hierarchical organizational structure. The matrix, says Obolensky, is a transitional state into a more project-oriented structure, which he calls the Complex Adaptive System organization.*

In such an organization, leadership responsibilities will be delegated, either formally as dictated by organizational governance or informally as necessity requires, to the lower levels of an organization where the work is actually accomplished. Therefore, the need for leadership development throughout the organizational structure, and not just for those individuals who are designated as managers, will be required to facilitate the work to meet the objectives of the project or program. The need for leadership delegation in increasingly complex projects appears to be obvious when looking at workflow and workflow demands. A single project manager is finding it more difficult to have the needed technical knowledge to cover the increasing knowledge requirements as more areas of expertise are required in a complex project. While the project manager will continue to occupy an overall leadership function, effective leadership will need to be delegated to individuals on the project or program management team whose functional and technical areas are of greater import in the project or program at any point in time during the lifecycle. As project team members work with one another more frequently, self-managing teams operating with oversight from project managers should become the norm in more organizations. One can see this system of self-management operating in groups such as string quartets and, in some cases, symphony orchestras, where the team members are so familiar with each other that each member knows when to pick up the leadership position and when to hand it off to another member. Another example are dance teams where lines of dancers know when the lead has changed based on changes in the thematic music or firefighters who have various expertise based upon the types of fire, weather conditions, and other variables. The squad commander is still in charge, but the head of the fire jumpers may be in the lead over the trenchers at any given time.

With that in mind, the framework for the competencies, skills, and attributes required for each project manager and team member will now be explained.

---

* *ibid.*, p. 23.

The Cognitive Readiness Framework

As noted in Chapter 1, the primary focus of project management standards has, until quite recently, focused on the development of hard skills, such as charter development, work breakdown structure, schedule, or risk management. The soft skills that appear in these standards are so described because it was difficult to provide hard or empirical data to support the theories and outcomes associated with those skills. Even within the hard skills, the discussion of soft skills required to accomplish actions within the processes were only mentioned, such as in risk management where one should involve the team in risk identification.

Other references for soft skills have been handled using names of various theories. For example, there have been many approaches to leadership, such as Theory X, Theory Y; Hersey-Blanchard Situational Leadership Theory; or Burns Transformational Leadership Theory. But these theories have little other than anecdotal evidence to support them.

Numerous books and articles exist on how to improve decision-making skills, but most approach the subject from the perspective that human beings make decisions based on a rational thought process, taking little account of the biases that exist in every human brain. (See the discussion in Chapter 4 on biases.) One should note that many of these theories have found their way into the standards, solidifying them as valid or foundational approaches for how to approach the process of decision-making and leadership, despite the lack of empirical data, especially for team approaches. It is only relatively recently that studies and books on the irrationality of human decision-making have been published or books questioning how much the situation or fact bases drives the decision process. It is with this background in mind that the co-editors of this book developed the Cognitive Readiness Framework depicted in Figure 2.1.

Neuroscience Background

Neuroscientific studies form the core of the cognitive readiness framework. In the past ten to fifteen years advances in neuroscience have enabled professionals to gather hard evidence from repeatable experiments to support new theories around the biological bases of human decision-making, interpersonal relationships, and leadership. Psychologists and neuroscientists can watch in real-time how the brain responds to various stimuli through the use of functional magnetic resonance imaging

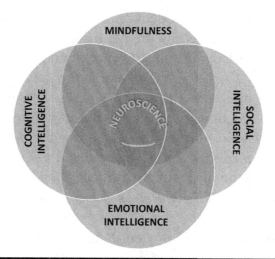

Figure 2.1   The cognitive readiness framework.

(hereinafter known as fMRI) devices. fMRI is capable of measuring brain activity by detecting changes in cerebral blood flow and neuronal activation.

An example of this biological foundation has been the identification of what are known as mirror neurons in the brain. These neurons influence the actions of individuals to replicate the actions they observe in others. As Daniel Goleman and Richard Boyatzis, two co-authors of Chapters 6 and 7 in this book, note in a Harvard Business Review article, "Mirror neurons have particular importance in organizations, because leaders' emotions and actions prompt followers to mirror those feelings and deeds. The effects of activating neural circuitry in followers' brains can be very powerful."* One can now pinpoint the types of neurons activated in many such circumstances and the areas of the brain in which this activation takes place. One can also trace the path this neuron activation follows from one area of the brain to another. Project managers and team members can use this research and other similar study information to help prepare them to make better decisions, have more effective team member and stakeholder interactions, and better lead their team members with confidence. The data gathered through the use of fMRIs and repeatable psychological experimentation forms the basis for the information contained in Chapters 3–7. Therefore, neuroscientific research and data accompanied by related psychological studies form the foundation for the Cognitive Readiness Framework.

---

* Goleman, D., and Boyatzis, R. March 12, 2018. Social intelligence and the biology of leadership. *Harvard Business Review*, September 2008 (Harvard Business Publishing, Cambridge). Accessed online at https://hbr.org/2008/09/social-intelligence-and-the-biology-of-leadership.

There are four pillars in this model upon which cognitive readiness rests, and each pillar is informed by the neuroscientific foundation of the framework: mindfulness, cognitive intelligence, emotional intelligence, and social intelligence. These four pillars are interrelated, thus making the foundation of the model stronger. For example, there appears to be a relationship between emotional intelligence and mindfulness that is explored in another article by Daniel Goleman and his co-author Matthew Lippincott. "It is through improvement in competencies related to emotional intelligence, in fact, that mindfulness makes executives more effective leaders."* In this book, Chapters 3 and 4 address two areas of neuroscientific contribution to project management.

Chapter 3 provides a look at how neuroscience can help increase one's understanding of the human brain to increase one's ability to better understand oneself and others, thereby contributing to one's leadership abilities. For the project or program manager this understanding means that their ability to understand themselves and others on their team will facilitate their ability to lead the team. This leadership ability should be vested in the numerous soft skills such as listening, written and oral communication, stakeholder interactions, and risk communication.

In the discussion of how the brain works, the chapter offers a view of how the brain developed responses to an external environment that is now considerably changed from what it had been during most of the human brain's evolution. The tardiness of these changes can cause reactions that may not be appropriate, and may even be destructive in today's environment with the various environmental factors that exist such as ethical, social, and group mores. The brain tends to have a protective bent that favors threat perception over opportunity perception. There are a number of domains in which these threats exist, and Chapter 3 covers each of those domains and their relationship to project or program leadership. Humans are social beings, and depriving humans of social connections can have detrimental effects on the brain. The pain that humans experience from social deprivations or problems uses the same neural networks as those neural networks involved in physical pain. Despite the need for sociality, the brain has developed segregation biases that favor members of kin-groups, those individuals who share the same strains of DNA, and eventually those biases extended to favor others who share similar ideologies, preferences, and preferred outcomes.

---

* Goleman, D., and Lippincott, M. September 2017. Without emotional intelligence, mindfulness doesn't work. *Harvard Business Review*, (Harvard Business Publications, Cambridge).

The next portion of Chapter 3 deals with three areas that are of import in any discussion of complexity: stress, resilience, and insight. On the subject of stress, it turns out that not all stress is detrimental. The optimal arousal-curve conversation looks at how various levels of stress affect individual performance. Strategies to enable project or program team members and the project or program manager to reduce stress through emotional regulation are examined including situation selection/modification, attentional deployment, cognitive change, and response modulation. The effects of managing and the ability to switch between two neural networks, the default mode network and the task positive network, are reviewed, as are their import on project leadership. Resilience in the face of the uncertainty caused by the ambiguity that attaches to a complex environment is discussed. The resilience of a project or program team and its project or program manager can have a direct impact on a project or program's failure or success. Strategies for developing resilience are reviewed, including mindfulness meditation, computer-based cognitive training, physical exercise, sleep, incremental stress exposure, and positive mood. One last area that can influence the outcome of a project or program is the way in which the project or program team solves problems or mediates risks. The typical approach used is the analytical method, in which once the problem is defined, various solutions are arrayed and the "optimal" solution is selected. A good example of this approach is the use of a decision-tree analysis. However, in complex situations there may be no viable alternative available. In these cases, the use of insight comes into play. The brain process through which insight takes place is discussed, as are ways to enhance the process.

The effects of bias in project decision-making will be examined in Chapter 4. In order to enable individuals to navigate through their daily activities, the brain over time develops many shortcuts. These shortcuts, or heuristics, are rules that the brain follows for many of the simpler, automatic actions a human performs during the course of a typical day. The shortcuts can range from recognizing the shape of a toothbrush, so one does not try to brush one's teeth with a razor, to doing simple multiplication in one's head. These heuristics help one to drive a car and speak on the phone simultaneously. A human could not effectively get through the day without them. For a project or program manager, recognition and interpretation of stoplight charts or standard lines on an earned value report can become part of the heuristics to help them manage projects or programs.

Unfortunately, some of the heuristics that developed to help humans deal with threats during the early period of the development of the human species still occur in situations in which actual, rather than perceived, threats no longer exist. For instance, when one is at a party and hears something that is perceived as a threat to one's self-esteem, the physiological effects, such as a racing heart rate and increased blood pressure, still occur despite the lack of any potential physical harm that might result from facing down a huge grizzly bear in the woods. The heuristics that produce these types of reactions, reactions that could "lead to severe and systematic errors,"* are called biases.

Project team members and managers routinely experience biases. The more familiar and pernicious of these biases in a project or program setting include optimism bias and planning fallacy, both of which contribute to underestimating project costs and durations; anchoring bias, which reduces one's ability to readjust one's expectations from an initial incorrect estimate to a subsequent and more correct estimate; cognitive dissonance and confirmation bias, both of which work to the dismissal of any information that contraindicates a previous poor decision and to search out only information that supports it; sunk-cost bias, which hinders one's inclination to terminate an obviously failing project despite, or perhaps because of, the money that has already been spent; framing effect, in which project decision-making can be significantly influenced solely by the way in which the decision is approached or presented; and ingroup/outgroup bias, which can adversely affect the functioning of a newly formed project team, particularly in virtual, global projects. These biases are examined in Chapter 4, along with ways in which these biases or their effects can be minimized so as to produce better outcomes.

Mindfulness

One of the basic practices of mindfulness meditation is to focus on one's breathing, becoming more and more aware of it until, as it is said in Zen, one gets lost in it. As this focus increases, one becomes more aware of one's thoughts, feelings, emotions, and reactions to both internal and external stimuli. Through the practice of mindfulness meditation, the project or program manager is able to maintain focus on three fundamental aspects: recognizing one's inner feelings and emotions, recognizing others feeling and emotions, and becoming better attuned to one's external environmental factors.

Mindfulness meditation has received much attention in the media over the last few decades, but only since the turn of the century have its effects

---

* Tversky, A., and Kahneman, D. September 27, 1974. Judgement under uncertainty: Heuristics and biases. *Science*, New Series, 185 (4157), pp. 1124–1131.

on the human brain and body been extensively studied. A 2015 Harvard Business Review article reported mindfulness meditation affects two brain areas, the anterior cingulate cortex and the hippocampus. Located behind the brain's frontal lobe, the anterior cingulate cortex is associated with self-regulation. Self-regulation involves the brain's ability to monitor and control thoughts, emotions, and behavior to suit situational demands. For instance, while one might have the impulse to become physically violent towards someone who appears to be verbally threatening, one suppresses such impulses through the activities of this brain area. The article notes that "[s]cientists point out that the (anterior cingulate cortex) may be particularly important in the face of uncertain and fast-changing conditions,"[*] a critical ability in complex situations. In the authors' studies, meditators exhibited greater brain activity in this area, as well as a greater ability to self-regulate and avoid distractions. Participants in the authors' mindfulness program also showed an increase in gray matter in the hippocampus, which is part of the limbic system associated with emotion, memory, and resilience.

While scientific studies to determine the effects of mindfulness meditation are helpful, myths and unproven statements both for and against those benefits still exist, although foundational neuroscientific studies have begun. The need to conduct multiple identical experiments to ascertain repeated similar findings, known as "replicability" in scientific circles, is one key to determine the validity of a particular outcome. There is also the need to separate causation from correlation. In other words, the demand for rigor in scientific testing needs to be applied in order to gain the empirical data to validate the findings.

In their book *Altered Traits*, authors Daniel Goleman and Richard Davidson decouple the proven benefits from the merely theoretical benefits.[†] Nonetheless, the proven benefits which they write about seem impressive. In one series of tests, the respondents reported a range of improvements: "from less anxiety to an overall sense of well-being, including emotion regulation as gauged by reports of recovering more quickly from upsets and more freedom from impulses."[‡] Goleman and Davidson also report that long-term meditation can reduce the amygdala's reactions to stressors and a strengthening between the brain's pre-frontal cortex and the amygdala.[§] Readers will learn in Chapter 3 that the amygdala is a group of nuclei

---

[*] Congelton, C. et al. January 2015. Mindfulness can literally change your brain. *Harvard Business Review*, (Harvard Business Publishing, Cambridge).
[†] Goleman, D., and Davidson, R. 2017. *Altered States*. (Penguin Books, New York).
[‡] *ibid.*, p. 94.
[§] *ibid.*, p. 97.

located in the temporal lobes of the brain and one of the tasks associated with its functions is the initiation of the management of adverse impulses such as fear, anger, aggression, and anxiety.

Other benefits can accrue from mindfulness practices, including maintaining attention span, working memory, and training oneself to be more empathic. This list includes additional health benefits provided by long-term meditation practices, such as maintaining telomeres (see Chapter 3 for additional information), thereby slowing cellular aging and reducing cytokine molecules, which contribute to inflammation. In psychotherapeutic settings, meditation was shown to help to reduce anxiety, depression, and pain.

So what exactly are the implications of this research into mindfulness for project and program leadership and project and program management teams? How might mindfulness meditation help project managers and team members during a project or program effort? Mindfulness appears to be able to

- Enable faster switching between the brain's default mode network and task positive network, which is believed to be a hallmark of more effective leaders
- Reduce stress during times of uncertainty in a project environment, such as periods of changing requirements or cost and schedule baseline changes
- Increase resilience during times of rapid project change, such as continuing multiple change requests or unforeseen risk manifestation
- Enable project leaders throughout the team to listen more effectively and to be more empathetic to, and forge tighter bonds with, team members, thereby promoting team cohesiveness and aiding the formation of high-performing teams, as well as being more empathetic to or listening more effectively to stakeholders, both internal to the project or program and external
- Reduce the project or program manager's fear-based need to micromanage other team members, thereby enabling individual creativity and problem solving through insight
- Increase one's situational awareness to enable a greater understanding of multiple issues involved in decision-making and thereby possibly decreasing framing bias
- Promote a positive mindset, which in turn enables greater resilience and ingenuity in project or program managers and the project or program management team.

Cognitive, Emotional, and Social Intelligences

The cognitive, emotional and social intelligence are outlined below and described in detail in Chapters 7 and 8, two companion chapters in which the authors discuss these intelligences in two contexts. The first context describes the emotional and social intelligence model and the neurophysiological base upon which they were developed and explains how one can increase one's capacities in, and effect use of, these intelligences through the use of the "intentional change process," which the authors then describe in some detail. The second context involves understanding which specific competencies have been found to be of greatest significance in distinguishing outstanding from average project and program management performers. Interestingly, not only do these include competencies in the emotional and social intelligence realms but also in that of cognitive intelligence.

Some definitions of terms:

- *Cognitive intelligence* is generally defined as one's mental capabilities, including but not limited to reasoning, understanding complex ideas, solving problems, abstract thinking, experiential learning, and related concepts.
- *Emotional intelligence* is defined by Daniel Goleman as "a crucial set of human capacities within us as individuals, our ability to manage our own emotional and our inner potential for positive relationships."[*]
- *Social intelligence* is further defined by Goleman in relationship to emotional intelligence, as "beyond a one-person psychology...to a two-person psychology: what transpires as we connect."[†]
- *Competency* is defined by Richard Boyatzis, as "an underlying characteristic... that leads to or causes effective or superior performance."[‡]

Each of these three intelligences has a group or cluster of competencies, which comprise those competencies that have been identified as differentiating

---

[*] Goleman, D. 2006. *Social Intelligence: The New Science of Human Relationships.* (Bantam Dell, New York), p. 5.

[†] *ibid.*

[‡] Boyatzis, R. 1982. *The Competent Manager: A Model for Effective Performance.* (John Wiley, New York) as cited in Boyatzis, R. et al. 2010. Emotional and social competencies of effective project managers, in Cleland, D., and Bidanda, B. (eds.). *Project Management Circa 2025* (Project Management Institute, Newtown Square).

outstanding project or program management performers from merely average performers. Each of these competency groups or clusters is outlined in the following discussion and is described in more detail in Chapter 7.

Cognitive intelligence competency is "an ability to think or analyze information and situations that leads to or causes effective or superior performance."* The differentiating cognitive intelligence competency cluster consists of pattern recognition and systems thinking.

■ *Pattern Recognition*: The capacity to recognize underlying schemas or models among information or situations that seem causally related, identify similarities, and use analogies to describe concepts. For example, a project or program manager's ability to schedule activities in related ways to fully use human resources that are in a matrix situation to them rather than organizationally aligned. Having resources in a full-time employment situation is preferable and a better use of a resource and can be achieved by identifying similarities in activities that aligned to fully use the time of a human resource and their availability.

■ *Systems Thinking*: The ability to explain complex situations and understand the role of different factors; how they influence each other; the cause-effect relationships implied in a certain situation; and the results they bring. This ability to explain complex situations impacts the project or program managers' ability to communicate to the broad range of stakeholders that generally exist on complex projects and programs and allows them to understand and maneuver through the complex relationships that may exist among the various stakeholders.

Both the emotional intelligence and social intelligence competency cluster are divided into two aspects: awareness and actions. As mentioned earlier, emotional competencies involve one's self and social competencies and one's interactions with others (see Figure 7.1 in Chapter 7).

Emotional intelligence competency is "an ability to recognize, understand, and use emotional information about oneself that leads to or causes effective or superior performance."† It is further described in Chapter 7, as managing "one's own moods, impulses, and emotions in a way that facilitates rather than interferes with the task to be performed."

---

* Boyatzis, R. et al. 2010. Emotional and social competencies of effective project managers, in Cleland, D. and Bidanda, B. (eds.). *Project Management Circa 2025* (Project Management Institute, Newtown Square), location 5888 in Kindle edition.
† *ibid.*

■ *Emotional self-awareness*: Understanding how one feels at any given point in time; using those feelings to guide decision-making; having a realistic assessment of one's skills. The project or program manager should understand what their skills are and supplement their management team with members who have skills that will complement them. The project or program manager who feels they must do it all or feels they can save budget by doing it all is not realistically assessing their skills against the needs of the project or program, nor are they realistically using their feelings about the budget to guide that decision. Errors in such judgments will generally be costly for the project or program.

■ *Emotional self-management*: Emotional self-control; positive outlook; drive to achieve; adaptability. The project or program manager that possesses the drive to achieve and a positive outlook will often project such an attitude on to the team. The issues will be approached as manageable and not insurmountable. Positive outlook does not mean one does not acknowledge the risk and the potential consequences of the risk, but one is not overwhelmed by the risk and the team approaches the risk with the attitude that a mitigation strategy is possible and achievable.

Social intelligence competency is "the ability to recognize, understand and use emotional information about others that leads to or causes effective or superior performance."*

■ *Social awareness*: Empathy or understanding others by understanding and perceiving their emotions; organizational awareness or identifying social and power networks and the underlying values that drive groups. This awareness allows the project or program manager to understand the connectedness of the stakeholder network and the myriad issues that might result from such connectedness. It also mentally prepares the project or program manager for the consequences of unintended miscommunications that inevitably occur in a complex environment.

■ *Relationship management*: All competencies used to persuade and guide, negotiate, resolve conflicts, and achieve collaboration. These competencies are acknowledged by most writers on project and program management as a key to stakeholder management, as well as team management. The competencies of persuasion, negotiation,

---

* *ibid.*

conflict resolution, and collaboration are difficult to teach. They arise from the empathetic self, and mindfulness meditation and mentoring can assist the project and program manager access this competency. But while the skills of negation and collaboration can be taught, the art and feel for the competency comes from the individual.

Summary

The basics of the Cognitive Readiness Framework are mindfulness, cognitive intelligence, emotional intelligence, and social intelligence, all based on a solid foundation of neuroscientific research. As one will have noticed, the pillars of this process are clearly interconnected. For instance, mindfulness meditation practice can help develop the positive outlook noted in the emotional intelligence competency cluster. Similarly, mindfulness meditation can lead to one recognizing one's feeling and emotions, as well as understanding others' feelings and emotions. Mindfulness meditation practice can also help an individual recognize when certain biases are occurring, so that one can intervene to counteract the bias prior to the actions the bias might otherwise prompt. Understanding and reducing biases can promote better decision-making and promote inclusion of out-group members in a project team.

However, in addition to giving the reader a framework for understanding the need for cognitive readiness in project teams, the reader is provided practical suggestions for how to go about developing the capabilities associated with cognitive readiness. Discussions in the book set forth ways to

- Understand and manage stress;
- Increase resilience;
- Develop positive mood;
- Reduce the effects of bias in project decision-making and interpersonal relationships; and
- Develop one's cognitive, emotional, and social intelligences by using the intentional change process.

Chapter 3

Introduction to Neuroscience and Project Leadership

Carl Belack and Dan Radecki, PhD

Contents

Introduction

The scientific foundation for project cognitive readiness rests on clinical studies performed by neuroscientists, psychologists, and behavioral economists over the last four decades. Project leadership and effective team membership both require the ability to engage in rational decision-making and productive interpersonal relationships. Unfortunately, as numerous and repeated clinical studies have shown, human decision-making is not always rational, nor are human interpersonal relationships necessarily productive. In fact, two individuals have won Nobel Prizes in economics during the last 15 years for their work showing just how irrational humans can be when they make decisions.* There are methods, processes, and techniques which, if properly employed, can improve both the rationality of decision-making and the productivity of interpersonal relationships within a project setting. These methods, processes, and techniques will be explored throughout this book. However, one should first establish a requisite baseline of knowledge about the inner workings of the human brain.

This chapter will first cover fundamentals of the human brain's evolutionary development. It will then examine the ways in which the brain perceives threats. Next it will examine how the preponderance of an individual's actions are governed by non-conscious activity in the brain, and the problems that arise as a result. Human interactions will be explored in the section on sociality. Finally, the importance and advantages of human resilience, insight, and positive emotions in a complex business environment will be considered.

Brain Fundamentals

The Brain's Evolutionary Lag

One principle about how the brain works is that the speed of its evolution lags behind the speed of societal change. While there is still some debate on the precise pathway that led to the evolution of *Homo sapiens*, the lineage can be traced back at least 1.5 million years to the species *Australopithecus robustus* and perhaps even farther, some 3–4 million years, were one to include evolution from the time of *Australopithecus afarensis*. Despite the long period of evolution to its current state, some experts argue that the human brain has developed more slowly than have technologies that humans have created. Edward O. Wilson, known to many as the father of sociobiology, has observed, "the real problem with humanity is the following: we have Paleolithic emotions, medieval institutions, and god-like technologies."†

---

* Daniel Kahneman, a psychologist, received the award in 2002, and Richard Thaler, a behavioral economist, in 2017.
† Edward O. Wilson in a conversation on National Public Radio with Robert Krulwich and James D. Watson, 9 September 2009.

In the 1960s, neuroscientist and physician Paul MacLean posited the Triune Brain Model, which suggested three stages to the development of the human forebrain: (1) the earliest, a reptilian brain; (2) wrapped in a paleomammalian brain; which was (3) wrapped in a neomammalian brain, its current state.

While this model is now viewed by many neuroscientists as overly simplistic, it does reflect Wilson's description of the early origins of the human brain and it provides a glimpse into why human emotions, rooted in pre-hominin species and affecting human decision-making processes, may contribute to the human brain's difficulties in keeping pace with current technological and environmental developments.

Safety First

A second principle of the brain and how it works is that it is exquisitely focused on monitoring for and reacting to potential threats in our environment. The human brain values the safety of its owner above all else. Its chief concern is to ensure the sustained propagation of its owner's DNA into the human gene pool through offspring: the "brain drives one's behavior to minimize threat. [It is also] hypervigilant in detecting danger."* To further the propagation of one's DNA, this hypervigilance leads one to protect offspring, their offspring, cousins, and others who share some of the same DNA. One must keep in mind that while, for the most part, human beings today live in safer circumstances than they have in the not-too-distant past, their brains still assume that if something seems like a threat, it probably is. When human beings roamed the savannah to get from point A to point B and heard a rustling in the brush off in the distance, they did not have time to consider if a mouse or a lion caused the rustling. The brain had to assume it was a lion because if they decided it was a mouse and they were wrong, their life span might be significantly truncated. In furthering the human organism's safety, the brain has developed a negativity bias. While the brain has neural circuitry for recognizing both threats and rewards, *the circuitry for threat detection is estimated to be many times greater than that for reward recognition.*[†]

---

* Hull, L., and Radecki, D. 2018. *Psychological Safety: The Nonconscious Drivers of Individual Behaviour and Team Success.* (Academy of Brain-based Leadership, San Francisco).

[†] Gordon, E., Palmer, D.M., Liu, H., Rekshan, W., and De Varney, S. Online cognitive brain training associated with measurable improvements in cognition and emotional wellbeing. *Technology and Innovation*, 15 (1), 53–62.

Many different types of threats are perceived by the brain. The Academy for Brain-based Leadership has developed a model that shows the different domains to which the brain is threat-sensitive.* Their SAFETY™ model lists these areas: Security, Autonomy, Fairness, Esteem, Trust, and You.

■ *Security* represents the brain's craving for predictability. It is represented by consistency, commitment, clarity, and certainty. When these are not present, the brain may interpret its environment as unsafe.† As noted in earlier chapters, complex projects are riddled with ambiguity, which in turn leads to uncertainty. Project managers, team members, and other stakeholders may feel threatened to varying degrees by such uncertainty.

■ *Autonomy* is the perception that one is in control of one's environment. The actual degree of control may be real or merely perceived. The brain feels rewarded when it is able to make choices among multiple alternatives. Conversely, a lack of choice over time can lead to a "victim" mentality, which can have negative cognitive, emotional and physical implications.‡ A complex project's periods of ambiguity may lead the project manager to reinforce his or her desire for control by micromanaging all or some of those members in the project team. This reaction, of course, leads project team members to feel that the project manager is impinging on their own autonomy, leading to subsequent conflict between the team and the project manager.

■ *Fairness* represents the desire that the brain has for exchanges that occur within our environment to be fair to all involved. The brain uses the same networks in perceiving disgust that it does when perceiving unfairness in the environment.§ With all of the decisions that the project manager has to make during the course of a project, coupled with the various stakeholder groups with their occasionally competing agendas, the perception of fairness may be difficult to maintain in a project environment. Additionally, when team members perceive others,

---

* Hull and Radecki, *op. cit.*

† Davis, F.C., Neta, M., Kim, J., Moran, J.M., and Whalen, P.J. 2016. Interpreting ambiguous social cues in unpredictable contexts. *Social Cognitive and Affective Neuroscience*, 775–782.

‡ Stern, S., Dhanda, R., and Hazuda, H. 2009. Helplessness predicts the development of hypertension in older Mexican and European Americans. *Journal of Psychosomatic Research*, 67, 333–337.

§ Cheng, X. et al. 2017. Anterior insula signals inequalities in a modified Ultimatum Game. *Neuroscience*, 348, 126–134.

particularly other team members, as being treated unfairly, they may similarly experience a visceral disgust response.

■ *Esteem* reflects how one views oneself, how one compares oneself to others, and how one thinks one is perceived by others.* If team members are involved in a project in which they feel they been given an opportunity for intellectual and professional growth, their esteem will increase. However, if they are given tasks that are not within their areas of expertise and feel they have no possibility of being successful, or if they are given tasks that someone much junior to them should have been given, they may feel threatened. Moreover, if a project manager berates a team member in a public forum, there is a high probability such action will create a hypersensitive stress response in the team member, further hindering creativity and cognitive capacity.

■ *Trust* addresses the human need for sociality. Humans thrive in tribes or groups. Those who are not already a part of one's group are initially viewed as a threat and part of an "out-group."† Complex projects typically involve many individuals and groups of individuals, who temporarily come together to interact with one another. Those individuals who are working together or have worked together in the past may view themselves as part of an in-group. Those individuals who are not or have not been working together will be viewed as part of an out-group. The next chapter will deal with the detriments of in-group and out-group biases. Project managers need to understand the origin of these biases and how to effectively manage them within the project.

■ *You*: Refers to how each of the previous areas affect a specific individual. No two individuals' threat-sensitivities are identical. Each person will experience threat-sensitivities that are unique, based on biases, hormones, personality, socialization, past experiences, current situation and outlook, and hopes for the future.‡ It is important that the project manager understand that she has SAFETY™ drivers and learn to recognize them when they occur in order to understand when she may be driven by them. Once that ability is in place, she can then understand and begin to reappraise others' SAFETY™ drivers when they

---

* Hull and Radecki, *op. cit.*

† Mobbs, D., Meyer, M., Yu, R., Passamonti, L., Seymour, B.J., Calder A.J., Schweizer, S., Frith, C.D., and Dalgleish, T. A key role for similarity in vicarious reward. *Science*, 324, 900.

‡ Hull and Radecki, *op. cit.*

emerge. One difficulty this approach presents to the project manager is that each team member's threat-sensitivities, as well as those of other significant stakeholders, need to be understood in order to enable productive personal interactions. Another difficulty presented is that an individual's threat-sensitivities may change over time. The project manager cannot therefore assume that a team member with whom she has previously worked has the same SAFETY™ profile as in the past.*

Individual threat-sensitivities at any given time will determine how one perceives a potential threat and will influence the actions one takes to defend against that threat. Since each individual has a different SAFETY™ profile, when two people are interacting with one another, what one perceives as a perfectly harmless action or declaration may be perceived quite differently by the other. Despite the innocent intentions of one person's actions towards the other person, if the other's brain perceives them as a threat, the brain of the person will react automatically and defensively.

Preponderance of the Non-Conscious

A third organizing principle of the brain is that humans are driven by the non-conscious operations of the brain. The human brain never ceases to function during an individual's lifetime. Its operations are essential in regulating the many sub-systems of the human body. The human brain receives approximately 11 million bits of data per second from the body's senses but is only able to consciously process about 40 bits per second. The rest are processed non-consciously.† The brain's non-conscious operations involve using heuristics, which are automatic short-cuts, and biases to help humans navigate their daily encounters. These heuristics are non-conscious drivers to help us interpret the world. They are prevalent in the majority of our decisions. Daniel Kahneman has described the brain as a "coherence machine" trying to make sense of the billions of bits of data it receives every day. Because it craves coherence, it builds simple stories. When it encounters difficult questions such as "should I hire this person?" it instead substitutes

---

* At the time of the writing of this chapter, a basic SAFETY™ profile assessment was available free of charge at the Academy of Brain-based Leadership's website (https://academy-bbl.com/safety-assessment/). Two levels of more detailed profiles were available for purchase.

† Wilson, T.D. 2002. *Strangers to Ourselves: Discovering the Adaptive Unconscious.* (Harvard University Press, Cambridge).

easier questions such as "do I like this person?" (Kahneman, 2014). The reader may read more about heuristics and biases and how they affect decision-making and personal interactions in Chapter 4.

The interplay of the amygdala and the pre-frontal cortex illustrates the importance of non-conscious brain operations.* The amygdala is part of the Triune Brain Model's paleomammalian brain and the pre-frontal cortex is part of its neomammalian brain. The amygdala plays a significant role in decision-making, storage, processing, interpretation of memory, and emotions. It also plays a role in aggression, fear, and anxiety. When an individual hears a sudden, unexpected, loud noise, the processing within the amygdala makes that person jump and directs her attention toward the direction of the noise. It is the amygdala that contributes to fight, flight, or freeze responses that humans experience. In short, the amygdala plays a significant role in immediate, automatic responses. While much of this automaticity acts to help individuals protect themselves, it frequently raises false alarms that continue to produce the anxieties associated with fight, flight, or freeze. This automaticity is also responsible for detrimental project management decisions and actions associated with the biases discussed in the next chapter.

The pre-frontal cortex plays a significant role in executive function, or differentiating among choices, social control and behavior moderation, and complex decision-making such as considering potential outcomes of current actions.† When at its best, the pre-frontal cortex can act as a braking system on the amygdala's adverse reactions.‡ However, it takes much more effort by the pre-frontal cortex to counteract the detrimental effects of the amygdala because of the automaticity of the amygdala's actions. As a result, the pre-frontal cortex requires and consumes a great deal of energy. It is also important to note that significant amounts of stress can adversely weaken the pre-frontal cortex's ability to act as a braking system, while simultaneously strengthening the amygdala. If a project manager is not aware of his team members' SAFETY™ drivers, he may inadvertently induce stress, thereby leading to a downward spiral in their ability to manage their own emotions.

---

* Because of the complex pathway interconnections in the brain, some neuroscientists generalize this dynamic as the interplay of the sub-cortex (the limbic system) and the cortex.

† Arnsten, A.F.T. June 2009. Stress signaling pathways structure and function. *Nature Review Neuroscience*, 10 (6), 410.

‡ Lieberman, M. 2013 *Social: Why Our Brains are Wired to Connect*. (Crown Publishers, New York).

The Need for Sociality

Human beings are social animals. This sociality may have begun, not surprisingly, as a safety mechanism. Exclusion from a group or tribe would raise one's probability of being vulnerable to predators, either animals or members of other tribes. In a 2015 paper, psychologist Naomi Eisenberger showed that the brains of those experiencing social pain showed activity in the same brain areas as they might have if they were to experience physical pain. In the paper, she noted that previous laboratory experiments, using a game called Cyberball, showed the pain experienced by individuals when they were purposely excluded from participating in the game with two other individuals.* Anyone who has experienced a broken romantic relationship, cyberbullying, the death of a loved one, or other forms of social exclusion knows full well the actual pain one can feel during and after the event. In functional magnetic resonance imaging studies of responses to social rewards, such as having one's name associated with positive impressions like "competent," "likeable," and "trustworthy," the reward area of the brain showed an increase in activity that was even greater than that associated with physical rewards like money or food.† How others perceive one clearly matters to the human brain. Eisenberger's team also showed that social pain can elicit a more pronounced and more protracted response in the brain's pain areas when compared to responses to physical pain. Interestingly, studies have also recently shown that there is a pharmacological intervention, Acetaminophen, that can be used to reduce both physical and social pain.‡

Social deprivation can have significant detrimental effects on the brain. Laboratory studies on rats in forced social isolation resulted in disruption to the limbic system and the medial pre-frontal cortex. Additionally, the human brain is hard-wired to quickly distinguish between those who are members of our own group or tribe, our in-group, and those from outside of our group, the out-group.§

The significant size of the brain's cortex in primates is thought to be due, in part, to its increased need and ability for managing social networks.

---

* Eisenberger, N. 2015. Social pain and the brain: Controversies, questions, and where to go from here. *Annual Review of Psychology*, 603.
† Phan, K.L., Sripada, C.S., Angstadt, M., and McCabe, K. July 2010. Reputation for reciprocity engages the brain reward center. *PNAS*, 107 (29), 13099–13104, https://doi.org/10.1073/pnas.1008137107
‡ Durso, G., et al. April 10, 2015. Over-the-counter relief from pains and pleasures alike. *Psychological Science*.
§ Mobbs, D. et al., *op. cit.*

This ability includes the management of social skills for relationships with those in the in-group. It also includes skills to remember details about those individuals who are in one's in-group and significant others who may not be a part of the in-group. Interestingly, there is a special part of the human brain that is dedicated to social network interactions, particularly when emotions are involved, which is not shared with other types of memories such as political or technical facts, mathematics, or other non-social memories. In-group and out-group biases are significant among human beings. Studies such as the *Stanford Prisoner Experiment* and the *Robbers Cave Experiment* attest to the fact that, when brought together, even people who are originally unknown to one another will form their own in-groups and out-groups with potentially adverse results. In literature, William Golding's *Lord of the Flies* is a perfect example of the in-group and out-group bias and its consequences. All is not lost however. Clinical experiments on humans show that different parts of the brain process information when the subject who is being tested is thinking about herself as opposed to when she thinks about an unknown person. As the subject becomes more familiar with the once unknown person, her brain shifts to engaging the same brain area used to think about herself. If those in the out-groups can become more familiar to those in the in-group, some of that bias may be diminished.* In fact, there is compelling research showing that familiarity may not be necessary: simply exposing in-group members to those in out-groups may diminish that bias. (Cao and Contreras-Huerta, 2015) This research is instructive for project managers who are managing global teams. Frequent exposure of team members to one another, whether by phone or, more preferably, through virtual meeting platforms where team members can see each other, may help reduce this bias that exists in all human beings to some extent. Similarly, it may be helpful to bring the entire team together for an initial face-to-face meeting and then move to virtual meetings to help achieve that end. By reducing this bias, team members' trust in one another may also increase.

The in-group and out-group dynamic can be particularly pernicious in a project environment. Projects are, by definition, temporary endeavors. Project teams are formed to implement the project and are disbanded once the project is completed. The following describe some of the issues that may arise in and among project teams and stakeholders as a result of the in-group/out-group bias dynamic.

---

* *ibid.*

- Project team members may be simultaneously assigned to multiple projects and project teams, thereby compounding the in-group and out-group dynamic.
- Multiple teams may be competing within a single project, for instance within a research and development environment.
- A single project team may also be composed of a majority of members who are co-located, but with a minority who work remotely, thus setting up the possibility for in-group and out-group dynamics within the project team itself.
- In-group and out-group issues may also arise among sets of project stakeholders with competing agendas.
- And finally, bias can also be attributed to a lack of diversity on the project team, thereby reducing the team's potential creativity and its ability to look at problems from varying perspectives.

Managing issues associated with this bias may be the one area on which the project manager will have to spend the bulk of her time.

Complexity, Stress, Resilience, Insight, and Positive Mindset

As discussed in earlier chapters, one of the areas that accounts for complexity in projects is the ambiguity associated with complex systems. One consequence of project ambiguity is uncertainty. As noted in the previous section, the security area of the SAFETY™ model suggests the brain's need for predictability. Such predictability may not be possible during the periods of uncertainty that occur in a complex project environment, setting up a high probability of threat perception by project team members. Exposure to this uncertainty and other threats in a complex environment may result in chronic stress for a number of team members. In chronic stress, the amygdala is strengthened, resulting in an increased fear response and emotional reactivity. If that were not enough, the activities of the pre-frontal cortex, which as noted above plays a role in moderating the excesses of the amygdala, is slowed down, resulting in poorer decision-making, cognitive rigidity, and memory and attention deficits. Finally, chronic stress can result in mood and motivation diminishment and has an adverse impact on the brain's network integrity and plasticity, its ability to change and learn.*

---

* Crum, A., Akinola, M., Martin, A., and Fath, S. 2017. The role of stress mindset in shaping cognitive, emotional, and physiological responses to challenging and threatening stress. *Anxiety, Stress, and Coping*, http://dx.doi.org/10.1080/10615806.2016.1275585

Helpful and Destructive Stress Levels

Of course, stress does not always have a deleterious effect. If managed properly, stress can result in greater productivity or what is known as "optimal arousal."

The inverted U-curve in Figure 3.1 depicts the link between performance and stress, shown in the figure as "arousal." Little or no stress tends to promote apathy, disorganization, and distraction leading to substandard performance. As stress increases so does performance. A beneficial amount of stress is known as eustress. At the highest point on the curve, performance is focused and organized, but it begins to decrease as the amount of stress gets to be too great, ultimately leading to high stress and burnout. Those who have been involved in complex projects in either management or team member roles are typically familiar with team burnout. Individuals experience different sources of stress and have varying tolerances for stress. In order to manage his team more effectively, the project manager will try to understand both stress sensitivities and tolerances of each member in his team for varying stresses.

Among other issues, detrimental amounts of stress can result in diminished brain plasticity. Plasticity refers to the ability of the brain to learn from repeated stimulation. There has been found to be an increase in the production and reception of neurotransmitters between two neurons following one week of repeated stimulation. This repeated stimulation produces what is known as long term potentiation, shown as LTP on the figure. Long term potentiation results in learning. One result of this

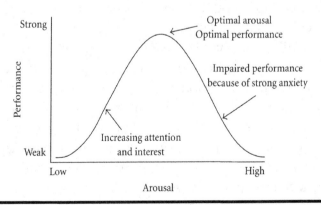

Figure 3.1 Optimal arousal curve. (Diamond, D.M. et al. The temporal dynamics model of emotional memory processing: A synthesis on the neurobiological basis of stress-induced amnesia, flashbulb and traumatic memories, and the Yerkes-Dodson Law. *Neural Plasticity*, 2007, Article ID 60803. doi:10.1155/2007/60803.)

diminished brain plasticity is the brain's inability to learn and adapt to new situations, important needs for project team members amidst the uncertainties of a complex project environment.

Emotional Regulation Strategies

Various strategies can be employed to manage emotions, thereby reducing the stress endemic in complex project environments. There are five phases in the emotional regulation process as described by James Gross.* Each is listed sequentially below:

- Situation Selection
- Situation Modification
- Attentional Deployment
- Cognitive Change
- Response Modulation

In each of these phases an individual can exert control over her emotions. Examples of each are given below. It should be noted that this process can be a cyclical. One can have emotions about having emotions. For instance, one may be angry at one's spouse only to consequently feel guilty about having been angry.

- *Situation selection/modification*: One can choose to avoid or modify situations during which stressful emotions typically arise. Example: if John fears public speaking, he may choose to avoid opportunities at which to speak in public. This strategy is the most proactive, but it has pitfalls. While John avoids the stress of speaking in public, it also deprives John of sharing his ideas with large groups of people and may ultimately hinder his professional career. John may alternatively choose to modify the situation by only presenting his ideas to large groups of people on a pre-recorded, virtual platform. He gets to convey his presentation to many people, but he will not have face-to-face contact with them or feedback from them during the presentation. Interestingly, the drawback that this alternative presents is precisely the lack of face-to-face contact with a live audience.

---

* Gross, J.J. 1998. Antecedent- and response-focused emotion regulation divergent consequences for experience, expression, and physiology. *Journal of Personality and Social Psychology*, 74 (1), 224–237.

- *Attentional deployment*: This strategy is one of the first strategies that humans develop during their lifetimes. If one cannot modify the situation in which one finds oneself, one can distract oneself from that which causes one negative emotional responses by focusing on different aspects of the situation or by distracting oneself in other ways. Example: Fatima enjoys going to movies but she cannot stand to watch gory scenes. When a gory scene arises, she can either cover her eyes or distract herself by looking at the strange hairstyle of the person sitting in front of her, thereby minimizing or eliminating the emotional response. One downside of self-distraction is that it is associated with significant memory loss.

- *Cognitive change*: This strategy is employed after the emotional reaction has occurred. It involves re-appraising the situation to reduce the probability that the emotion will arise. An excellent example of this strategy is described by Walter Mischel in an interview at the Long Now Foundation while discussing his book, *The Marshmallow Test: Mastering Self-Control*.* The strategy involves changing one's perspective about the situation to minimize or eliminate the emotional reaction. For example, if Diego is on a diet while shopping in a market and someone is giving away free pastries, Diego could have decided to look at the pastry not as something that smells delicious and tastes wonderful but rather as something that will add inches to his waist and cause him to die sooner than might otherwise be expected. Athletes may use this strategy as well prior to a significant event by interpreting the "butterflies" in their stomach not as being a sign of nervousness but rather as a sign that they are getting psychologically and physically prepared for the event.

This re-appraisal strategy has been shown to have more beneficial results than another strategy frequently employed by the brain, namely suppression. Suppression involves waiting until the emotion occurs, and then using the cortex to actively suppress the actions that would result from such emotion. Both re-appraisal and suppression can result in similar short-term results, such as Diego's not eating the pastries to which he has been exposed. However, re-appraisal, because it is a strategy to reinterpret a stimulus, takes place earlier in the process, reducing not only the emotion itself but also the release of the harmful neurotransmitters associated with the emotion. Since suppression takes

---

* http://longnow.org/seminars/02016/may/02/marshmallow-test-mastering-self-control/. Website accessed on October 19, 2017.

place only after the emotion has already occurred, the damage from the neurotransmitters has already begun to occur and will continue even after the activity associated with the emotion has been suppressed. (Ochsner and Gross, 2014)

■ *Response Modulation*: This strategy involves directly modulating the emotion after it has already appeared. This strategy can be achieved through many methods. One can use pharmaceuticals or alcohol to ameliorate one's emotions. One may also use exercise as a way of working off stressful emotional responses. Frequently, people suppress their emotions which, while initially achieving the desired result, ultimately may end up producing significant detrimental memory loss, as was the case with the self-distraction strategy.*

These strategies can be employed by project managers and team members during the course of their project activities to regulate the destructive effects that can result from an overactive amygdala. Such over-activity results in adverse effects on both their decision-making abilities and their abilities to interact productively with other team members or stakeholders.

Neural Networks and Leadership Roles

In many theories about project leadership roles, two different roles are noted, people-oriented roles and task-oriented roles. Interestingly, the brain has two antagonistic neural networks, each of which underlies these separate leadership roles, the default mode network and the task positive network. The default mode network is active when the brain is not focused on accomplishing a specific task. It is the predominant network that is active much of the time an individual is awake, which is why it is called the default mode network. It plays a central role in emotional self-awareness, social cognition, and ethical decision-making. The predominant network is also linked to creativity and insightful problem-solving. It is the network that is active when people are daydreaming, thinking about problems from the past, and considering potential threats they might face in the future.

---

* Goldin, P.R. et al. March 2008. The neural bases of emotion regulation: Reappraisal and suppression of negative emotion. *Biological Psychiatry*, 63 (6), 557–586.

The task positive mode is important for leaders in analytical problem-solving, focusing attention, decision-making, and control of action, in other words, getting specific activities accomplished.

The two networks do not work simultaneously. When one is active, the other network tends not to be. Both networks are essential for various leadership roles. The former is essential for relational leadership roles, the latter for task leadership roles. Leaders use the default mode network for their emotional and social intelligence abilities, for solving problems with insight, and for seeking more creative approaches to project issues. For example, when interfacing with team members in instances that require empathy and ethical decision-making, the default mode network is engaged. When the project manager is focused on the task-oriented project management hard-skills, such as trying to select one of a number of qualified vendors for the awarding of a subcontract or reviewing a work breakdown structure to insure its completeness, the task positive network is engaged.*

Resilience

Project stops and restarts, reformulations of end-product requirements, the need to explore, train team members on, and employ new technologies during the course of the project, and changes due to the political strategies of significant stakeholders, result in frequent setbacks for the project manager and team, causing notable stress. Extended periods of uncertainty associated with these and other aspects of a complex project environment promote chronic stress for many of those team members involved.

Resilience has been defined as, "the ability to adapt and cope despite threatening or challenging situations and it is associated with the resumption of normality following excessive stress"† The importance of individual and team resilience cannot be overstated. Resilience is a competitive advantage for organizations executing complex projects.

---

* Boyatzis, R. et al. March 2014. Antagonistic neural networks underlying differentiated leadership roles. *Frontier in Human Neuroscience*, 8, Article 114.
† Agaibi, C.E., and Wilson, J.P. 2005. Trauma, PTSD, and resilience: a review of the literature. *Trauma Violence Abuse*, 6, 195–216. CrossRef Medline as cited in Ogeil, R., and Baker, K. January 28, 2015. The interaction REM sleep with safety learning in humans: Could a good night's sleep alter a traumatic experience? *Journal of Neuroscience*, 35 (4), 1337–1339.

Research has shown that there are ways to make the brain more resilient. They include mindfulness meditation training, computer-based cognitive brain training, physical exercise, and sufficient levels of sleep.[*]

■ Once viewed as a practice associated primarily with Eastern religions, *mindfulness meditation* has proven its efficacy even in a business environment. A number of businesses across the globe, such as Google, Aetna, IBM, and General Mills, have fostered the integration of mindfulness practices into their workers' daily lives, and for good reason.
  – Mindfulness meditation can buffer the impact of stress by decreasing the gray matter in the amygdala, while increasing the activation of the pre-frontal cortex.[†] Studies have shown that 2.5 hours of mindfulness meditation a week can, over an 8-week period, reduce individual burnout.[‡]
  – Mindfulness-based stress reduction practice has also been shown to increase the robustness of telomeres. Telomeres have been likened to the plastic protective tips at the end of shoelaces. They occur at the cellular level in the human body and consist of nucleotide sequences on the ends of chromosomes that protect against the chromosomes' deterioration over time or their fusion with neighboring chromosomes. Chromosome deterioration is linked to aging.[§]
  – Mindfulness also helps in the task-oriented leadership role by strengthening the brain's braking system, thereby enabling a purposeful reduction in the activity of the default mode network discussed earlier and subsequently allowing the task positive network to predominate.[¶]

---

[*] An excellent review of these and other methodologies that promote resilience in individuals can be found in Tabibnia and Radecki. 2018. Resilience training that can change the brain. *Consulting Psychology Journal: Practice and Research*, 70 (1), 59–88.

[†] Hülsheger, U.R., Alberts, H.J., Feinholdt, A., and Lang, J.W. March 2013. Benefits of mindfulness at work: The role of mindfulness in emotion regulation, emotional exhaustion, and job satisfaction. *Journal of Applied Psychology*, 98 (2), 310–325. doi: 10.1037/a0031313. Epub 2012 Dec 31.

[‡] Krasner, M.S., Epstein, R.M., Beckman, H., Suchman, A.L., Chapman, B., Mooney, C.J., and Quill, T.E. September 2009. Association of an educational program in mindful communication with burnout, empathy, and attitudes among primary care physicians. *JAMA*, 302 (12), 1284–1293. DOI: 10.1001/jama.2009.1384.

[§] http://dx.doi.org/10.1016/j.psyneuen.2010.09.010

[¶] Hölzel, C. et al. March 2010. Stress reduction correlates with structural changes in the amygdala. *Social Cognitive and Affective Neuroscience*, 5 (1), 11–17. Doi.org/10.1093/scan/nsp034.

■ *Computer-based cognitive brain training*, such as that cited at the end of the section on a positive mindset below, has proven helpful in strengthening the brain's pre-frontal cortex-based "braking system." The proper and repetitive use of this training has been associated with measurable improvements in cognitive and emotional well-being. Computer-based cognitive brain training additionally been associated with strengthening of inhibitory control network activity, though research into this field is still in its infancy and conflicting data exist as to the robustness of "brain training."*

■ Aside from its other well-known benefits, *physical exercise* can mitigate the negative impact of stress on the brain.† One way that it does this mitigation is by increasing the brain-derived neurotropic factor in the brain. Brain-derived neurotropic factor increases plasticity, which is necessary for learning and adaptive changes in the brain.‡ It is part of the family of nerve growth factors which mindfulness meditation has also been shown to help increase by counteracting the effects of stress. Physical exercise has also been shown to have a positive effect on promoting restful sleep; and, like mindfulness meditation, it has been shown to promote telomere growth.§

■ *Sleep* is another factor in promoting resilience. Rapid eye movement (REM) sleep is associated with the development of cognitive resources to manage stress and hyperarousal.¶ REM sleep typically occurs during the second half of a full night's sleep, which is 7–8 hours for most individuals. If an individual gets only 4–5 hours of sleep each night, much of the brain activity that occurs during REM sleep is truncated, resulting in a diminished ability to manage other brain activity associated with both memory and emotional arousal.

One other approach to increasing resilience has been demonstrated among individuals who work in specific fields in which they regularly

---

* Berkman, E.T., Kahn, L.E., and Merchant, J.S. January 1, 2014. Training-induced changes in inhibitory network activity. *Journal of Neuroscience*, 34 (1), 149–157. DOI.org/10.1523/JNEUROSCI.3564-13.2014.

† Tabibnia and Radecki, *op.cit.*

‡ Nokia, L. et al. 2016. Physical exercise increases adult hippocampal neurogenesis in male rats provided it is aerobic and sustained. *Journal of Physiology/Neuroscience*, 594.7, 1855–1873.

§ https://www.sciencedaily.com/releases/2017/05/170510115211.htm

¶ Payne, J.D., and Nadel, J. 2004. Sleep, dreams, and memory consolidation: The role of the stress hormone cortisol. *Sleep & Memory/Review*, 11, 671–678. www.learnmem.org/cgi/doi/10.1101/lm.77104.

encounter excessive amounts of stress. As Russo et al, note in their article in *Nature Neuroscience,* "it seems clear that moderate degrees of stress exposures during early life, adolescence and adulthood can shift an individual's stress-vulnerability curve to the right or broaden the curve by increasing the range of tolerable stress for the organism... Stress resilience is enhanced in specific populations, such as military personnel and rescue workers, through controlled exposure to stress-related stimuli."*

Military and emergency workers routinely undergo training designed to increase their stress inoculation to promote more positive outcomes in times of conflict and in other emergency situations. While there is no reason to believe that similar outcomes cannot be attained with appropriate training for project team members, further investigation needs to be done to ensure the validity of such training for a complex business and technical environment. Additionally, traditional organizations are reluctant to spend the amount of time necessary to inoculate team members through exposure to stress over time, as do those organizations involved in the military with training exercises.

Insight

The last area this introduction to neuroscience and project leadership will examine is insight. Insight is a critical part of creativity, which is a significant factor in efforts that need to address problems in novel ways, a hallmark of complex projects. Human beings use two approaches for problem solving: (1) the analytical approach; and (2) insight. The analytical approach was introduced earlier, during the discussion of the task positive neural network. It is focused and normally involves a specific process used to solve the problem at hand, such as mathematics to resolve a budget issue or a work breakdown structure to decompose the work that needs to be accomplished to produce a desired project deliverable. During the analytical process, the task positive network is activated and visual attention to the problem at hand increases until the process had been completed and the issue has been resolved.

From a brain perspective, insight is achieved in a different manner. While there are no predefined problem-solving processes to follow, achieving

---

* Russo, et al. November 2012. Neurobiology of resilience. *Nature Neuroscience*, 15 (11), 1478, 1482.

insight does appear to have a predictable process in the brain, as described in depth by Kounios.*

- First, the brain achieves a resting state in which distractions from an inward focus are minimized.
- Second, areas of the brain start to search and gather applicable memories from the past that might aid in devising a new strategy for attacking the problem at hand.
- The next step involves sensory gating or shutting down sensory input to focus non-consciously on the matter at hand. For instance, the person involved in the process may be seen closing or diverting her eyes upward in order to limit visual sensory input to the brain. The brain's electrical activity is dominated by alpha wave activity, at a frequency of 8–13 hertz, indicating that it is in a relaxed state. When queried about situations in which creative solutions occur to them, many individuals reply that they occur when exercising or while in the shower, both activities that produce an alpha wave state, which leads to the final step, gamma wave production.
- Just prior to achieving insight, the electrical activity switches to gamma waves, which occur at a much higher frequency, 25–100 hertz, indicating increased activity as the brain pushes to assemble its applicable stored memory to arrive at a unique solution. Shortly thereafter, the insight occurs, and the gamma wave production continues for a short period longer and then begins to drop. Upon reaching the insight, the neurotransmitter dopamine is released as a reward.

This process can be enhanced in people through a specific behavioral mindset—that of having a positive mood—which leads to solving more problems and using insight to solve more problems. Those individuals with higher anxiety solve fewer problems and fewer still using insight; in other words, they are less able to use their creativity. Mind-Body-Stress-Reduction has been shown to increase positive mood and decrease anxiety, thereby enhancing one's ability to solve problems through insight.†

---

* Kounios, J., and Beeman, M. 2014. The cognitive neuroscience of insight. *Annual Review of Psychology*, 65, 71–93. DOI: 10.1146/annurev-psych-010213-115154.

† *ibid.*

Positive Mindset

Having a positive mindset not only helps increase individual resilience and insight, it contributes other benefits as well. In a 1981 study, Harvard psychology professor Ellen Langer took two separate groups of men in their seventies and eighties to an old monastery in the wilds of New Hampshire in the United States. The surroundings inside and outside the monastery had been changed to resemble an environment similar to the late 1950s. The first group was taken a week prior to the second group. When the first group arrived, they were instructed to imagine themselves and act as they were as younger men living in the 1950s during their time at the monastery. The second group was only instructed to reminisce about the 1950s during their stay. The monastery was filled with mementos of the 1950s; black and white television, magazines from the period, an old radio. Their entertainment included discussions of political and sports events of the period, watching movies from the period, and listening to radio shows from the period. At the end of each group's stay, she ran physiological and psychological tests on those involved and compared them to the same tests she had run prior to their stay in the monastery. The results showed that those in both groups improved in both sets of tests; however, those in the first group improved significantly more than those in the second group. Those individuals who acted like they were younger appeared to have bodies mirroring that youth. (Feinberg, 2010)

Psychologist Barbara Fredrickson has studied the effects of both positive and negative mindsets. She has found that a negative mindset tends to narrow an individual's perceived options, for example, attack or flee. On the other hand, a positive mindset tends to broaden an individual's perceived options, such as play, explore, savor, and integrate. She has named this ability to perceive various options as one's "thought-action repertoire." (Fredrickson, 1998) In a 2011 paper, she and her co-author, Christine Branigan, described experiments that showed that positive emotions have other benefits as well. They note that while

> Past research has shown that people who experience and express positive emotions cope more effectively with chronic stress and other negative experiences...Fredrickson and Joiner (2002) found that people who experience positive emotions show a style of broad-minded coping in which they step back from their current problems and consider them from multiple angles. The broadened

scopes of attention and thinking inherent within such broad-minded coping, we speculate, might also underlie the three types of coping...linked to the occurrence and maintenance of positive emotions during chronic stress: positive reappraisal, goal-directed problem-focused coping, and the infusion of ordinary events with positive meaning. Together with positive emotions, these coping strategies have been linked to thriving despite adversity

(Fredrickson & Branigan, Positive emotions broaden the scope of attention and thought-action repertoires, 2005).

Finally, in another 2005 paper, Fredrickson and Kareem Johnson noted experiments that indicate that a positive emotional state reduces the likelihood of own-race bias, the in-group and out-group bias noted above, in facial-recognition studies. (Johnson & Fredrickson, 2005)

The benefits of a positive emotional state for both the project manager and team members are clear. In the uncertain environment of a complex project, stress will frequently push team members past eustress, the positive stress noted earlier, and into adverse stress. This stress may adversely affect not only team member interactions but also interactions among team members and stakeholders. As is wont to occur in a complex system with reinforcing feedback loops, additional unnecessary stress may thereby be generated. Project managers and team members need to understand the importance of maintaining a positive emotional state throughout the project, particularly during ambiguous periods of the project.

But how does one go about developing a more positive emotional state? There are resources available for those project managers and team members interested in achieving this emotional state. Meditation alone can help an individual focus on the positive things that are occurring in the present during everyday life. MyBrainSolutions.com is a clinical-based website* that offers numerous exercises shown to help individuals develop positivity, reduce stress, practice relaxed breathing, and meditate. For those project managers and team members who may be acting as organizational coaches, a positive psychology toolkit is available that provides assessment, exercises, metaphors, and other positive psychology aids.† And numerous

---

* Located at https://www.mybrainsolutions.com/index.aspx
† More information is available at https://positivepsychologytoolkit.com/
  join/?_ga=2.84849561.1476918721.1511879576-1858629479.1511879576

books on positive psychology are available were one to choose that path to understanding how to develop a more positive outlook.*

Summary

The human brain has evolved over millennia. Evolution over such a long period has left its imprint for better and for worse. There are four principles that need to be remembered when considering how the brain works:

- The brain has evolved more slowly than human society and technology. The complexity of the business and technological environments may have an adverse or complicating effect on the brain's decision-making capabilities.
- The primary concern of the brain is to ensure individual safety. There are approximately five times as many neural networks searching for threats as there are for rewards. The Academy for Brain-based Leadership has developed a model, the SAFETY™ model, that represents the six domains in which the brain searches for threats and opportunities:
  – Security
  – Autonomy
  – Fairness
  – Esteem
  – Trust
  – You
- The preponderance of the activities of the brain happen non-consciously and automatically.
- The human brain has a need for sociality, a need to interact with other humans. Negative results may obtain when that need is not met.

Today's complex business environment and the ambiguity inherent therein present the project manager and project team with a direct challenge to the "security" and other domains of the SAFETY™ model. The result is increased, sometimes chronic, stress for those involved in complex projects.

---

* Martin Seligman, who many view as the founder of the positive psychology movement in the United States, has written a number of books on the subject that are currently in print and also available electronically.

It is important that the project manager and her team members understand and are aware of the inverse U-curve to understand when they are moving from a productive level of stress to a debilitating level.

The brain's neural networks work in two different modes, the default mode network, and the task positive network, both of which play their part in an individual's ability to provide leadership to those around him. The former is people-oriented and the latter task-oriented.

Because of the frequent changes, stops, and restarts caused by ambiguity in complex projects, resilience is an important capability for project managers and team members. Four things have been shown to increase an individual's resilience: mindfulness meditation, sufficient sleep, exercise, and computer-based cognitive brain training. Additionally, some studies suggest that gradual levels of exposure to stress over time may also increase resilience.

Project complexity may also require innovative approaches to solving issues that arise during the course of a project. Developing the ability to use one's insight may help in resolving these issues. Neuroscience has enabled an understanding of what goes on in the brain in achieving insight. Insight can be improved through stress reduction and a positive emotional balance.

A positive emotional balance has other benefits as well. It has been shown to improve one's health, broaden an individual's perspective of available options, and reduce own-race bias, all of which are beneficial to the individual and the organization during the course of a complex project.

Chapter 4

Minimizing the Effects of Bias in Project and Program Decision-Making

Carl Belack

Contents

Introduction

Project and program managers make decisions many times during their typical working day. These decisions may include which human resources to put on activities, what steps need to be taken to make up lost time due to an activity that overran its scheduled duration, how to identify and enhance a project opportunity, or how to approach a stakeholder to obtain their support for a project or program. One would like to believe that these decisions are made thoughtfully and rationally without any other interference in that thought process. Unfortunately, this situation is frequently not the case. One reason is that human brains acquire and maintain biases, and these biases account for much of the irrational decision-making that occurs both in life generally and on projects and programs specifically.

The previous chapter briefly contained a discussion of what biases are and how they have evolved. This chapter initially contains a discussion about some myths around the rationality of human decision-making. A model of two processes is provided through which the brain makes decisions: one automatic, the other more laborious and thoughtful. The chapter then continues with a discussion about a number of biases that are most identifiable in organizations both prior to and during the project or program management life cycle, including optimism bias, loss aversion bias, and others. While discussing biases may be informative, such discussion does little to help project or program managers in addressing the adverse effects they may experience on their projects or program components or with interactions with their project or program stakeholders. Therefore, several approaches to help the project or program manager recognize and minimize the adverse effects of these biases will be discussed.

Automaticity and the Brain

Animal brains, including those of human beings, have evolved over time. As the reader learned in the previous chapter, in its evolution the human brain developed heuristics to aid in the aspects of existence. These heuristics are shortcuts to facilitate decision-making throughout each and every day of a typical human lifetime. The positive effects of these heuristics are too plentiful to enumerate in this text; however, it should be noted that these mental shortcuts allow the human brain to cope with the amount of information it is required to process in a typical day and even more so when under stress. An individual's brain engages heuristics from the time a person opens her eyes in the morning, until the time she falls asleep at night. Her brain also uses heuristics during periods of sleep. An individual's heuristics determine when she is in a safe environment, and more importantly, they alert her almost immediately when she is about to encounter danger. They make fight or flight decisions for her. As noted in the previous chapter, many of these behavioral decisions are passed on from generation to generation through the process of evolution. It is astonishing to consider how effective the human brain has become by incorporating heuristics; in other words, it has become increasingly more frugal as greater demands for decision processing have been placed upon it. One need only think about what happens in the brain when it sees someone performing an act that results in a sound—like a girl bouncing a basketball. Even though the speed of sound is slower than the speed of light, the brain synchronizes the perception of both, so the viewer sees the ball hit the ground and hears it hitting the ground simultaneously*—truly amazing!

Nonetheless, some of the brain's reactions to sensory input cues, which have developed to alert the limbic system to danger, now trigger the brain when such danger no longer exists. Additionally, of the 11 million bits of sensory information that reach the brain each second, it can only consciously process about 50 bits per second.[†] So the brain needs to be selective about those relatively few bits of information to which it pays attention. Doing otherwise would slow one's decision-making process to a slow crawl. Despite what one might like to think about how well the human brain works, it has significant gaps in how it perceives the information it receives, or how capable it is of processing the information it has received. The behavior resulting from this cue reaction and other legacy triggers may run counter to an individual's best interests and to the interests of those with whom that individual interacts. These reactions are due to heuristics gone bad, also known as biases.

As two prominent psychological researchers have noted "these heuristics are highly economical and usually effective, but they lead to systematic and predictable errors."[‡] Good magicians, illusionists, and con artists support themselves and their families by fooling their audiences' brains for both good and ill by thoroughly understanding and exploiting these biases. While studying advanced physics at Columbia University, magician Alex Stone "began to notice a number of connections between magic and science—especially psychology, neuroscience, mathematics and physics. Magic at its core is about toying with the limits of perception."[§]

---

* This occurs as long as the distance between the viewer and the ball is 33.5 meters or less. In other words, as long as the two sensory inputs (the sight of the ball hitting the ground and the resulting sound) are received within 80 milliseconds of each other, the brain can effectively make them seem like they are happening simultaneously. But once the viewing distance exceeds 33.5 meters, they appear to be asynchronous.

† https://cienciaemnovotempo.wordpress.com/categorias/fisica-neurociencia/how-much-information-processing-the-brain/, accessed on August 29, 2017.

‡ Tversky, A., and Kahneman, D. 1974. Judgment under uncertainty: Heuristics and biases, *Science*, 185 (4157), pp. 1124–1131.

§ Stone, A. 2012. *Fooling Houdini*. (Harper Collins, New York), p. 5.

The use of the word "perception" is critical. Many definitions of the word "perception" incorporate the term "opinion," which has at its root a series of biases. As the reader will see, these limits of perception can have disastrous effects for project and program managers and their teams.

How human brains have evolved and how they work has been the subjects of much discussion, study, theorizing, and clinical experimentation. For a number of centuries, human beings were thought to be able, for the most part, to make rational decisions, particularly when it came to economic decisions.* For the last 15 years, functional magnetic resonance imaging has allowed neuroscientists to understand which areas of the brain are engaged by different types of stimuli, and how stimulated areas interact to undertake certain tasks. This technology has enabled neuroscientists to see what areas of the brain are engaged and to what extent when under duress in stressful situations. However, even before the advent of functional magnetic resonance imaging, psychologists Daniel Kahneman and Amos Tversky posited their now-famous *prospect theory* that discussed irrationality in human decision-making under conditions of risk.† In this now famous paper,‡ the authors delivered a critique of expected utility theory, which suggests that reasonable people make rational choices in decisions most of time. In contrast, they argued that "utility theory…is not an adequate descriptive model and we propose an alternative account of choice under risk."§ In their paper the authors discuss how individuals choose among alternatives in contexts involving risk or uncertainty. They suggest that such decisions are made with respect to a reference point rather than potential absolute outcomes.¶ Certain types of decisions made under risk are clearly suboptimal. Despite the absolute equality of outcomes for gains and losses along the "outcome" axis, losses are perceived as having a greater impact along the value axis. This perception frequently results in risk-taking behavior, particularly for project, program, and portfolio managers, due to

---

* For further information see *rational choice theory* in game theory and *expected utility theory* in economics.
† Kahneman, D, and Tversky, A, 1979. Prospect theory: An analysis of decision under risk. *Econometrica*, 47 (2) (The Econometric Society), pp. 263–291.
‡ Daniel Kahneman received the 2002 Nobel prize in economics for this paper. Amos Tversky died in 1997 and Nobel prizes are not given posthumously.
§ Kahneman, D., and Tversky, A. 1997. Prospect theory: An analysis of decision under risk. *Econometrica*, 47 (2) (John Wiley and Sons, New York), p. 263.
¶ https://commons.wikimedia.org/wiki/File:ValunFunProspectTheory2.png#/media/File:ValunFunProspectTheory2.png, accessed on August 24, 2017.

decisions that are influenced by *loss-aversion bias*, also known as *sunk-cost bias*.

Sunk-cost bias has been used to posit theories for decisions made for countries continuing war, or continuing economic and legislative positions, beyond where the value proposition would justify the continuation of action. It has also been used to explain why individuals may stay in relationships beyond when the relationship is beneficial to either party. The phrase often used in such situations is "I have already invested so much time and money." It is a phrase often heard when organizations continue to invest in a project or program components that appear to be failing.

Kahneman went on to co-author a number of other influential papers in this area or on related topics, some of which will be discussed further in this chapter. However, in his 2011 book, *Thinking, Fast and Slow*, he posits that there are two metaphorical systems the brain uses to process information and make decisions (Kahneman, 2011).* System 1 is the system that does the quick, reflexive, almost immediate decision-making, with much of this work being done in the sub-cortex, primarily in the limbic system, the area of the brain that largely supports the emotional and behavioral responses. System 2 does the more intricate thinking and decision-making, and that work is primarily done in the cortex, specifically in the prefrontal cortex, as described in the preceding chapter.[†]

Kahneman uses the following example to illustrate the difference between the workings of the two systems. He suggests that the reader use his intuition to solve the following problem that consists of three statements:

A bat and ball cost $1.10.
The bat costs $1.00 more than the ball.
How much does the ball cost?[‡]

For many people, their intuition will quickly, but incorrectly tell them that the answer is 10 cents. That is because the brain's System 1 quickly does the following mathematical calculation:

---

* This book is essential reading for project or program managers who want to understand in some detail how their brains make decisions, and the effects that biases have on those decisions and on our interpersonal actions.
† The reader is referred to the interplay between the limbic system and the pre-frontal cortex described in the previous chapter.
‡ Kahneman, D. 2011. *Thinking, Fast and Slow.* (Farrar, Straus, Giroux, New York), p. 44.

$$1.10-1.00 = 0.10.$$

However, were the reader to give this problem a bit more thought, using System 2, he would realize that there are three mathematical statements that define the problem:

$$x + y = 1.10,$$

where x is the bat and y is the ball

$$x-y = 1.00$$

$$y = ?$$

When the second equation is subtracted from the first, the result is $2y = 0.10$. Therefore $y = 0.05$. Most brains typically opt for the first method that employs System 1 rather than using System 2.[*] Why might that be? Kahneman suggests that a significant purpose of System 2 is to act as a controller over System 1, to monitor its activities and to step in and take over when more concentrated effort, rather than merely intuitive reacting, is necessary. Unfortunately, System 2 tends to be lazy because its use requires a great deal of energy, which the brain ultimately tries to conserve, and subsequently it reverts to using System 1.[†] "Though it accounts for only 2% of body weight, [the brain] accounts for 20% of the body's resting metabolic rate" (Jabr, 2012).

In their book *Willpower*, Roy Baumeister and John Tierney report that making compromises (decision-making) takes willpower, and using willpower expends brain energy:

> When your willpower is low you're less able to make these tradeoffs. You become what researchers call a "cognitive miser" hoarding your energy by avoiding compromises.[‡]

Baumeister and Tierney continue to provide the example of what one typically experiences when purchasing a car. For most people the decision

---

[*] Over 50% of the students at Harvard, MIT, and Princeton gave the answer of 10 cents rather than the correct answer. Over 80% gave the incorrect answer at less selective universities, according to Kahneman. *ibid.,* p. 45.

[†] Kahneman, *op. cit.,* p.44.

[‡] (Baumeister & Tierney, 2011) Baumeister, R., and Tierney, J. 2011. *Willpower.* (Penguin Press, New York), p. 102.

to purchase a car is a difficult one at best. Buying a car requires a significant monetary investment. The brain will use a lot of energy just to make the decision of which car to buy. However, as if that was not difficult enough, after the decision to buy a particular make and model has been made, the salesman will purposely go through a long list of options that the buyer then needs to consider in the decision process. The energy used in these decisions will eventually wear down even the most seasoned negotiator. When studying this process, researchers found that a clever car salesperson could get the average buyer to spend €1,500.00 (approximately $1,950 USD) more than the original purchase price merely by manipulating the order in which she presented various options to the buyer.* The salesperson does this knowing full well that when a brain's energy source is depleted or near depletion, it can also lead to one's inability to adequately engage System 2, which might otherwise put a stop to this excessive spending. Before one is consciously aware, one has agreed to options one may not have agreed to purchase earlier in the negotiation decision process.

For project and program managers, the corollary is the negotiation for major procurements. Subcontractors often offer to provide a variety of services to make the work move faster, smoother, and cheaper; however, when the bottom line is realized after the negotiations, the cost of the procurement has escalated from the initially projected cost for the work when planning the project or program component. Even though a project or program team including subcontract professionals may do the negotiation, the human brain is still only able to process so much material and so many options.

In *Behave: The Biology of Humans at Our Best and Worst*, Robert Sapolsky, professor of biology, neurology, and neurological sciences at Stanford University suggests that there are many interlacing systemic causes affecting decision-making and behavior. He examines these causes using a timeline suggesting that specific behavior may be influenced by: cognitive biases that occur within a second of a particular behavior; sights, sounds, and smells that may occur seconds to minutes prior to the behavior; hormones that may have acted hours to days prior to the behavior; an environment that may have affected the structure of the brain weeks to years prior to the behavior; the effect childhood upbringing may have had on the brain; genetic and perinatal effects; and finally, by cultural behavior

---

* *ibid.*, p. 104.

effects of the group or groups to which that individual belongs. In all, his examination is an exhaustive and enlightening one. (Sapolsky, 2017)

Regardless of the causes of these biases, one is left with fact that these biases exist and affect our behavior continuously. Biases result in the brain defaulting to the use of System 1, the brain's legacy system; when System 2 would be better engaged in the decision-making process. This accounts for the biases that adversely affect our abilities to make optimal decisions. Some of the more obvious biases, which result in the greatest harm to project and program management, are explored in the following section.

Some Significant Biases

There are well over 150 biases that have been identified to date. Any one or more of these biases may come into play during the course of a typical project or program. This section provides an examination of a number of the more recognizable biases that project or program managers and teams will regularly encounter throughout their working careers. These biases, in the order in which they are presented in this book (not the order of importance or impact to any one project or program), are the following:

- Optimism bias and planning fallacy
- Anchoring bias
- Cognitive dissonance and confirmation bias
- Loss-aversion (also known as sunk-cost bias)
- Framing effect
- Ingroup/outgroup bias

Optimism bias and *planning fallacy* may affect the project from its very inception and continue throughout the project life cycle. *Optimism bias*, sometimes referred to as *the rose-colored glasses bias*, occurs because human beings have a tendency to "overestimate the probability of positive events and underestimate the probability of negative events."* An example in our private lives would be underestimating the risk of being in an automobile accident or having a heart attack, as compared to other people.

---

* Sheppard, J. et al. Exploring the causes of comparative optimism. *Psychologica Belgica*, 42, p. 65, © 2002.

A closely related bias compounds this bias. The *planning fallacy* was identified and named by Kahneman and Tversky, and it describes "plans and forecasts that are unrealistically close to best-case scenarios."[*] These biases result in situations familiar to project and program managers, such as projects whose time and cost expectations are significantly underestimated and whose benefit expectations are significantly overestimated by executives and senior managers, even before the projects are chartered. Two examples are: the Sydney Opera House was originally planned for four years and $7 million AUS, but was finished in fourteen years and $102 million AUS; and the "Big Dig," an underground highway and bridge system in Boston, was originally estimated to cost $2.4 billion USD but ended up costing over $14 billion USD. The reasons for this optimism include:

- A "tendency of individuals to exaggerate their own talents"
- A "tendency to misperceive the causes of certain events…to take credit for positive outcomes and to attribute negative outcomes to external factors, no matter what their true cause"
- A "tend[ency] to exaggerate the degree of control we have over events, discounting the role of luck."[†‡]

As anyone who has been involved in projects or programs is aware, there will be deleterious effects from trying to meet unachievable cost and time expectations. Further the effects produce equally unachievable benefits and wreak unimaginable havoc on the project or program component teams. The project or program manager and team members are constantly taking shortcuts that are inevitably counterproductive and place even greater stress on team members and stakeholders, much of which is due to the automaticity with which the human brain works.[§] The results of project schedule and costs overruns due to this optimism are legendary in project and program management, particularly in these documented complex projects:

---

[*] Kahneman, *op. cit.,* p. 250.

[†] Lovallo, D., and Kahneman, D. July 2003. Delusions of success: How optimism undermines executives' decisions. *Harvard Business Review,* (Harvard University Press, Cambridge) p. 2.

[‡] This last item cannot be emphasized enough. Most people greatly underestimate the role that chance, or luck, plays in project outcomes and in life outcomes as well. For an excellent perspective of that role, the reader is directed to Taleb (2006) in the bibliography.

[§] It should be noted that not all initial project underestimates are caused by unconscious biases. As Bent Flyvbjerg, Director of Oxford University's BT Centre for Major Programme Management, notes, forecasters and planners intentionally underestimate costs and overestimate benefits of their projects in order to gain an advantage over competitors (Flyvbjerg, 2008).

- The Sydney Opera House
- The Boston Central Artery Project, also known as "The Big Dig"
- The Scottish Parliament Building
- Three Gorges Dam
- The Denver International Airport
- The Channel Tunnel
- World Trade Center Transportation H
- Montreal Olympic Stadium
- Budapest Metro Line 4

All of these efforts had significant cost and schedule overruns, many of which exceeded their original budgets by over $1 billion USD (McCarthy, 2010). These projects, of course, are extreme examples of well-documented, public sector construction projects. Nonetheless, they are representative of what most project and program managers and teams will encounter, albeit on a somewhat smaller scale, at some point in their careers. It should be noted that even when other stakeholders are part of the decision process, they are often affected by the optimism bias. For example, when a government authorizes large construction projects, government officials are often part of the decision or authorizing process for budgets and schedules but may even influence this authorizing process with the infusion of more optimism about how well the project will proceed from the time of initiation to closure. In fact, project or program managers have experienced having their overly optimistic budgets and schedules affected by becoming even more optimistic, thus creating even smaller budgets with shorter timelines with increased risks.

But wait, one might say, the project or program manager and project or program team have a chance to correct these unrealistic expectations when they develop a detailed work breakdown structure, schedule, budget, and resourcing plan, or when the program manager reviews the integrated schedule impacts. This detailed plan will theoretically bring realism into the process and reset the executives' and other project and program stakeholders' expectations. Unfortunately, as reassuring as this idealized process may sound, it rarely works that way. The process does not work that way because **anchoring bias** is "one of the strongest and most prevalent of cognitive biases."* Once early estimates are established, regardless of how inaccurate or random their method of development might have been, people will

---

* Lovallo, D. and Kahneman, D., *op. cit.,* p. 3.

tend to "anchor" on those estimates, even when terms such as "based on a conceptual design" are used. In other words, once project schedule, cost, and benefit expectations are initially established, it is difficult to get stakeholders and team members in whose minds the initial baseline expectations were established to substantially revise them. Project and program managers in reviewing the lessons learned from projects and programs during closure often find that the development of the plan was based upon the initial data gathered to the exclusion of data that arrived later, even if received prior to submittal of the final plan. For example, there were many risks identified in the mid-planning stages of the "Big Dig," such as environmental and political risks, as well as urban planning, that were ignored in favor of the initial cost and schedule figures that were submitted to the team. With the Channel Tunnel, the lowest bidder's submission became the anchor bias even when prior to submittal to the final plan several items, including the need for air conditioning, issues regarding financing models, and communication, became apparent as not being accounted for in the budget and schedule. Each of the projects listed have similar stories: the projects were tied to an optimistic initial estimate or estimates of one or more planning element; in other words, the projects were subject to anchoring bias.

Numerous studies have been done to validate how anchoring bias works. Kahneman cites many of these studies in his book, including the following two. In the first, two groups of students were successively gathered around a roulette wheel, which was rigged for the ball to stop at either 10 or 65. One group saw the wheel stop at 10, the other at 65. The students were asked to write down the number on which they saw the ball stop. Shortly thereafter, they were asked to estimate the percentage of African nations among the United Nations member states. The average answers of each group clearly reflected the anchoring to the number on which they saw the ball land on the roulette wheel: the group that saw 10 on the wheel had an average estimate of 26%, and the group that saw 65 on the wheel had an average estimate of 46%. Another experiment involved two groups of people, one a group comprised of real estate professionals, and the other comprised of business school students with no real estate experience. Each group was divided in half, shown a house and property on which it resided, and each group was given a booklet describing a house that was actually on the market. The booklets included a list of property attributes, including the asking price. One of each group's booklets had a lower asking price, and the other had a higher asking price. Each group was then asked to give their opinions about what they believed a reasonable asking price would be. Both real estate professionals and students gave prices that were clearly affected by the "anchors" in the booklets they were given. Interestingly, the students admitted that their estimates were affected by the prices in the booklets, while the real estate professionals insisted their estimates were not affected! This example just goes to show that even experts are not immune to anchoring bias. In other experiments, it was also shown that when given a chance to adjust their initial estimates after seeing information that ran contrary to those estimates, experts were less inclined than non-experts to appropriately adjust their estimates.*

Clearly optimism bias, the planning fallacy, and anchoring present significant problems for project managers, team members, and stakeholders. In Chapter 1, the butterfly effect, a result of sensitivity to initial conditions, was said to have a direct impact on complex systems. Such is the case with the initial condition of unachievable outcome expectations for almost any kind of project or program, but it is certainly even more so for a complex project or program. The final section of this chapter provides a discussion of a specific method, reference-based forecasting, for mitigating the adverse effects of these biases in developing initial project estimates. However, since project schedules, budgets, and expectations are frequently re-estimated throughout the duration of the project and program components, optimism bias and the planning fallacy will continue to affect new estimates.

There are two other common, pernicious biases that seem to work synergistically with one another throughout a project or program as well, **cognitive dissonance** and **confirmation bias**. *Cognitive dissonance* is well described in the Simon and Garfunkel song, "The Boxer," when it notes, "still a man hears what he wants to hear and disregards the rest" (Simon, 1969). When an individual makes a decision and subsequently receives facts that run counter to that decision, it provokes discomfort in the brain. The occurrence of cognitive dissonance activates the anterior cingulate cortex responsible in part for attention, reward anticipation, and decision-making; and the anterior insula involved in such functions as emotion, perception, and cognitive functioning. These areas of the brain, which share connections between the amygdala and the pre-frontal cortex, are involved in the roles of emotional reaction and behavior moderation respectively and were discussed in Chapter 3. The activation of these areas of the brain causes the discomfort noted. In order to reduce or eliminate the discomfort upon seeing the new facts, the individual's brain will block or

---

* Kahneman, D. *op. cit.*, pp. 118–126.

disregard information that runs counter to the beliefs that led to his decision. Thus, this action reinforces his beliefs. The same individual will continue to only seek out information that confirms his decision, *confirmation bias.* Strikingly, the more important the decision and beliefs, the stronger both biases seem to act.

One can see these two biases at work throughout everyday real-world encounters. People are bombarded non-stop by what others would like them to believe. Media promoting beliefs in products, religions, political perspectives, and other ideologies are ubiquitous in today's technological, media-driven world. Kahneman says, "System 1 is gullible and biased to believe. System 2 is in charge of doubting and unbelieving, but System 2 is sometimes busy, and often lazy."* The result is that when System 2 is otherwise engaged, or the brain is tired and depleted of energy; it cannot effectively expend the resources to undertake the effort required to undo the belief of a falsehood. As an example, when multiple electronic devices divert the brain with multiple messages, the brain is engaged and cannot divert its limited resources to undertake the effort required to undo the belief of a falsehood.

The implications of these two biases during the course of a complex project or program are obvious. The ambiguity that attends complex projects or programs requires the project or program manager and team members to be flexible and adaptable. Both necessitate the regular re-examination of beliefs, assumptions, and decisions that are made during the normal course of a project or program. Both cognitive dissonance and confirmation bias act against an individual's willingness and perhaps ability to conduct these needed re-evaluations to the detriment of the project or program components. For the project and program manager, both biases mean asking questions that may make the team uncomfortable. Such discomfort arises because the questioning challenges team members' biases. The questioning should also seek to understand the level of existing disagreement and to promote discourse; conflicting data should be reviewed and discussed in earnest with the team and affected stakeholders. If this discussion and discourse causes issues with egos, one generally will know that it is challenging the confirmation bias.

Loss-aversion, or **sunk-cost bias**, was one of the biases identified by Kahneman and Tversky during their work leading up to the development of prospect theory. Their experiments brought to light what Kahneman

---

* Kahneman, D. *op.cit.,* p. 81.

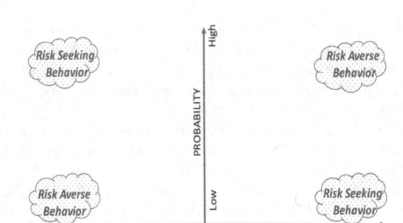

Figure 4.1   The fourfold pattern.

calls the *fourfold pattern*, which represents predictive patterns of behavior that human beings exhibit when making decisions in uncertain or risky situations.

Kahneman and Tversky's findings show that, in certain situations, people are loss averse—that is, they dislike losses more than they appreciate equivalent gains, and people are therefore willing to take risks to avoid those losses.* An example of this bias is when one has invested in a huge house that now has foundation issues, one invests money to fix those issues. Then the electrical is discovered to be inadequate and must be replaced to meet code, so one invests additional money to fix those issues. The next issue arises and one feels because one has sunk so much money into the huge house that one must fix the next issue and the next—the sunk cost.

The significance from a project and program management perspective is the risk-seeking behavior shown in the upper left corner of Figure 4.1. In a project context, this typically represents a large project to which significant resources, funding, time, and energy have been allocated but which, nonetheless, seems to be hopelessly failing. Regardless of the high probability that the project will fail, management continues to pour additional funds and resources into the project precisely because of this cognitive bias, loss-aversion. Most project managers have been witness to the "zombie" project, the failing project that refuses to die. Unfortunately, this phenomenon extends well beyond the project setting and into the international political system as well. The battlefields of the world have been

---

* Kahneman, D. and Tversky, A. *op.cit.*, p. 287.

littered with the remains of brave individuals whose leadership refused to recognize the futility of their situations due to loss-aversion bias. The effects of this bias continue to play out on the world stage to this day.

The way in which an issue or problem is presented, or *framed*, directly effects the decision one makes about the issue. In everyday parlance, one sometimes refers to this occurrence as the glass half full or the glass half empty. Technically this presentation is known as the ***framing effect***. Kahneman and Tversky exposed this bias in a paper they published in 1981:

> The psychological principles that govern the perception of decision problems and the evaluation of probabilities and outcomes produce predictable shifts of preference when the same problem is framed in different ways. Reversals of preference are demonstrated in choices regarding monetary outcomes, both hypothetical and real, and in questions pertaining to the loss of human lives. (Kahneman and Tversky, 1981)

One of the experiments Kahneman and Tversky cited to prove their findings was the now famous Asian disease experiment and poses the following scenario. Imagine that a town in the United States is preparing for the outbreak of an unusual disease that originated in Asia. Two alternative programs have been proposed to address the disease. A first group of respondents were given the following scientific estimates of each program:

- If Program A is adopted, 200 people will be saved.
- If Program B is adopted, there is a 1/3 probability that 600 people will be saved, and a 2/3 probability that no people will be saved.

Respondents were then asked which of the two programs they would favor. A second group of respondents were shown the exact same scenario but were given the following scientific estimates of each program:

- If Program C is adopted, 400 people will die.
- If Program D is adopted, there is a 1/3 probability that no one will die, and a 2/3 probability that 600 people will die.

Respondents were again asked which of the two programs they would favor. The reader should keep in mind that *statistically* the outcomes of all four programs are identical: the probability is that 200 people will live regardless of which of the four programs is selected. The results of the experiment showed that the first group of respondents selected Program A, the risk averse choice. The second group selected Program D, the risk seeking choice. The major difference is that in the first scenario, the estimates are framed in the context of how many lives will be *saved*. In the second, the estimates are framed in the context of how many lives will be *lost*. Again, in the authors' words:

> The majority choice in decision (i) is risk averse: a riskless prospect is preferred to a risky prospect of equal or greater expected value. In contrast, the majority choice in decision (ii) is risk taking: a risky prospect is preferred to a riskless prospect of equal expected value.*

These results are informative in two respects for project and program managers, who make multiple decisions every day: (1) the need to be careful of how they frame decisions for project teams so as not to inadvertently favor one alternative over another; and, (2) the need to carefully examine the way in which decision scenarios are presented, so they can be aware of how the scenarios may bias their impending decision.

For a project or program manager, the manner in which a risk is framed will affect how its mitigation strategy is designed. An example of this is when one is at a stakeholder meeting on a critical issue facing the project or a series of program components and the project or program manager is leading the discussion. The framing of the discussion topics, questions, and issues can change the meeting from one that is positive, negative, or neutral or a mixture of the three. As the project or program manager, the need to think through the framing of the topics, questions, and issues for that meeting is critical and the understanding that framing can be tiered from one discussion to the next is essential.

The last bias to be examined is the ingroup/outgroup bias. As biases go, this is probably one of the most insidious, at least from a sociological perspective. There are at least two possible theories as to why this bias exists. As mentioned in Chapter 3, one of the driving forces for human beings is to make sure that their own genes are replicated and perpetuated throughout the human gene pool. However, an individual's genes are drawn from one's parents, and some of those genes are shared not only with

---

* Kahneman, D. and Tversky, January 30, 1981. The framing of decisions and the psychology of choice. *Science*, 211, 454.

siblings and children but also with aunts, uncles, cousins, and other kin. So, human beings genetically favor kin groups over other groups.* The other theory about this bias is that the human body has two immune systems, one proactive and one reactive. When one is infected with a disease, the reactive immune system goes into action, developing antibodies and raising body temperature to destroy the body's invaders. However, the bias against people from outgroups is believed to be a function of the proactive immune system. As humans have evolved, individuals from the same kin group typically shared the same environment, ate the same foods, were exposed to the same kinds of diseases, and developed immunities to those same diseases. When exposed to outgroups who carried diseases against which an ingroup had not developed immunological protections, these new diseases could easily devastate those in the ingroup. As a protective device, the brain therefore developed a behavioral immune system in the guise of a bias against those in outgroups (Schaller, 2011).

The adverse effects of this bias are easily identifiable and have persisted throughout the evolution of *Homo sapiens*: ethnic, racial, religious, political, and philosophical conflict. It is conceivably the greatest individual cause of wars, terrorism, and other violent and non-violent conflict. While violent conflict may not exist in project environments, non-violent technical, ideological, and political conflict provides a continuing source of friction among project and program teams and other project stakeholder groups. While kin group conflict may have been one of the original sources for the ingroup/outgroup bias, this bias now takes on other dimensions of inclusion and exclusion. People today may belong to several groups, not just a kin group. For instance, those within one's social network may be considered to be among an ingroup.

The implications for project and program managers are significant. Team members within a project or program may view each other as their ingroup and those outside the project or program as outgroup members. Within a project team, those team members who are co-located may consider themselves as an ingroup, and those at other remote locations may be considered as part of the outgroup. Project stakeholders may form influence groups that may be in conflict with other groups. The list can go on and on, and the inherent difficulties for managing the project are compounded exponentially.

---

* A frequent saying among anthropologists that reinforces this theory is that "one sibling equals two cousins."

For program managers, the issues may manifest themselves internally to the program with project components setting up ingroup components and outgroup components. This manifestation may result in human resources not being shared with outgroup components by the ingroup components, causing scheduling difficulties, which may in turn cause budget issues.

With the previous discussion in mind, the next portion of the chapter examines ways in which project managers and team members can attempt to minimize the adverse effects that these biases have on project or program outcomes.

Bias Mitigation Approaches

A number of different ways of addressing biases have been recommended over the past few decades. There are three general ways of addressing biases that will be covered in this text:

■ A generic method for addressing biases
■ Methods for addressing sets of biases
■ Methods for addressing individual biases

Generic Method

A *generic method for addressing biases* involves three steps: (1) *acknowledging* that human beings have biases that can adversely affect their decision making and interpersonal behavior; (2) *recognizing* the bias as it occurs in the brain; and (3) *minimizing* or *mitigating* the effects of the recognized bias. This method can easily be recalled with the acronym *ARM*: acknowledge, recognize, and minimize.

Acknowledging that one has biases, that one is biased, can indeed be a difficult thing to do. In the English language, when one is described as "biased" such description typically has a negative connotation. Being called "biased" is equated with being called prejudiced, and, indeed, the brain has in fact evolved to pre-judge situations in order to enable the safety of the individual. Therefore, it may be difficult for one to admit to one's obvious biases. It is even more difficult admitting to biases that one does not even know exist, hence the purpose of this chapter. The first difficult step for project and program managers and team members is to admit the existence of these biases and resolve to take steps to minimize their negative influences. Some team building exercises that can be used during kick-off meetings will ask for team members to list thoughts or ideas that they have regarding the project or program components. The lists often highlight to the team many biases that are held. It is important this type of exercise be facilitated and that no team is identified with any one thought or idea, but that they admit they exist, so the next step can begin.

Recognizing and ***minimizing*** these biases are even more difficult to accomplish but can be done through diligent and thoughtful practice. There is a time lag of approximately 150 milliseconds between when the bias's electrical initiation occurs in the brain and conscious awareness of that action takes place. Within that interval, an individual can choose to counteract or minimize that impulse (Pychyl, 2011). As an example, Herman knows that he is overweight and needs to avoid eating high-caloric foods like pastries, cookies, gelato, and similar foods. One day he is at work and his teammate is having a birthday celebration. Naturally, high-caloric foods are involved in the celebration. Herman enters the room where the celebration is taking place, and his nose immediately picks up the aroma of freshly baked pastries and his brain makes a decision as it has evolved to do that it wants to consume a few of them. Herman can now recognize the decision his brain has made *prior* to his hand moving down to the plate to retrieve the pastries.

In this same manner, Herman can recognize when one of the biases discussed above has occurred in his brain during the conduct of his job as project manager. He may be managing a project that is a favorite of one of his senior managers, and which that senior manager has told him is important for the project to succeed regardless of the fact that the project was grossly underestimated with highly dubious benefits from its inception. Nonetheless, despite Herman's heroic efforts and those of the project team, Herman eventually gets information proving to him that this project, which is running significantly over schedule and budget, will never achieve its expected objectives or benefits. Yet the potential impact of his perceived failure as project manager triggers cognitive dissonance in his brain. He can train himself to *recognize* when this bias is occurring so he can intervene and prevent himself from dismissing this information, thereby *minimizing* or eliminating the effects of the bias. He can also foresee that with the funds, time, and effort that have been expended on the project, his senior manager's brain will probably also experience cognitive dissonance bias when Herman presents him with the bad news. Herman can also expect that his senior manager will go on to encounter loss-aversion bias, when Herman recommends terminating the project immediately.

Recognizing and minimizing are easier to describe than to accomplish. Accomplishment should be viewed in two stages. First, Herman could accomplish recognizing and minimizing his experience. Second, he could attempt to assist his senior manager, as well as the project team, in also doing so with the understanding that this second stage is not fully within his control.

Training one to recognize when a bias is occurring requires self-awareness. Developing self-awareness can be achieved with mindfulness. Mindfulness can be developed in a number of ways. The most prominent of these ways is through the practice of meditation. There are various types of meditation, one among the several is mindfulness meditation. It encourages one to pay close attention to one's thoughts as they drift through the mind. "Through mindfulness meditation, you can see how your thoughts and feelings tend to move in particular patterns. Over time, you can become more aware of the human tendency to quickly judge an experience as good or bad, pleasant or unpleasant. With practice, an inner balance develops" (GAIAM, n.d.). As discussed in the previous chapter, aside from helping to develop mindfulness, meditation has other ancillary benefits.

There are other methods to achieve mindfulness as well. Social psychologist Ellen Langer's work focuses on developing mindfulness without using meditation. She defines mindfulness as "the process of drawing novel distinction [which] keeps us situated in the present. It also makes us more aware of the context and perception of our actions than if we rely upon distinctions and categories drawn in the past" (Langer and Moldoveanu, 2000). Regardless of the method one uses to develop mindfulness, once one becomes more self-aware of one's prevalent biases, they can become more easily recognizable as they occur. Chapters 5 and 6 will discuss mindfulness in more detail.

While recognition of a bias, when it occurs, takes training and patience, minimizing or counteracting the impulse of the bias takes *willpower,* resolute determination. Like self-awareness through meditation, willpower can also be developed and strengthened. In a talk he gave to the Long Now Foundation, psychologist Walter Mischel suggests that the way in which we represent or frame our decisions may hold a key to developing willpower. Mischel is famous for conducting what has come to be known as the "marshmallow test." It involved the experimenter seating a child in a room in front of a table with a plate that held a marshmallow. The child was told that the experimenter would be leaving the room for a period of time, and if the child would refrain from eating the marshmallow for that period of time, she would be given an additional marshmallow when the experimenter returned. Needless to say, it was difficult for many of the children to restrain themselves from eating the marshmallow placed in front of them. While the experiment is entertaining to observe, the willpower required to exert self-restraint is considerable.

Mischel suggests that one strategy for developing this willpower lays in how one frames the dilemma. During the marshmallow tests. the experimenter might initially describe the marshmallow to the child as sweet and delicious; on the other hand, it might be described differently, as looking like a ball of cotton. The first description will almost certainly reduce the child's willpower with the second strengthening it. Mischel calls these two descriptions hot ideation and cool ideation. The hot ideation creates more of a desire, thereby reducing willpower, and the cool reduces the desire with the opposite effect (Mischel, 2016). This framing mechanism can be used in other situations. In the example of Herman's problem project, when he receives the adverse project status information, he appears to be viewing it with a hot ideation. In other words, he is only considering that the failed project will adversely reflect on others' perceptions of him as a project manager. Instead, he might choose to view it with a cool ideation. His recommendation to terminate a project, which the entire organization knew would never succeed, could be viewed positively in that it would save the organization from throwing even more time and money into a failed effort. The action would also show that he had the courage to make a recommendation that others might not have had, thereby enhancing his reputation as a good project manager.* In such an adult situation, it may be a matter of how Herman decides to frame his view of his decision with his senior management and his project team: whether hot or cool ideation.

Categorizing Sets of Biases

There are two methods that address how to mitigate the effects of various sets of biases. Both suggest the importance of accepting that humans are all flawed and are affected by biases, both inherited and developed over time. The difference between the two methods involves how the biases are chunked or categorized, so they can be further addressed.

---

* For another excellent perspective on this subject, please see the Baumeister and Tierney book, *Willpower*, in the bibliography.

The first, developed in a paper published by the NeuroLeadership Institute, suggests that all biases can be divided into five categories, with all biases in a single category being able to be mitigated with similar tactics. It is called the SEEDS model and its categories are the following: similarity, expedience, experience, distance, and safety. For instance, the first category, similarity, addresses an individual's self-interests and his perception of himself and the groups with which he is affiliated. The reader will recognize the major bias in the group, the ingroup/outgroup bias. The authors recommend the following actions to mitigate the effects of this group of biases:

- Increasing awareness of the biases in this group
- Implementing methods to counteract biased hiring, team assignment, and so forth
- Taking steps to increase communications, resolve conflicts and differences, and take different perspectives*

The project and program manager will note that many of the steps for mitigating the effects of the biases in this group are those characteristics of leadership such as good communication skills, conflict management, and team building.

The second method posits that leaders make decisions based on "unconscious processes that neuroscientists call pattern recognition and emotional tagging. These processes…can be distorted by self-interest, emotional attachments, and misleading memories." The authors of this second method suggest that good leaders need to recognize those individuals in their organization who are most likely to be affected by these "red flag conditions" and to address the conditions when they arise. The reader will undoubtedly notice that the first category, self-interest, is like the NeuroLeadership category, similarity (Campbell, Whitehead, and Finkelstein, 2009). The authors suggest the following seven-step process to identify red flags:

1. Lay out the range of options.
2. List the main decision makers.
3. Choose one decision maker to focus on.
4. Check for inappropriate self-interest or distorting attachments.
5. Check for misleading memories.

---

* Lieberman, M. et al. November 2015. Breaking bias updated: The SEEDS model. *NeuroLeadership Journal*, Six (NeuroLeadership Institute, New York), p. 8.

6. Repeat the analysis with the next most influential person.
7. Review the list of red flags you have identified and determine whether the brain's…pattern recognition system and emotional-tagging process might be biased in favor of or against some options. If so, put one or more safeguards in place.*

   The authors described a case study in which three safeguards might strengthen the decision process:

- Injecting fresh experience or analysis.
- Introducing further debate and challenge.
- Imposing stronger governance.†

Addressing Individual Biases

At the time of the writing of this chapter, there are two methods that can be used to mitigate specific biases. The first is described in the Lovallo and Kahneman paper cited earlier in this chapter, "Delusions of Success." The second is video and gaming training to reduce individual biases. The method Lovallo and Kahneman propose for addressing optimism bias/ planning fallacy for developing more accurate estimates for complex projects is called *reference-class forecasting*. Before a senior manager or management team develops its initial expectations for project costs, schedule, and benefits (note: the reader should recall the power of anchoring bias), the authors suggest that he, she, or the team follow a five-step process to acquire an outside perspective of probable project outcomes.

1. Selecting a reference class of projects, a set of similar projects that have been done before and whose outcomes are known. These projects can be within the subject organization or may have occurred within the industry in which the organization sits.
2. Assessing the distribution of actual outcomes within the selected reference class.
3. Intuitively predicting where the new project falls within the range of outcomes of the reference class based on similarities of size, complexity, and other appropriate factors.

---

* *ibid.*, pp. 12–13.
† *ibid.*, pp. 10–11.

4. Assessing the reliability of the prediction in step 3 through estimates of predictability. It may, the authors say, be wise to consult a skilled statistician for this step.
5. Correcting the intuitive estimate based on the results of step 4.[*]

Bent Flyvbjerg has also recommended this method for use on major projects and programs in his paper cited earlier in this chapter (Flyvbjerg, 2008). Programs can use similar methods for new project components.

The second method involves single intervention, 60-minute training sessions that target six specific biases, two of which were discussed earlier: confirmation bias and anchoring bias. Two versions of the training were tested, a video game and an interactive video presentation. The experimenters report that "[p]laying the game reduced the three biases by about 46% immediately and 35% over the long term. Watching the video reduced the three biases by about 19% immediately and 20% over the long term." (Morewedge, 2015)[†] Needless to say, this research is quite promising for organizations, project-based or otherwise, that wish to improve decision-making by reducing the effects of these specific biases.[‡]

Summary

Biases are a fact of life. Human beings regularly exhibit many of them. Biases help successfully navigate everyday life but can also impede one's ability to make optimal decisions and interact effectively with project stakeholders. A number of the more easily relatable biases and their potential adverse effects were discussed, including

- Optimism bias and planning fallacy
- Anchoring bias
- Cognitive dissonance and confirmation bias
- Loss-aversion (also known as sunk-cost bias)
- Framing effect
- Ingroup/outgroup bias

---

[*] Lovallo, D. and Kahneman, D. *op. cit.,* p. 7.
[†] For the research article from which this information was derived, please see "Debiasing Decisions" in the bibliography (Morewedge et al. 2015).
[‡] As of the writing of this chapter, subscriptions to commercial versions of these interactive games could be obtain through Creative Technologies, Inc. (https://cretecinc.com/).

In order to minimize the adverse effects of these biases, various bias mitigation methods were discussed.

- Using the *ARM method*, which recommends the following:
  - Acknowledging that biases exist and effect everyone without exclusion
  - Recognizing when one's biases occur through increased self-awareness using mindfulness as a vehicle to increase that awareness
  - Minimizing or eliminating the effects of bias by exerting one's willpower in the interval between when the brain processes the bias's impulse and when the effect of that impulse takes place.
- *Categorizing similar biases* and implementing recommended minimizing strategies:
  - The NeuroLeadership Institute's SEEDS model
  - The "red flags" categorization method.
- Implementing *processes to counteract individual biases* such as *reference class forecasting* to address optimism bias/planning fallacy, and interactive, bias-reducing game training.

Chapter 5

Mindfulness: The Foundation for Intelligence and Optimal Performance

George Pitagorsky

Contents

Project Management, Complexity, and Cognitive Readiness

Successfully bringing projects in on time and within budget while delivering a quality product that creates organization or business value is a challenge that requires mindfully applied intelligence. Intelligence, as it is described in this context, is a complex of multiple facets or "multiple intelligences," for example, cognitive, emotional, social and spiritual. One should also acknowledge that several researchers group intelligences into other groupings, but the breakdowns do not significantly change the overall thrust of the groups or the context of multiple intelligences and how they operate within project and program management, especially in the area of stakeholder management.

Managing the simplest project in terms of cost, schedule, and scope is a complex activity involving the coordination of people, often with diverse views, objectives, and capabilities to create an outcome that satisfies and respects stakeholder expectations and enables optimal performance in future projects, particularly where the same people or organizations collaborate on multiple projects over time. Project or program management requires the integration of a suite of leadership, technical, and business management understandings, skills and capabilities. Behavioral skills, such as the ability to respect, recognize, and appreciate the work of others, are essential to leadership.* For example, being able to recognize the technical and social skills of the communications manager on the project team, as they are related to external stakeholders, is essential to maintaining clear communication structures. Thus, the ability to respect the skill set of external communications is essential to the project or program and its measure of success. It should be noted that many projects and programs do not have stated metrics or fully acknowledged risks that address these skills, especially when they are less robust than required or when they are missing on the team. One could argue it is the lack of the ability to respect,

---

* See Porath, Christine, **The Leadership Behavior That's Most Important to Employees,**
  https://hbr.org/2015/05/the-leadership-behavior-thats-most-important-to-employees

recognize, and appreciate the work of the communication manager or the position that creates this issue on projects and programs.

Practicing and continuously improving behavioral skills relies on cognitive readiness. As noted in Chapter 1, cognitive readiness involves the mental preparation, including skills, knowledge, abilities, motivations, and personal dispositions, needed to establish and sustain outstanding individual and team performance in the complex and rapidly changing environment of project, program, and portfolio management. In short, it is the readiness of individuals and teams to confront their inner workings—the way they think, interrelate, and behave. Thus, the intelligences set forth and cognitive readiness set forth in Chapter 1 work together to provide the project and program manager, as well as the team members, the necessary base behavioral traits, as well as the skills, knowledge, abilities, motivations, and personal dispositions to perform in the complex and rapidly changing environments in which project and program objectives are accomplished.

Importance of Behavioral Skills and Mindfulness

Behavioral skills enable one to interact with others. Though there is no definitive list of behavioral skills (in general, for projects or programs), there is general agreement as to their importance.*

Behavioral skills relate to communicating, resolving conflict, empathy, accepting accountability, diplomacy, influencing and directing, patience, the ability to accept and adapt to change, self-confidence and self-awareness, stress management, personal time management, the ability to give and take criticism, and other human interactions. These behavioral skills are critical to building teams, solving problems, managing conflict, negotiating agreements, managing expectations, mentoring, coaching, and directing teams and work. Further, these skills are necessary for communicating to stakeholders, including both internal and external stakeholders. This communication skill goes beyond managing expectations to include the ability to communicate in the lexicon of the group of stakeholders to which

---

* See Jiang, J.J., Klein, G., and Margulis, S. 1998. Important behavioral skills for IS project managers: The judgements of experienced IS professionals. *Project Management Journal*, 29 (1), 39–43. https://www.pmi.org/learning/library/behavior-skills-information-system-nonverbal-communication-2067 which cites several sources to support this claim. Also, there are a large number of additional articles and studies that can be cited.

one is communicating, the ability to key into terms that will initiate the listening function in the group of stakeholders, and the ability to maintain an open channel for future communication on various issues and risks facing the project or program.

Behavioral skills are closely related to and overlap with cognitive style, which describes how people think, solve problems, learn, perceive, remember, and relate to others. An individual's or team's behavioral skills are a portion of what sums up to cognitive style. Within a project or program management team, the need for the project or program manager to understand the team members' cognitive style, as well as their own, cannot be overstated. The members of the team will approach the issues and risks from their individual cognitive style. No one cognitive style will be preferable over another one. The ability to understand and blend the cognitive styles and draw on the strengths of the individual styles will be one of the keys to the project or program manager's success in achieving the project or program management objectives.

These skills have their foundation in emotional, social, cultural, and spiritual intelligences, while technical and business capabilities have their foundation in cognitive intelligence. These aspects of emotional, social, cultural, and cognitive intelligence—the multiple intelligences—interact in individuals, driving their behaviors and decisions. For example, cultural intelligence, the ability to manage relationships across cultural divides, combines cognitive intelligence, knowledge of the factors that differentiate one culture's norms from another's, and emotional and social intelligences. This type of cultural intelligence would become important on a virtual, global project, as an example. The project manager may be managing individuals on the team from multiple countries, bringing multiple cultural experiences and backgrounds to bear on the project. The project manager must find a way to balance those cultural experiences and backgrounds to attain the best inputs from them for the project in problem solving, issue resolution, and risk management.

Through observation and the collection of anecdotal material, a general observation has been pulled together: project managers and business people tend to subordinate behavioral skills to technical and business skills. People in general avoid critical analysis of their own conscious and unconscious mental models—the beliefs, ideas, images, and cognitive biases that drive their behavior. As an example, project meetings seldom discuss the softer side of the project, such as communication issues, but spend time on the technical even when there is consensus that there are communication issues with a stakeholder group that are impinging on technical issues. In many ways, there is an acceptance of a risk the project team is creating for itself by avoiding the critical analysis of its own conscious or unconscious mental model that is driving its behavior. Biases are discussed in Chapter 4 of this text.

A project is a collision of factors that have varying importance at different times in the project. In this context it is widely recognized* that the ability to lead and work effectively with the team and stakeholders is one of the most important factors in achieving project success. The project manager, who has been successful, works to cultivate the qualities of open-mindedness, empathy, self-awareness, and clarity that enable him or her to perform optimally while working well with others. He or she applies them in team building, project reviews, managing expectations, negotiating estimates and schedules, and managing conflict and organizational change.

Cognitive style includes perception, but in order to focus and manage our perceptions and to filter and orchestrate the handling of the perceptions of the team members one needs a tool. Mindfulness presents one such tool comprised of three parts according to Shauna Shapiro, a psychologist and proponent of mindfulness, and her co-author, Linda E. Carlson, in their 2017 book, *The Art and Science of Mindfulness: Integrating Mindfulness into Psychology and the Helping Professions.* The three parts are: intention, attention, and attitude. Said another way, "Mindfulness is awareness that arises through paying attention, on purpose, in the present moment, non-judgmentally," says Kabat-Zinn. "It's about knowing what is on your mind."† Mindfulness is both a process and, as Kabat-Zinn's definition implies, an outcome to be achieved. Throughout, mindfulness will be used both as the end result of being mindful and the practices that lead to it. The emphasis is on the process used by the project and program manager and the team to achieve the outcome of mindful awareness.

Managing perceptions begins with the ability to objectively observe one's mind to filter out biases and mental factors that get in the way of perceiving things clearly. One key to managing perceptions is the

---

* Ward, J.L. 2013. Fourteen project leadership skills to boost your career. Paper presented at *PMI® Global Congress 2013—EMEA*, Istanbul, Turkey. Newtown Square, PA: Project Management Institute. https://www.pmi.org/learning/library/project-leadership-skills-boost-career-5796

† Mindful Staff, Jon Kabat-Zinn: Defining Mindfulness, https://www.mindful.org/jon-kabat-zinn-defining-mindfulness/

acceptance that each of us has biases, as well as acknowledging biases once they become apparent to us or they are pointed out to us. It is important also to acknowledge group biases to enable the group to manage perceptions.

Mindfulness, the ability to objectively see things as they are, is a foundation for these qualities and for intelligence, at least in the sense of knowing one's mind. The key to being able to appreciate the power of mindfulness is to see for oneself. For those needing motivation to see for themselves, there are a growing number of scientific studies that have validated this claim.* For project managers, this ability to objectively see things as they are may mean setting aside preconceived notions of groupings of stakeholders and why they are communicating the way that they appear to be. The ability to set aside these preconceived ideas or judgments may allow the project manager and the team to have more open and fluid communications that may allow the discovery of new or different motivations behind the words or actions of stakeholders. Another example of setting aside preconceived notions for a project team is the ability not to be overly focused from the beginning on a technical solution prior to confirmation of the technical requirements. The issue of focusing on a technical solution prior to establishment of the requirements with the customer has cost many a project, thus customer, both budget and schedule.

Mindfulness training at first develops focused attention and subsequently develops an open monitoring of internal and external stimuli, resulting in an increased capacity to perform. "Overall, reviewed studies suggested that early phases of mindfulness training, which are more concerned with the development of focused attention, could be associated with significant improvements in selective and executive attention whereas the following phases, which are characterized by an open monitoring of internal and external stimuli, could be mainly associated with improved unfocused sustained attention abilities. Additionally, MMPs [mindful meditation practices] could enhance working memory capacity and some executive functions."† Mindful meditation practices enhance the various skills and

---

* Davis, Daphne, PhD and Hayes, Jeffery, PhD, "What are the benefits of mindfulness" APA Journal, July/August 2012, Vol 43, No. 7 http://www.apa.org/monitor/2012/07-08/ce-corner.aspx
† Chiesa, A., , Calati, R., and Serretti, A. April 2011. Does mindfulness training improve cognitive abilities? A systematic review of neuropsychological findings. *Review Article, Clinical Psychology Review*, 31 (3), 449–464 http://www.sciencedirect.com/science?_ob=ArticleListURL&_method=list&_ArticleListID=-1104709995&_sort=r&_st=13&view=c&md5=6fdd76614d1a588e517866ff1084a28a&searchtype=a

intelligences by providing different ways of relating, being, and existing in relationship to the things and people in our lives or the projects and programs. It allows one to move from resisting to finding ways to exist with or engage with the people and things that exist in our lives, projects, or programs. In other words, rather than continuing to fight the budget cut by expending more budget in a fight that one knows will not be won; one finds a way to engage the internal stakeholder, the sponsor, to find ways to succeed within the budget one has. Another example is that one does not fight the immovable stakeholder that is negative about one or more of the project objectives. Instead, one acknowledges the stance of the stakeholder, acknowledges the risks the stance creates, and attempts to mitigate that risk, while continuing to communicate in a positive manner with the stakeholder in order to exist with the stakeholder as the stakeholder will not go away. They are, after all, immovable. One makes the stakeholder aware that he or she has been heard; the stakeholder is still a vital member of the stakeholder community; and the stakeholder is still visible within the bounds of the project, as one is still interacting with him or her in regard to risk.

Optimal Performance

Optimal performance is to sustainably act in the most desirable way under prevailing conditions. It implies the ability to balance multiple, often conflicting objectives while satisfying expectations in an ever-changing environment. Optimal performance is the result of bringing together intelligence, mindfulness, and concentration with the factors shown in Figure 5.1 below—Optimal Performance Factors. These factors build on one another and reinforce one another.

Figure 5.1   Optimal performance factors. (Pitagorsky, G. 2017. *Managing Expectations: A Mindful Approach to Achieving Success*. (More Than Sound Publishing, MA), 19.)

The quest for optimal performance begins with sufficient mindfulness to have a realistic point of view—seeing things for what they are, impermanent, changing, and imperfect, and acknowledging one's values and motives. While stakeholders each have their own perspectives and perceptions, to think that things are not impermanent, changing, and imperfect is not in keeping with reality and must be confronted. The project manager who seeks optimal performance rises above the individual perspectives by taking a systems' view and then promotes a common understanding of the situation at hand.

Mindfulness also allows one to be open to what is arising in the present. It allows one to avoid the desire to constantly be pushing and pulling on people, situations, and factors to try to have what is conform to what one desires reality to be. When a project or program manager can demonstrate to a team the ability to work within the reality of a situation following a situational analysis, the team will generally be able to avoid fighting the reality and be able to achieve optimal performance.

Optimal performance also relies on concentration, the ability to focus on a chosen interconnection of ideas or thoughts, tasks, or objects. Concentration without mindfulness is not sufficient. Mindfulness provides the awareness needed to respond effectively to the challenges arising in the moment. For example, an antelope drinking at the river is not fully absorbed in the drinking; it reserves a bit of awareness to flee when a crocodile attacks. Just as the project manager should not be fully absorbed in tracking performance metrics to the exclusion of the political environment in which the project is being conducted and in which the funding for the project may be threatened. Further, the program manager should not be so focused on the integrated schedule that he or she is not listening to the stakeholders of one or more of the related projects or related other work such as operational work units into which the projects will transition. Failure to listen to such operational units may mean that the projects within the integrated schedule may successfully meet their milestones but may never be transitioned into the operational unit, because requirements that changed were never heard and were never integrated into the scope baseline.

Beyond Intellectual Understanding to Experience and Action

The description of sugar brings with it an intellectual understanding of what sugar looks like, where it grows, how it is processed, and its many variations and their attributes. However, until one tastes sugar, one doesn't really "know" experientially what sugar is.

Together, intellectual understanding and personal experience gives one the opportunity to know things as they are in a new light. Everyone has experienced mindfulness, concentration, and the application or misapplication of behavioral knowledge and other skills. The challenge is to do what can be done to continuously apply knowledge and experience to continuously improve skills, capabilities, abilities, and one's personal dispositions as a project or program manager.

Living Above the Line: Project Management as a Zen Art

Productively exploring cognitive readiness, mindfulness and intelligence goes beyond analysis and academic understanding. It implies taking a hard look at oneself, as a project manager.

Is one living above the line or below it? Living above the line means that one is aware of one's thoughts and feelings and has the possibility of being responsive, as opposed to reactive. Living below the line means that one is unaware of unconscious impulses, habits, mental models, thoughts, and feelings that drive behavior.

In the Zen tradition, Zen arts are used as vehicles for increasing the amount of time spent above the line to promote self-learning. By objectively observing one's behavior, seamlessly, as the practitioner performs his or her art, he or she gets to see when he or she is habitually reacting rather than responding. The performer increasingly sees, without self-judgment, when he or she is making errors and has an opportunity to avoid or minimize their impact. He or she sees his or her impulses, biases, habits, and reactions.

Project management is the Zen art of focus. One aspires to perfection while one realizes that one will probably not achieve it. One realizes that one can achieve optimal performance.

> All you have to do is start with the intention to cultivate optimal performance, using every experience as fuel for the effort, and then to do your best, be mindful of your thoughts, feelings, physical sensations and everything that is happening around you. When you realize that you are distracted or behaving in a way that is not in keeping with your goals, step back, reflect and move forward skillfully, learning from each experience. Relax and use

each experience as a means for getting increasingly peaceful and clear, seeing things as they are and performing optimally.*

With the intention of using every experience as fuel for the effort of self-learning, one becomes a warrior. Not one who aggressively fights others with the intent to kill, but one who applies kindness, courage, and focused dedication to the acquisition of self-knowledge, then dedicates that knowledge to bringing peace, optimal performance, and sanity to others. The warrior has the courage to look in the mirror and see him or herself just as he or she is, with his or her imperfections, accept them, and then work to purify them.

For example, the warrior project manager skillfully confronts his or her fear to push back against irrational demands. He or she fully experiences the fear and transforms it into the resolve that is needed to convince the demanding project sponsor that a realistic plan should be far more effective than one that supports the illusion of hitting an ideal but impossible target. The motivation is to perfect oneself, while working to satisfy the stakeholders: sponsors, clients, managers, workers, and anyone else who can be influenced by or influence the project.

The ideal to perfect oneself should not be confused with perfecting others. The Zen project manager should avoid trying to perfect others in his or her image. The perfection is solely for the individual. It is the individual that is confronting his or her fears and irrational demands.

Multiple Intelligences

Intelligence is an important performance factor. Who does not want intelligent people on their projects? Yet, sometimes the ones with the highest intelligence quotients (IQs), also known as cognitive intelligence, turn out to be the most impossible to work with, because their emotional intelligence (EQ) is low, or they lack social skills (Social Intelligence, SI), or the motivation and mindfulness to put their intelligence to work.

Howard Gardner in the 1980s changed the common view of intelligence by introducing his Theory of Multiple Intelligences. He defined intelligence as *"the capacity to solve problems or to fashion products that are valued in one or more cultural setting."*† His theory went beyond the idea that

---

* http://www.projectinsight.net/blogs/project-management-tips/zen-and-the-art-of-optimal-performance
† Gardner, H. 1983/2003. *Frames of Mind. The Theory of Multiple Intelligences.* (BasicBooks, New York), p. x

intelligence was limited to the cognitive realm, instead arguing that it consists of seven distinct, separate intelligences.

The intelligences Gardner identified in 1983 are linguistic, logical-mathematical, musical, bodily kinesthetic, spatial, interpersonal, and intrapersonal. In his 1999 book, he identified three "new" candidate intelligences: naturalist, spiritual and existential.*

Please note that the intelligences all operate interactively in a complex relationship in which they affect one another. Recognizing multiple intelligences enables the cultivation and improvement of each and breaks down the fixation on cognitive intelligence to the exclusion of other meaningful factors.

It should be noted that most employment functions or hiring protocols do not account for multiple intelligences. Interview processes seldom account for more than a superficial review of social and emotional intelligence, if at all. It is not until the employee is in the job function for a period of time that the various intelligences are measured and in some jurisdictions one must be careful how one establishes metrics for each outside of the cognitive intelligence area due to various legal constraints.

The project or program manager, if allowed or if it is part of their job function, should consider metrics for the various team members that relate to the multiple intelligences and how they relate to the project or program and the other team members. It will also enable the project or program manager, if they request to have such metrics applied to their performance also.

Four Intelligences: Cognitive, Emotional, Social, Spiritual

Stephen Covey summarized the intelligences: physical (PQ), mental (IQ), social/emotional (EQ), and spiritual (SQ).† Covey's approach was established to develop a holistic approach to an effective person.

Over the years, several models have been defined. In this chapter, we will focus on cognitive, emotional, social, and spiritual intelligences. Physical intelligence (Gardner's bodily-kinesthetic) is the ability to use one's body in highly differentiated and skilled ways. While this intelligence is important, it is less likely to be applied in most project management situations; therefore, it will not be addressed in this text. However, there are some cultural and

---

* Gardner, H. 1999. *Intelligence Eframed: Multiple Intelligences for the 21st Century.* (Basic Books, New York), p. 47.
† Covey, S.R. 2004. *The 8th Habit: From Effectiveness to Greatness.* (Free Press, NY), p. 50.

regional based projects where the application of physical intelligence should be applied and integrated with the application of the other intelligences. An example of a project where physical intelligence may be important would be working in a remote, harsh climate area where the ability to find shelter or other amenities is limited or nonexistent.

Cognitive Intelligence

Intelligence, as the term is connotatively used, per fifty-two leading intelligence researchers,

> is a general mental capability that, among other things, involves the ability to reason, plan, solve problems, think abstractly, comprehend complex ideas, learn quickly and learn from experience. It is not merely book learning, a narrow academic skill, or test-taking smarts. Rather it reflects a broader and deeper capability to for comprehending our surroundings—"catching on," "making sense" of things or "figuring out" what to do.*

This is cognitive intelligence. Cognitive intelligence is a complex of elements. It is typically a measure of spatial, mathematical, and language abilities, as well as memory and recall. In addition to these definitional qualities, cognitive elements include motor skills, attention, perception, and executive skills. Executive skills are the ability to integrate multiple skills and perceptions, self-regulate, overcome biases, and make decisions.†

Cognitive intelligence relates to the intellect, analysis, and the integration of perceptions and concepts. It is what we commonly refer to as "brain power." Most project managers and the project teams tout their technical, skill, or degree backgrounds to let individuals know that they possess this type of intelligence. It is the signature quality of each project or program members' resume or curriculum vitae. Each project or program member lists the training, education, degrees, work experience, and publications they possess. In other words, it is the statement of their cognitive intelligence.

---

* Mainstream Science on Intelligence, Wall Street Journal, December 13, 1994
† For a description of the elements of cognitive intelligence and IQ see https://blog.udemy.com/cognitive-assessment/

Emotional Intelligence

Emotional intelligence complements cognitive intelligence by bringing in the skills to consider, understand, and manage one's own emotions and recognize, to be cognizant of, and influence the emotions of others.

The ability to understand and manage one's own emotions is a critical factor for healthy interpersonal relationships and managing stress. Healthy relationships are critical to success in any endeavor involving more than one person, such as projects or programs.

There are negative or afflictive emotions like anger, fear, jealousy, and depression, and positive emotions like compassion, love, and happiness. Each emotion has a continuum of intensities and ranges within each intensity band. For example, fear may manifest as mild anxiety or intense paralyzing horror and all gradations between these extremes. Happiness has the range from simple contentment to ecstatic joy. Both afflictive and positive emotions are normal, unavoidable parts of life. Each project or program manager, team member, and stakeholder will experience and carry forward experiences of these emotions. The interplay of those experiences and the emotions that they evoke will create further emotional responses or reactions that the project or program manager will need to be able to recognize, to be cognizant of, as they emerge within the team or in actions with stakeholders, and be prepared to influence, especially in conflict resolution. The dynamics of each situation will vary depending upon the range of the emotional responses and may change over time, which is another element of which the project or program manager will need to be aware.

Emotions are mental states in which there is a complex of feelings that are distinct from other mind states such as cognition, volition, and the awareness of physical sensations. Emotions are experienced as a localized or general felt sense. When in conflict with a team member or customer over an estimate, there may be tension in the abdomen, throat, or chest. A success may be experienced as a widespread feeling of pleasure for the positive emotions; failures bring forth negative emotions felt as tension and pain.

Managing one's emotions relies on the ability to be aware of them as they arise, which is self-awareness, and to be able to moderate behavior to avoid being reactive, which is self-management. One should note the difference between being reactive, thoughtlessly acting as a result of a stimulus, and being responsive, thoughtfully acting in a situationally appropriate way.

As a project or program manager, one may be aware of one's own physical or mental cues, but team members or stakeholders may not. One needs to learn, where possible, the cues that signal emotional responses of team members or other stakeholders. It is part of the larger need of the project or program manager to get to know the team members from each of the intelligence perspectives, in order to serve the achievement of the objectives of the project or program and to achieve a healthy, functioning team.

Managing emotions is *not* about suppressing or denying them. The person with a high degree of emotional intelligence can experience deep and intense emotions, while being able to control tendencies that may not be appropriate in certain circumstances or with certain groupings of people. Consider the management of anger: anger can be felt fully as an intense, unpleasant complex of physical sensations. Lashing out at another or breaking things are ways of avoiding those feelings. Suppressing the feelings by denying their presence is also an avoidance technique. Managing the emotions means being able to experience and acknowledge them while not behaving reactively or employing an inappropriate avoidance technique. For the project manager, it may mean stating to the team that he or she is upset by the budget reduction that they just received. Acknowledging the upset or anger tells the team that the emotion they are experiencing from the project manager is not directed toward them but is real and they were reading the emotions in the room correctly. Another example would be issues of frustration with suppliers not delivering goods or services on time or in a timely manner. The frustration experienced by the project manager should be stated to the supplier's customer representative but in a controlled manner. The project manager demonstrates emotional intelligence by being able to maintain a controlled stance in the face of the schedule delay. The project manager is acknowledging the emotion to him or herself and the customer representative, but in a controlled manner, which is only possible through the awareness of the emotion.

There are four dimensions of emotional intelligence. In addition to *self-awareness* and *self-management*, there is the ability to be aware of other people's emotions, *social awareness* and *social intelligence*, and the ability to work with one's own and other people's emotions in negotiations, coaching relationships, team activities, leadership, consulting, and relationship management.* Note, in the prior example the project

---

* *Primal Leadership: Realizing the Power of Emotional Intelligence* by Daniel Goleman, Richard Boyatzis and Annie McKee, Harvard Business School Publishing, 2001.

manager was self-aware of his upset over the budget reduction and knew it was being projected. His social awareness allowed him to know that he needed to communicate to the team about that emotion to clarify that the emotion was not directed toward them. In this case, the project manager should also note to the team that the emotion is directed toward a situation and not any one person. Directing anger in an organization or outwardly toward a funding source accomplishes nothing and may set the stage for members of the team to pre-judge individuals rather than forming their own opinions.

For a more detailed description of the components of emotional intelligence, the referenced work of Goleman, Boyatzis, and McKee and the other works for Goleman regarding the subject should be used as foundational reference documents.

Social Intelligence

Social intelligence is the capacity to play and work well with others. Or, put another way, it is the ability to develop relationships with other people and to handle social or public environments. There is a continuum associated with social intelligence to measure where a person ranks on the spectrum. People at the lowest end are those in the autistic disorder spectrum. Those individuals with the highest level of social intelligence are often exemplified as great leaders or charismatic individuals.

Social intelligence is a component of emotional intelligence. Goleman breaks emotional intelligence into two dimensions: the intrapersonal, self-awareness and self-management, and the interpersonal or social intelligence, social awareness, and social facility or relationship management. Social awareness consists of primal empathy, empathetic accuracy, listening, and social cognition. Relationship management breaks down onto synchrony, self-presentation, influence, and concern.*

Current understandings of emotional and social intelligences have been influenced by neuroscience, which has studied the interplay between social interaction and brain structure and brain chemistry. Neuroscientific studies point to a relationship between good leadership and social intelligence.

> The notion that effective leadership is about having powerful
> social circuits in the brain has prompted us to extend our concept

---

* Goleman, Daniel, *Social Intelligence*, p.331.

of emotional intelligence, which we had grounded in theories of individual psychology. A more relationship-based construct for assessing leadership is social intelligence, which we define as a set of **interpersonal competencies built on specific neural circuits (and related endocrine systems) that inspire others to be effective**.*

Researchers have found that when leaders exhibit empathy and become attuned to others' moods, this action affects their own brain and the brain of their followers, as if their minds are part of a single system, as opposed to two or more brains reacting to one another.† One can therefore extrapolate that it is likely that this same dynamic operates in almost any social interaction. Projects are social interactions with some stakeholders working together to accomplish their objectives. Examples of this statement are project teams, which are comprised of a set of stakeholders working to achieve agreed upon project objectives, or customer stakeholders, who share a common interest in the deliverable or deliverables of the project.

The field does need scientific studies to understand and substantiate the importance of the dynamics of social intelligence. This need extends specifically to project and program teams, as well as to stakeholder group interactions. It is important to look to one's personal experiences to begin to understand how social intelligence works. How does it feel when one is working with someone who listens, is empathetic, understands where one is coming from, synchronizes with you, presents him or herself in a suitable way for the situation, and shows concern for others? How much more productive is a team of people with higher social intelligence than one that is influenced or directed by members with low social intelligence?

The need for project managers to be able to understand how social intelligence may improve team dynamics and general leadership dynamics should drive further research. Project managers may currently be able, through self-awareness and the interplay of empathy, understanding, and situational awareness, to demonstrate greater leadership skills, thus a higher degree of social intelligence.

---

* Goleman, Daniel, Boyartzis, Richard E, Harvard business Review, September 2008, https://hbr.org/2008/09/social-intelligence-and-the-biology-of-leadership
† *ibid.*

One step project and program managers can take to increase their social intelligence is to become more self-aware of the impact of their words and actions in their interactions with team members. One often finds that one reacts to words or situations without thinking through how the reaction may be received. By learning more about the team members and other stakeholders, the project and program manager will have the capability to be more empathetic, thus understanding how their words and actions will be received. Such knowledge and the ability to control their words or actions should provide the project or program manager the ability to shape the outcomes of the interactions with team members and other stakeholders.

Spiritual Intelligence

The idea that no one is an individual alone but is part of a unified system interacting with one another has emerged from neuroscientific studies of the influences of social interaction on the brain. This point is where the more concrete intelligences or intelligences that can be subjected to metrics or empirical evidence—cognitive, emotional, and social—begin to flow into the realm of spiritual intelligence.

Project managers, particularly in volatile, uncertain, complex, and ambiguous projects, do well when they operate with a higher degree of spiritual intelligence. It helps them to see the big picture and be less likely to be biased in their decision-making or interactions. Biases are discussed in Chapter 4.

Spiritual intelligence is *not* linked to any religion. It is a fundamental capacity, like any intelligence, which can be cultivated and enhanced. It encompasses "wisdom," knowing the nature of the universe, including one's own inner workings, ethics, and acting skillfully to do no harm and help, if one can. Spiritual intelligence is the capacity to go beyond the concrete material realm into the transcendent. It involves the ability to transform the experiential knowledge of self and the nature of the universe into skillful, practical, compassionate action, while being calm and accepting under most conditions.

Spiritual intelligence is becoming increasingly part of the mainstream in the discussion of the basic intelligences, as neuroscientists are influencing psychologists and validating some of the ancient wisdom carried in spiritual philosophies. The psychologists and philosophers are bringing spiritual intelligence into organizations, as a means for influencing values such as the acceptance of diversity, win-win conflict management, social responsibility, stress management, and teamwork.

> Spiritual intelligence is the central and most fundamental of all the intelligences, because it becomes the source of guidance for the others.*

The spiritually intelligent person recognizes a universal consciousness that is behind their individual identities, thoughts, and mental concepts. They are comfortable with paradox, irrationality, setbacks, and continuous change.

Robert Emmons boils spiritual intelligence down to five capabilities: transcending the physical and material; experience of heightened states of consciousness; seeing day-to-day experience as sacred; using spiritual methods such as prayer, meditation, and contemplation to address problems; and a tendency to be virtuous and oriented to the benefit of others as well as oneself.† For the project manager, the ability to treasure the day-to-day experiences involved in project work is necessary for inner wellbeing, as well as the wellbeing of the team. The project manager avoids emotional disruptions within the team, as well as self, by focusing on the benefit of the others and the whole, the team. By focusing on the experience of the day-to-day and maintaining an acceptance of the learning that comes from such experiences, the project or program manager conveys to the team a leader that is less erratic, more centered, and more focused on the team and stakeholders than the issue of the day. Such project or program managers are often viewed as leaders, problem-solvers, or those individuals in control because of the calm demeanor that is conveyed from the view of the experience of the day-to-day being sacred.

Danah Zohar, who coined the term, identifies twelve principles of spiritual intelligence. The principles are:

1. *Self-awareness*: Knowing one's own values and beliefs
2. *Vision and value led*: Basing action on principles
3. *Positive use of adversity*: Using adversity as a learning opportunity; being resilient
4. *Holistic*: Seeing everything, including oneself, as part of a complex system of interacting people, places, and things

---

* Covey, S. 2004. *The 8th Habit: From Effectiveness to Greatness.* (Simon and Schuster), p. 53
† Emmons, R.A. 2000. Is spirituality an intelligence? *The International Journal for the Psychology of Religion.* 10, 27–34.

5. *Compassion*: Feeling what others feel as if you were feeling it; seeing them as part of you
6. *Celebration of diversity*: Accepting and valuing diversity among people
7. *Field-independent*: Possessing, expressing, and defending one's own views in the face of resistance from others; self-assurance
8. *Ask fundamental "why" questions*: Needing to know why things are as they are
9. *Ability to reframe*: Assessing problems and issues in the context of the big picture
10. *Spontaneity*: Transcending beliefs and mental models responsive to the needs of the moment
11. *Sense of vocation*: Desiring to be of value to others; to serve
12. *Humility*: Understanding and acknowledging accurately one's place as one player among many in the universe*

When one analyzes spiritual intelligence, one can see its complexity and holistic nature. There are assessments of spiritual intelligence that rely on the subjective reporting by individuals. Whether you measure or assess it or not, one can explore for oneself how one's world view, ingrained beliefs, and well-intentioned openness influence one's ability to remain calm and centered in the face of adversity or, in the case of a project or program manager, risk events that occur such as the loss of key staff or significant scope change.

This ability to remain calm and centered in the face of adversity is a critical factor in the management of projects. Projects experience issues and face risks on a daily basis or more often. The ability to remain a calming influence within the team and for the other stakeholders will often avoid the creation of other risks or the escalation of the current risk, which is being handled, including communication risks or actions being taken outside of the planned mitigation strategies. The ability of the project or program manager to draw on his or her own insights from whatever inner core or contemplation method one may use should allow the project or program manager to feel more centered or self-assured about the decisions and actions he or she is conveying to the team or taking with the team. The conveyance of calm, self-assuredness, and positive use of adversity in the face of a risk realized should allow the project or program team to implement the mitigation strategy while communicating to the other stakeholders the importance of the steps being taken, thus reducing or avoiding secondary risks.

---

* Zohar, Danah, Q's for Great Leadership: 12 Principles of SQ, http://danahzohar.com/ www2/?page_id=146

Mindfulness as a Foundation for Intelligence

Intelligence is a complex of capabilities and abilities that supports the continuous improvement and optimization of performance. Mindfulness is a foundation for intelligence.

Goleman discusses the high and low roads of cognitive operation in this quote:

> The low road operates on automatic, outside our awareness, and with great speed. The high road operates with voluntary control, requires effort and conscious intent and moves more slowly.*

One operates on conscious and unconscious levels. The unconscious level takes one through a day with a minimal amount of extra mental effort. In such a day there are stimuli and responses. One is on autopilot. This approach to a day may be fine and efficient in some circumstances for a person. For example, digestion, normal breathing, and more occur on the low road. However, one needs conscious awareness when confronted with a challenge, a desire to continuously improve performance, the need to make a critical decision, or, for a project or program manager, to identify and handle a risk.

> Between stimulus and response there is a space. In that space lies our freedom and power to choose our response.†

What Mindfulness Is

As with intelligence, mindfulness has many operable definitions. One article‡ presents eleven definitions gathered mostly from psychologists. Mindfulness, as assimilated from these definitions, is the quality of being aware of what is happening in the present moment.

> "Mindfulness is awareness that arises through paying attention, on purpose, in the present moment, non-judgmentally," says Kabat-Zinn. "It's about knowing what is on your mind."§

---

* Goleman, Daniel, Social Intelligence, p.321
† Covey, Stephen, The 8th Habit, p. 42
‡ https://pasadenatherapist.wordpress.com/2008/06/11/11-definitions-of-mindfulness/ Chapman, Kalea, PsyD, June 11, 2008, Mindfulness, Psychology in the Media
§ Kabbat-Zinn, Jon, Defining Mindfulness, http://www.mindful.org/jon-kabat-zinn-defining-mindfulness/

> The practice of maintaining a nonjudgmental state of heightened or complete awareness of one's thoughts, emotions, or experiences on a moment-to-moment basis; also: such a state of awareness.*

Have you ever done something, like driving from point A to point B, with no recollection of how you did it? You were not mindfully aware; you were on autopilot or, as it is sometimes styled, a creature of habit. When mindfully aware one sees more of the unconscious drives, beliefs, and habits that influence behavior. In project and program management, one makes presentations on a regular basis to senior management, customers, or other stakeholders about the status of the project or program. One can present the material in a non-mindful manner; just presenting the facts of future risks, performance management measurements, and other project-related material without experiencing the moment or situation in which one is engaging one will miss the subtle feedback and response. Another example of non-mindful project or program management is the team meeting where the project or program manager is not listening, viewing the slides presented, or watching the interactions of the team members. The information lost in both experiences, as well as the person-to-person interactions, were invaluable, and the losses may in fact result in later risk.

While there may be people who are not mindful at all, most are mindful at least some of the time. For instance, reflecting on when one was (1) immersed in some activity while effortlessly observing the experience, such as a physical activity like running or playing a sport or a work-related activity; then, (2) was consciously aware of risks and skillful practices to make for a more effective performance. For the project manager, the presentation of a report before immediate management may be the activity similar to going for the daily run, but when the same report is to be presented to the external customer he or she is consciously aware of the need to be artful and skillful in the words to be used and how schedule or cost variations should be presented. In other words, the active, participatory, open attention on the present—in this case, the presentation.

In the context of emotional intelligence, enhanced mindfulness enables the early recognition of stimuli and their effects needed to increase self-awareness. Emotional intelligence enables the use of the space between stimulus and response to choose, thus supporting self-management. For example, if someone criticizes one's performance or an idea one holds

---

* https://www.merriam-webster.com/dictionary/mindfulness

dear and with which one identifies, it is a sign of emotional intelligence to sense the arising of a negative emotion like anger or fear and follow this recognition to decide how to respond. Does one argue, and yell; or, withdraw or engage in a dialogue that might start with a statement similar to, "Well that is an interesting perspective. Tell me more about …?" Since many items in project and program management require the identification of an owner, such as the owner of a risk or the owner of the risk mitigation strategy, the alignment with one's performance is significant. Ownership makes the actions taken in regard to something one owns personal and by definition negative critiques are personal. One must be self-aware enough to recognize that it is the ownership of the action that is triggering the sign of a negative emotional response, and capturing it allows one to respond effectively.

Mindfulness can result in greater social intelligence, sensitivity to the way others are feeling, and the space to make the moment-to-moment decisions that are the foundation for managing relationships. Managing relationships, whether with stakeholders, customers, functional managers, or team members, is a critical part of the project or program manager's job. It is through well-managed relationships that cost and schedule estimates are negotiated, decisions and agreements made, and the team motivated to excel.

Mindfulness enhances cognitive intelligence by promoting the clear, focused thinking required to make decisions, solve problems, remember things, and apply skills and knowledge to accomplish activities or milestones of a project. Awareness of the need for managing risk and promoting the use of the most situational appropriate strategies are forms of the kind of mindfulness that supports cognitive intelligence.

Enhanced mindfulness supports spiritual intelligence. It provides the *experiential* knowledge of the interconnectivity and ever changing, impermanent nature of mind and the external environment. It forms the basis for being receptive to this knowledge, which results in the ability to be self-aware and enables insight into one's self-identity. It enables one to be aware of a stable calm inner sense that is non-judgmental affecting one's attitude and resilience.

Mindfulness Meditation

Meditation is a method for exercising the mind. It trains concentration and mindfulness. Concentration is the ability to choose an object, sound, physical sensation, aphorism, task, or other item, to which one pays attention, and to stay with it in the face of distractions. Concentration calms and quiets the mind, and with intensive practice brings about an experience of calm quiet spaciousness that ultimately supports transcendence. Mindfulness is the ability to see what is happening in and around one.

Mindfulness meditation, also called insight meditation, increases both concentration and mindfulness, and the practice of mindfulness meditation has been around for thousands of years. **Mindfulness meditation does *not* try to stop thoughts**, but simply trains the mind to objectively and unobtrusively notice anything and everything that is occurring in the moment. In other words, awareness is one of the hallmarks. If one wants to cultivate concentration, one notices when the mind has moved away from the chosen object. Otherwise, one simply keeps noticing, as one goes about one's business without judging where one is concentrating one's attention or noticing without attaching value or importance to the same.

There are many mindfulness meditation techniques. Some are formal and require dedicated time and a quiet location that is relatively free from interruption. Others are informal and can be practiced throughout the day.

The following method is one of many forms of meditation one may choose to practice. It is presented as an example only and is not meant to endorse one methodology over another.

How to Meditate

Formal Practice

Choose a relatively quiet place where one will not be interrupted and a convenient time of day. Choose a duration: one can start with five or ten minutes. Over time, extend one's practice to twenty or thirty minutes. Set a timer. Extend the time only when one is comfortable with the period of time one is meditating currently. As with a form of exercise, if one overextends oneself, one will not generally continue with the practice.

The most important aspect of meditation is to be relaxed. One should not think one can or should stop thinking. Just see what happens. Watch the process, as if it was a movie.

- Sit comfortably erect and relaxed.
  - Hands and arms resting comfortably.
  - Body balanced and stable. Lips slightly apart, a subtle smile.

- – Head gently reaching upward, imagine a string pulling gently upward from the crown; chin slightly tucked, head, neck, and spine relaxed and erect. Tail bone slightly tucked forward.
- – Shoulders hanging loosely, chest open.
- ■ Feel the sensations of one's body. Let one's body rest actively.
- ■ Take note of one's breath. Just notice the inhalation and exhalation, wherever it is most prevalent, at the nostrils, the rising and fallen of the chest.
- ■ Notice thoughts, feelings, sensations, sounds, sights, smells as they occur.
- ■ Accept everything with a friendly accepting attitude, whether it is pleasant, unpleasant, or neutral, just notice it and let it be.
- ■ If one becomes distracted, lost in thought, as soon as one realizes it, bring one's attention back to the body, the breath, and begin again, just noticing.

Informal Practice

Whether one has a formal practice or not, one can practice informal meditation, every day and, ideally, every moment. There are many possibilities for when one can choose to practice. For example, when the phone rings or a ping tells one there is text message or email, take a moment to count two breaths, sense one's body, then respond or just get back to what you were doing.

Walking from one place to another, choose to focus on one's movement, notice the physical sensations and thoughts and when one gets pulled away to obsess about, become attracted to, or disgusted by something one thinks, sees, or feels.

At a meeting, focus purposefully on the content. Notice when one's mind wanders and bring one's attention to one's breath for a moment before focusing on the meeting content.

Western and Eastern Views

The Source of Mindfulness Meditation

Mindfulness meditation was the principle meditation technique taught by the Buddha over 2,500 years ago. It was meant to be used along with wisdom and skillful behavior to achieve freedom from suffering. Meditation practitioners who were trained in Buddhist meditation techniques and Eastern philosophy have fueled mindfulness meditation in the United States and Europe.

Joseph Goldstein, Jack Kornfield, and Sharon Salzberg were the first Westerners to teach mindfulness meditation and spearheaded the spread of it in the West. They were trained in Southeast Asia and brought the practice back within the context of Eastern spiritual teachings. Jon Kabat-Zinn, founder of Mindfulness Based Stress Reduction, a secular, medically-oriented mindfulness meditation program, was also influenced by Eastern spiritual traditions, particularly Buddhism. The Mindfulness Based Stress Reduction work set the stage for secular mindfulness meditation.

Enabling Distinction Making and Unbiased Decisions

As mindfulness meditation has become popular and used in organizations, including the United States Army, Google, and business consultants in the West, psychologists and others have drawn distinctions between Eastern and Western approaches. The Western mindfulness expert's focus is on effective decision making and action. Many of them, unfortunately, have the idea that the Eastern approach promotes silence, inaction, and mindlessness. Some Eastern mindfulness experts complain about the secularization of a technique. To the Eastern mindfulness experts, such an approach belongs in a spiritual context and the quest for enlightenment.

The Western experts do a disservice to the active managers and performers they serve by dissuading them from a useful tool. The more orthodox Eastern experts do a disservice by denying the benefits of meditation to lay people who are interested in stress relief, increased concentration, and mindfulness. Neither strict construction is serviceable for those wishing to practice mindfulness meditation to allow more effective decision-making and directed action.

Taking an either-or attitude, Western experts seem to dismiss meditation and the focus on internal awareness, missing the opportunity to use mindfulness meditation to cultivate the very distinction making and effective action they value. For example, one writer, summarized the difference between Eastern and Western traditions as follows: *"the Eastern perspective of Mindfulness can be described as enhanced attention, while the Western perspective can be viewed as distinction making."**

---

* Feldbauer, Robert, Mindfulness: East versus West—Silence vs. Action, http://www.mpmglobal.com/

Good decisions come from the ability to objectively distinguish among choices and to recognize the things that get in the way of making a decision, for example biases, emotional attachments to positions, and other barriers, which are often self-imposed.

How can one make distinctions without enhanced attention? Distinction making is needed to make decisions. Attention is enhanced through mindfulness practice. The practitioner trains the mind to be more attentive of the things going on in and around himself or herself. Attention is a capability that decision makers should not do without. Attention and distinction making complement one another.

Project managers are constantly making decisions, often collaborating with others. For example, the decision to select a particular product design or vendor is made more easily when the decision makers step back, pay attention to their decision process to mindfully identify prioritized selection criteria and objectively compare alternatives, while being aware of one's own preferences and biases.

The view of Ellen Langer, who is credited for developing the current Western perspective of mindfulness, is summarized as follows:

> Rather than the focus on internal awareness and meditation, this perspective focuses on switching one's thinking from a "mindless" state to one which actively engaged noticing new things. An example of thinking mindlessly is making poor decisions due to mental traps.*

This statement is an example of either-or thinking that results from high-cognitive intelligence, with a left-brain, analytical, bias. Both-and thinking and the acceptance of paradox, coupled with the need to know why, are parts of spiritual intelligence. They complement and enhance cognitive capacity and provide a strong foundation for social intelligence, particularly in the realm of conflict management and decision making.

As a project manager, making decisions based solely on the numbers is dangerous, since numbers such as key performance indicators rarely tell the whole story. The mindfully aware project manager will add a dimension of subjective evaluation—intuition—into the process. The numbers validate the intuition or gut-feel. The intuition validates the numbers.

---

* *ibid*

There will also be an awareness that in many complex situations there are no clear cut, obvious decisions. For example, with both-and thinking, one avoids completely rejecting the use of a methodology because one fears loss of creativity and local autonomy. Instead, one finds a means for applying the methodology's principles and methods in a way that is appropriate to the situation.

Mindless vs. Mindful

Mindfulness training does *not* promote a *mindless* state. Mindfulness meditation allows the movement of the mind. It does not seek to stop thoughts. It is an open and aware state.

Meditation *is* focused on internal awareness. It promotes attention to feelings, mental states, concepts, and thoughts as objects of mindfulness. It is by training the mind through meditation that one becomes able to tell if one is thinking *mindlessly* or not, and to manage one's attention.

Project and program managers who want to be free of mental traps when making decisions can cultivate mindful awareness, so they can be aware when they are falling into mental traps. The project managers may find that they are reacting to a situation based upon the appearance of a set of facts that they perceive they have experienced before without concentrating and seeking to understand through concentration the full depth of the activities and impacts related by those facts in the particular situation. The project manager who uses mindfulness may experience a greater sense of situational awareness and satisfaction with the decision-making process, as well as the outcomes that result.

One should not mistake a quiet, peaceful state of mind or a mind that is open for mindlessness. Meditation does promote recognition of a quiet, peaceful state. This state is a far better platform for action than a hyper-excited state of mind fueled by emotionality. "Thinking in the cold light of day is more likely to be based on more rational, knowledge-based inferences, whereas thinking in the heat of the moment is generally faultier and more likely to contain irrational justifications for risky, yet personally desired, behavior."*

The point of mindfulness meditation is to simultaneously step back and observe whatever is occurring, whether it is silence and non-thinking,

---

* Gutnick, L.A. et al. December 2006. *Journal of BioMedical Informatics*, 39 (6), 720–736 http://www. sciencedirect.com/science/article/pii/S1532046406000451

feeling, perceiving, thinking, obsessing, doing, or awareness itself. An experience of calm and peaceful mind may be experienced as a side-effect.

In projects and programs, making decisions based on objective evaluation, while considering feelings, may result in a higher degree of experienced success factors. For example, making a fear-based decision as to how best to address a delay in the project or a budget overrun is far more likely to result in decision-making based on reactionary judgments rather than fact-based, holistic views of the project with the team. One is wise to step back, calm down, and then face the realized risk.

Conclusion

This chapter has highlighted the need to address project or program management complexity and uncertainty through cognitive readiness. Experiential and analytical understanding are required to fully engage multiple intelligences in order to perform optimally.

Four intelligences have been highlighted—cognitive, emotional, social and spiritual. Mindfulness and mindfulness meditation were also defined, discussed, and techniques provided, as means for cultivating greater mindfulness. Mindfulness was seen as an enabler and enhancer of the intelligences.

Intelligence is a multi-faceted performance-critical success factor. Common terminology refers to multiple intelligences. Individuals have degrees of the various intelligences outlined. Project teams and organizations have degrees of these intelligences also resulting from the interaction of the intelligences of their members.

It is more accurate to frame intelligence as a complex of interacting capabilities. Someone with a high cognitive intelligence and low emotional, social and spiritual intelligence, may be perceived differently, depending on their values and preferences, than someone with a more balanced overall intelligence. Further, any strength in any of the intelligences may lead to different perceptions in a group setting such as a project team. The desire is to have a balanced, interactive team that possesses the complement of intelligences and is capable of recognizing and interacting based upon those strengths.

It is the overall resultant composite of the intelligences that translates into the ability to operate to solve problems or successfully complete project objectives.

Mindfulness supports and enhances intelligence. It provides the power to choose what to think, what to say, and how to act by promoting the ability to see the gap between stimulus and response.

To improve performance:

- Assess intelligence, measuring it as objectively as possible and evaluating it subjectively and anecdotally. For example, if there are continuous unnecessary conflicts with others, maybe that is a sign that some improved emotional and social intelligence is needed. Assess the collective intelligence of the team or organization.
- Plan an approach to improve intelligence in the context of personal and organizational goals, values, and objectives. Consider applying formal and informal mindfulness meditation as part of the plan.
- Act. Do what can be done to influence personal intelligence and the collective intelligence of teams and organizations.
- Monitor the results and proceed.

Chapter 6

From Mindfulness to Action: Applying Augmented Cognition to Project Management

Daniele Di Filippo, Ivano Di Filippo, and Rebecca Winston

Contents

Introduction

Both the Project Management Institute and the International Project Management Association have noted the significance of a cognitive component in the competency requirements for project and program managers. Since mindfulness contributes to that cognitive component, the purpose of this chapter is to present a new perspective to project and program managers and executives around the concept of mindfulness and its impact and application in projects and programs. However, the authors realize that some readers may approach the concept of mindfulness with a negative opinion or a bias* as to its usefulness in a business or organizational setting or even perhaps its usefulness in general. Nonetheless, the following pages will offer an explanation of the potential of mindfulness to help project and program managers achieve success in managing and leading teams through the challenges presented by today's complex projects and program components.

Complex project and program environments are often characterized by a need to mitigate the effects of frequently occurring unpredictable and unexpected events that impact the achievement of the objectives of the project and program components. These unpredictable and unexpected events, brought about by the ambiguity that accompanies a complex environment, frequently include evolving customer needs that result in continuous, or what appear to be continuous, change requests (because they appear each and every reporting period), which adversely affect project and program component outcomes with respect to cost, time, and scope. This situation is commonly known as "scope creep." These complex project and program environments require a facility on the part of the project and

---

* Please see Chapter 4 in this book.

program manager in adaptive decision-making and the flexibility to respond to emerging project and program risks.

At issue in this chapter is whether the acquisition of mindfulness can appropriately enable project and program managers to supplement those "hard" skills (for example, technical, word processing, or language knowledge skills) that are required for *managing* a project with the "soft," or cognitive, skills (for example, listening, persuasion, or critical thinking) that are required for successfully *leading* a project. Within this chapter, an approach to implementing mindfulness will be set forth to exploit its potential for use on the project and program "battlefield," within the day-to-day interactions that the project or program manager faces, to elevate the project or program manager's ability to solve problems, make decisions, and coordinate the numerous activities attendant to a complex environment.

The basis for mindfulness to be considered an "advanced competence" or an "augmented cognition" will be presented by relating the material presented by the International Project Management Association and the Project Management Institute in "The Eye of Competence"* and "The Talent Triangle,"† respectively. Mindfulness is not a competence to be viewed as just another tool, but an integrated competence within both of these modeled views of the competent project or program manager, and an important aspect for achieving success with a complex environment.

The most common biases against mindfulness will be addressed, as exemplified by the following questions:

■ Mindfulness is just an Eastern practice, is it not?
■ Mindfulness involves merely emptying one's mind and stopping one's thoughts, does it not?
■ Mindfulness is a religion or a part of a religion, is it not?
■ Mindfulness requires a huge block of time, does it not?

Through the words of John Kabat Zinn, creator of the Center for Mindfulness in Medicine, Healthcare, and Society at the University of Massachusetts Medical School, mindfulness will be explained. Additionally, some of the studies of Kabat Zinn will be reviewed and the results of those studies will be applied to the field of project and program management. The discipline of mindfulness will then be framed to demonstrate how it

---

* https://www.ipma.world/the-next-generation-of-competence-icb4-2/
† https://www.pmi.org/-/media/pmi/documents/public/pdf/certifications/talent-triangle-flyer.pdf

can help build advanced cognitive competencies to enable the successful application of project and program management. This demonstration will include three facets of the project and program manager's awareness: inner awareness, awareness of other human beings, and awareness of the external environment.

Practical examples of how mindfulness can be applied to create high-performance teams through the activation of mental "flow" will be presented to afford the reader with practical examples of the use of mindfulness in the field. The term "flow" represents the ability to enter into an optimal mental state where the augmented competencies can be expressed in their entirety through maximum performance, similar to being in the "zone," as the term is used in many sports commentaries. Finally, the neuroscientific studies associated with mindfulness will be set forth.

Common Biases Associated with Mindfulness

Enquiries were made of a chief executive officer (which for reasons of privacy may not be revealed in this book) of one of the world's largest brands, who already had a positive disposition toward cognitive readiness. This chief executive officer was asked how he believed other chief executive officers in other companies might react or accept implementing a cognitive readiness approach in their daily work or operating existence, if a team of experts on the subject supported them. Some of his overall responses, as well as a specific response demonstrating a specific bias, are shown:

- "A colleague of mine who is a chief executive officer is not a practitioner of *Eastern practices*, so I doubt that he would champion this type of work for his team." (A belief that mindfulness and cognitive readiness are part of a religious practice is a demonstration of a bias due to lack of a broader understanding of the subject matter.)
- In a more generalized response to the inquiry: "I do not think a 'team of experts *can impact the state of mindfulness* in an executive team. I believe that a team of experts would be completely ineffective in creating *what needs to be a personal practice* for each executive."
- A team of experts' work would be too generalized *and not practical enough* to generate the type of change required for executives... executives need to find their *own way to personal practice*.

■ An individual executive's willingness to engage *would be highly correlated* to his or her own personal circumstances and **the specific needs of the businesses within which they operate.**

■ "I believe personal coaching by people with a personal practice and an understanding of the skills necessary to lead complicated businesses is paramount. Academics very rarely, if at all, have the necessary experience and tools **to shift executive behavior change around leadership behaviors and personal practice.**"

From these limited responses, one can deduce that the executive would not be willing to engage with experts, nor would he probably be willing to have his staff of immediate executives engage with experts for the reasons stated. The statements also reflect that he believes many in his position, chief executive officer, hold the same beliefs and convictions as he. In other words, they also would not be willing to engage or to have their immediate staff executives engage for the same stated reasons. While his responses represent a bias toward mindfulness and perhaps training of certain soft skills, the statements also highlight two other critical factors:

■ Cognitive readiness may be viewed as only an Eastern practice merely because one of its pillars is mindfulness. If considered as an Eastern practice, it may be considered too foreign to incorporate into daily leadership and managerial activities of an organization.

■ In order to advance mindfulness in the project and program management profession, it is imperative to demonstrate practical examples of its beneficial effects in ongoing complex projects and programs or what the chief executive officer called "leading the complicated business."

At the time of these enquiries, the chief executive officer who was interviewed could not have been aware of the fact that, as shown in the Cognitive Readiness Framework in Chapter 2, mindfulness is only one of the components of cognitive readiness. Mindfulness is also becoming a more universally accepted practice. The bias of being viewed as just an Eastern practice and one that must be practiced only at an individual level rather than an organizational level is dissipating. As a result of these and other common biases, evidence will be presented to show that it is becoming a universally accepted practice, that it can be implemented at the organizational level, and that it can be applied in the day-to-day activities of a project and program manager, as well as team members, for overcoming many of the impediments of complex project and program management. (Note: when discussing project and program managers in the chapter, it should be assumed that the material also applies to senior executives as well.)

Mindfulness: Just an Eastern Practice?

Practicing mindfulness should not necessarily be seen as an "oriental practice," as it is often portrayed in movies where the monks of a Buddhist monastery sit on a pillow in the lotus position and emit the sound of "Om"* in their mantras.† Mindfulness should instead be seen as a form of mind training aimed at empowering the practitioner to be active and attentive in the present. When beginning the practice of this pillar of cognitive readiness, mindfulness, it is practiced with intention; in other words, one should be purposeful and plan to practice mindfulness. Over time, practice becomes a learning that tends to improve automatically in a progressive manner and should eventually become effortless or nearly effortless.

What this progressive practice towards automatic inclusion into the daily stream of one's activities means is that it allows the project or program manager to remain present in the course of his or her activities. It should also allow the project or program manager to cultivate a higher quality of the mind, so that the mindfulness changes from being a concept or elusive experience to a way of being or existing, one's daily practice. Depending upon the type of mindfulness practiced, the project or program manager may have no disruption in the flow of work or interactions, but experience a greater attentiveness to the present and the present activities and other stakeholders involved in the activities.

Are Mindfulness and Meditation the Same?

First, one should define meditation. Meditation is the practice of focusing one's mind on a particular object, activity, or thought to achieve a state

---

* Om is a sacred sound and a spiritual symbol in Hindu religion. It is also a mantra in Hinduism and Buddhism (Wikipedia).
† Mantra is a sacred utterance, a numinous sound, a syllable, word or phonemes, or group of words in Sanskrit believed by practitioners to have psychological and spiritual powers (Wikipedia).

of calmness and mental clarity. Now, as a means of mental focusing, stress reduction, and wellbeing, meditation, as defined in this manner, can be integrated with the practice of mindfulness, which is a form of meditation, but is more concerned with the present and awareness of the present and not a focus on one item to the exclusion of the present. However, in the context of project and program management the practice of meditation is only tangentially connected to mindfulness. The connection is that mindfulness is but one outcome of the practice of this form of meditation. This outcome of mindfulness can be achieved through other means than the meditation practiced traditionally by Buddhist monks.

In other words, mindfulness provides an outcome that enables the project and program manager to be more self-aware and attentive to what is happening within her environment. This increased attention enables her to be present and aware of changes in the project or program environment; changes she is personally experiencing; changes her team members are experiencing; changes among and between her team members and other stakeholders; and changes within the business or organizational environment within which her project or program is functioning. The project or program manager will additionally be more nimble in her reactions to these changes, so she can attempt to mitigate the threat risks and exploit the opportunity risks.

Mindful meditation or a program of meditation that includes mindful meditation, if practiced regularly and properly, can help cultivate mindfulness, which should result in the enhanced awareness that a project or program manager needs in order to navigate the complex environment in which many projects and programs are performed. As there are many ways in which meditation can be practiced, there are also different forms of mental training that will allow us to develop a careful, open attitude, but mindfulness must refer to a practice that allows project and program managers, as well as executives, to follow in the day-after-day performance of their course of actions. The practice of mindfulness should not distract, but should enhance. It should be able to be integrated into the day by allowing the project and program manager to focus on present moment of the meeting that is taking place with the stakeholders or the risk review meeting with the team rather than being distracted by concerns, such as performance appraisals, that are due or items to be handled after one leaves the office.

Is Mindfulness Emptying One's Mind and Stopping One's Thoughts?

In some forms of meditation, one may learn to "empty one's mind," such as Sahaja, where the goal is for thoughts to cease. For the project or program manager, the meditative state of being able to stop his thoughts might allow him to regenerate or consciously reset his mental state to view a situation with more clarity. Thus, the project or program manager might create the situation that in Zen is defined as a mental void, or "Ku," but this would happen only to achieve a specific purpose desired by the project or program manager to solve a problem; it is not a means of reaching the general, overall benefits that mindfulness can achieve.

The general, overall benefits of mindfulness that can be achieved from the mental training that the project or program manager would undertake are the awareness of one's own mental patterns, thoughts, emotions, and sensations. With continual practice, one can develop the ability to become aware of what distracts one's attention from everyday tasks during various work activities. Exercises and practice can take many forms, with most requiring one to focus. It is through the act of focusing that one begins to know one's thoughts, feelings, and other sources of distraction.

Recognizing the source of one's distraction and returning to the goal of focusing on what is important to the task at hand is one of the main benefits of mindfulness. Mindfulness also helps one to habituate the recognition of those thoughts that have distracted one, so one can more effectively return to the task at hand. Zen explains with a beautiful image how the mind can remain firm and focused without being distracted by thoughts, which involves looking at one's thoughts like the clouds passing in the sky, or looking at a stream and viewing the thoughts as pieces of paper floating by one. One simply watches them go by and then returns one's mind to a point of focus.

For project or program managers, becoming distracted by thoughts, emotions, or images, rather than the tasks before them, could be detrimental to the project, program, or one or more of the program's components. A project manager sitting in a meeting with a subcontractor, who fails to hear the subcontractor indicate that that the subcontractor is having problems finding sufficient technical human resources in a niche technical area for an upcoming critical project activity, will have missed a potential risk to the project. A project manager must be mentally present in meetings, not just physically present.

For the program manager, who is reviewing the stakeholders and trying to see commonalities for communication purposes and becomes emotional about several who are viewing a few of the projects in the program negatively, he has lost focus. He is not in the moment of reviewing the stakeholders for commonalities for communication purposes. He is lost to the moment. However, if he could recover through finding a path to mindfulness by focusing through one of several techniques, he could focus and again be in the moment to find the commonalities for the purpose of communication.

Is Mindfulness Just Paying Attention to the Breath While Sitting in Lotus Position?

Thinking of mindfulness as just being about paying attention to one's breath is a common misperception or misinterpretation of the writings on the subject. Often the practice of mindfulness is associated with the vision of the monk, sitting in his monastery or in any other place, with his eyes closed paying attention to his breathing. Yes, this act by a person can also be a means to practice mindfulness, and it is certainly one of the simplest and most effective ways to practice mindfulness, especially at the beginning of the training path. However, this form of practicing mindfulness is not the only path or practice exercise available. This form of exercise also does not lend itself to all forums in which the project or program manager might find him or herself during a long day or while travelling. In any case, as long as the practitioner, the project or program manager in this case, is seated or, if alone in a room where one will not be disturbed, is lying down in an attentive position, the act of focusing on the patterns of one's breath, the feel of the air coming into the nostrils and being exhaled through the nostrils, whether one's inhalations are longer or shorter than one's exhalations, the rhythmic expansion and contractions of one's diaphragm as one breathes, can effectively be used as a point of focus, recognizing the thoughts that inevitably float by in one's mind, and gently bringing one's mind back to the patterns of breathing. Other practitioners of mindfulness suggest one can begin by focusing on certain sounds, tastes, or even touch, such as stroking a soft cloth. Mindfulness can also be the practice of yoga, as long as one is completely focused on the physicality of the move. The important concept is focusing to the exclusion of other sensory or thought processes. However, if the other thoughts or senses do encroach one is not to feel bad or angered, but to refocus and not be distracted. The main concept is to be in the moment with the item one is focusing upon: breathing, taste, sound, or touch.

Is Mindfulness a Form of Religion?

Mindfulness has its roots in meditation, which has its foundation in the Buddhist and Hindu religions, as well as other religions; however, recently, mindfulness has had a secular revival. This secular revival may even have a basis in the interest in the religions that formed the foundation of meditation, but the recent practice of mindfulness within organizations and professions has for the most part separated itself from the religious past. Several current large companies have applied the practice of mindfulness to their executives and staff because they do not see it as a religious practice or directly associated with a religion, but a practice that brings significant benefits to the organization. Companies such as Google, Facebook, Twitter, LinkedIn, Apple, Intel, and General Mills have become advocates of the value and benefits of this practice to their organizations and leadership. Some have even developed their own mindfulness programs, perhaps the most notable being Google's Search Inside Yourself program created by Chade Meng Tan with support from CEO Larry Page. In fact, the program at Google became so popular, the program resulted in an outside institute called the Search Inside Yourself Institute, which is a non-profit corporation that trains teams in mindfulness.

What Is Mindfulness?

The academic definition of the term mindfulness, originating from Buddhism, may be summarized as a state of mind where the person uses an intentional, accepting, and non-judgmental focus of attention on sensation, emotions, and thoughts while they arise in the present moment.* For the purposes of this text, one should accept John Kabat Zinn's definition

---

* The concept of the three elements of sensations, emotions, and thoughts is part of that branch of Buddhist philosophy that studies the "void" and is referred to as "the three bamboos." The control of these three bamboos leads to the first stage of the meditator's consciousness.

of mindfulness, which is "awareness that arises by paying attention, on purpose, in the present moment, and non-judgmentally."*

Mindfulness is a competence that every project and program manager and executive should have among his or her competencies for job performance. It should be considered a skill to be applied every day during the project or program life cycle or during the normal business day. The practice of the skill of mindfulness should be a path of progressive growth, similar to that of learning a new language or any new skill set, so that it can be applied in one's project or program management career or everyday life. Through the practice of mindfulness in the workplace, project and program managers, as well as executives, become enabled to improve both their inner focus and outer focus with a positive attitude (assertiveness and stress reduction) and an awareness of one's own thoughts (metacognition, see references to emotional intelligence).

When one experiences certain basic human needs such as thirst or hunger, one often focuses singularly on that one need and the feelings physically and emotionally that result from that need. This focusing extends to the effects of satiating that need. For example, when one drinks that glass of water or eats that snack to satiate that thirst or hunger, one focuses on the coolness and liquidity of the liquid or flavor or texture of food. One also focuses secondarily on the emotions that result from the relief of satiating that need. One can, as a mindfulness exercise, choose to cultivate this faculty and refine it to ever-greater degrees through practice by bringing it into our daily lives.

One must consider the constant "chatter" in one's mind that one often hears, but which is not given a comprehensive explanation. The chattering takes place in one's mind most of the day often without one being consciously aware of it. Do humans experience this "chatter" throughout their lives? As a child, human beings are still close to what is considered the primordial state; however, as one matures, one better learns to use the left side of one's brain, which is dedicated to the rational processing of issues. Eventually this rational processing of issues becomes the prevailing manner of working out issues, problems, and situations in which those issues and problems present themselves. The question is what happens to the right side of the brain since the rational processing has overtaken this type of conscious decision-making? Is the right side of the brain no longer active?

---

* Jon Kabat-Zinn Defines Mindfulness: https://www.youtube.com/watch?v=wPNEmxWSNxg&t=13s

Yes, the right side of the brain is active, but the instinctual phase is somewhat diverted from the feelings and emotions that come from the primordial brain based in the amygdala, based in the temporal lobes of the brain, and acts automatically without conscious control. This change in brain location control prevents one from maintaining one's focus and can take one away from the present moment; in other words, one tends to think of the future, the past, and the conditional. Most humans have experienced the unpleasant experience of not being able to fall asleep at night because during the day their brain was constantly immersed in the rational processing of problems, such as work, financial, and relationship issues. For the project or program manager, leaving the review of the risk register or the budget at the office can prove to be impossible. The need to find the mitigation strategy for the recurring risk will cause the recurring tossing and turning at night. In this situation, one's every attempt to remove rational processing becomes ineffective and causes it to become a stronger response.

With the practice of mindfulness, it becomes easier for one to decide at a certain moment to ignore the mental paths that distract one. In Zen, it is said that in mental training, it is as if one was in a room where several monkeys try to divert one's attention from one's point of focus by jumping around in order to distract one. With mental training, one is looking at them without reacting, without judging them, which will lead them away. In our daily life, those monkeys are, for example, the emotional, financial, or relationship distractions. For the project and program manager, the distractions can range from changes in scope, budget, and schedule to issues and risks with stakeholders, human resources, procurements, and other items attached to the project or program components.

In neuroscience, the daily practice of mindfulness that leads one to maintain focus longer and longer with greater benefits is explained by the creation of new neural circuits, new synaptic inter-connections, and neuroplasticity. Numerous studies have been performed, including one by Canadian psychologist Donald Hebb who declared, "neurons that fire together wire together,"[*] which establishes the ability of neurons to reorganize and ignite at the same time. By practicing mindfulness, by focusing on the issues in the present moment as those issues are being presented, we develop the ability to step away from the habitual, often

---

[*] https://www.supercamp.com/what-does-neurons-that-fire-together-wire-together-mean/ and Hebbian Learning and Plasticity by Wulfram Gerstner: https://pdfs.semanticscholar.org/f9fc/99a5c5 2aa5df1b530dfdeb25dfb6b10bdecf.pdf (page 3 paragraph 9.1.3).

unconscious, emotional reactions to see to issues as they exist in the moment they are presented. One is responding to issues consciously, instead of reacting to them with the brain's automaticity, heuristic paths,* and biases.

The project and program manager practicing mindfulness focuses in the moment on issues in the meetings, and when the same project and program manager is ready to relax at home, he or she can focus on home, family, and relaxation. It is through practice that the project and program manager will find the act of focusing becoming less of a challenge and more of a normative act, whether it is breathing for a couple minutes to focus or focusing on an object or a taste for a couple of moments. Being able to be in the moment will allow the project and program manager to be more engaged in the meeting or review of documents.

Awareness, the Augmented Cognition from the Inner

When one's mind is invaded by thoughts and emotions, it becomes extremely difficult to become aware of one's inner and outer environments in the here and now. Mindfulness helps to focus one's attention on the present moment and to have the possibility to be fully present for what is transpiring in that moment. Being present allows one to perform a more efficient appraisal of where one is with respect to the project or the program and its components. Mindfulness or focusing allows one to more precisely evaluate and analyze earned value expected for interim milestones in the present, so one can move forward in the project or program components. An effective analysis of the earned value metrics enables one to provide more accurate forecasts of team member performance and project progress according to the planned value in the project charter or business plan. While many project and program managers successfully provide effective and efficient analysis of earned value metrics, the project or program manager, who is focused and not diverted, should be able to provide this analysis in a clear and perhaps more efficient, meaning quicker, manner or with less extraneous details. In this case the project or program manager, who practices being aware and being fully present, develops a new competence.

---

* Heuristics are the strategies derived from previous experiences with similar problems. They can see as mind shortcut to accede quickly at information when decision making urge for a rapid response. Heuristics are helpful in many situations because they allow to keep functioning while decision making without stopping to think of a specific issue or problem so also, sometimes they can be efficient some other times the led to cognitive bias as explained in Chapter 4 of this book.

The competence is that of being able to tune in and to connect with the team members, to create a mental bridge with those team members, to understand to which team member it is possible to assign additional tasks, or if it is necessary to redistribute those tasks already assigned. In addition, the project or program manager is refining this new advanced skill by continuing to focus on the team and the project or program.

Several scientists have been active in this research area. One scientific reference is that of Dylan D. Schmorrow, who endeavored to understand the optimization of human performance in complex domains through a better understanding of the cognitive, behavioral, and attitudinal aspects of cognitive readiness. Schmorrow's work, along with that of other scientists, led to interesting articles such as "Augmented Cognition: An Overview," wherein augmented cognition is described as, "a form of human-systems interaction in which a tight coupling between user and computer is achieved via physiological and neurophysiological sensing of a user's cognitive state."[*]

A project manager's augmented cognition leads one to connect with similar studies being carried out with augmented cognition in the military,[†] in which the head of a task force is connected via computer with his soldiers and perceives through sensors whether at the moment there is a requirement to reassign a task. The reassignment was a question whether or not the subject to which the task was previously assigned was under severe stress. In that case, such augmented cognition is computer assisted, outer control. In the case of a project or program manager the control takes place from the inside, inner control, without the computer interface. With the advent of more computer interfaces in a project and program manager's work environment, the positive potentialities in merging these two modes may lead to an ever-higher optimization of cognitive competence. The question is still to be researched and explored in a pilot program in the organizational environment.

With Attention

When the brain is operating on autopilot, it is very difficult for those who do not have training with mindfulness or much practice with mindfulness to

---

[*] Foundations of Augmented Cognition edited by Dylan D. Schmorrow, Cali M. Fidopiastis.
[†] Stanney, K.M., Schmorrow, D.D., and Johnston, M. First Published September 1, 2009. Research Article https://doi.org/10.1518/155723409X448062

block the flow of thoughts, emotions, and feelings that encroach from time to time during the day. One cannot control them with one's will. As stated previously, in Zen it would be like wanting to stop monkeys jumping from one side of the room to the other. The more one puts into doing this task, the more agitated the monkeys become. So, what one can do? According to the body of study into mindfulness one should train oneself to keep attention on the flow of one's thoughts, on the focus of the activity at hand or the item on which one is intending to concentrate. The monkeys should disappear and will gradually begin to calm down, so one's mind is free once more to put itself to the efficient use of focusing on the activity at hand.

There is a Zen narrative that describes the importance of emptying the mind from one's own thoughts, beliefs, and biases: *"Nan-in, a Japanese master during the Meji era (1868–1912), received a university professor who came to inquire about Zen. Nan-in served tea. He poured his visitor's cup full, and then kept on pouring. The professor watched the overflow until he no longer could restrain himself. 'It is overfull. No more will go in!' 'Like this cup', Nan-in said, 'you are full of your own opinions and speculations. How can I show you Zen unless you first empty your cup?'"** One should empty one's mind, so one can begin to experience mindfulness. Once one has begun to learn mindfulness, one can begin to fill the mind. As one focuses one's mind, one will know one's limits.

With Intention, on Purpose

When the art of mindfulness was extracted from Eastern religions, mindfulness was recognized as the main basis of transcendental meditation, but what was overlooked was an important aspect for those who practice mindfulness for the first time. Some individuals may have seen documentaries where potential disciples of Buddhism are made to stand at the door of a monastery with only those people who remain the longest at the door having the opportunity to be admitted to the monastery. Those people who are admitted have demonstrated a firm intention to achieve their purpose. Kabat Zinn stated that it is necessary to have the intention to achieve enlightenment; one cannot "fall into" enlightenment.

---

* 101 Zen Stories is a 1919 compilation of Zen koans including nineteenth and early twentieth century anecdotes compiled by Nyogen Senzaki,and a translation of Shasekishū, written in the thirteenth century by Japanese Zen master Mujū.

Being Non-Judgmental Is a Very Important Element of Mindfulness Practice; Does That Mean That a Project Manager Should Not Be Judging?

"Mindfulness is awareness that arises through paying attention, on purpose, in the present moment, non-judgmentally*" says Kabat-Zinn. Extracting the last piece of his mindfulness definition, "non-judgmentally," one could be confused because the first question that arises is "how can a project manager be completely detached from the typical issues, while leading a project while being non-judgmental?" It is indisputable that it is not possible to avoid "judging" new situations emerging at a given moment, or judging the skills of team members who may be more suited to one task or another. So how can project managers face a situation in which a team member is carrying out an inappropriate action without at least providing a judgment as to that action? Can one continue to be judging, if the requests for changes determine the need to revise the project baseline? Absolutely one can! In addition, one can make more effective decisions. So what does being non-judgmental mean and when is it operable?

If one can continue to provide judgment in limited sets such providing input to project baselines, why is there a continued emphasis on the non-judging aspect of mindfulness?

Kabat Zinn describes non-judging as, *"Mindfulness is cultivated by assuming the stance of an impartial witness to your own experience. To do this requires that you become aware of the constant stream of judging and reacting to inner and outer experiences that we are all normally caught up in, and learn to step back from it."[†]* Awareness is the first key word. When one starts to pay attention to what is on one's mind, one discovers that one judges almost everything, thoughts assume a steady-stream of judging by overgeneralizing, jumping to conclusions too early, and labeling one's own and others' behaviors. This apparent habit of judging and doing an act that one is not aware of doing tends to fill one's daily thought patterns. One's mindfulness objective is to recognize the judging activity as it is occurring in one's mind. When that recognition occurs, one needs to merely observe the process that is taking place without attempting to stop it, in other words, without judging that activity.

---

* https://www.mindful.org/jon-kabat-zinn-defining-mindfulness/
[†] Full Catastrophe Living: Using the Wisdom of Your Body and Mind to Face Stress, Pain, and Illness by Jon Kabat-Zinn - Random House Publishing Group, September 24, 2013.

This mental model also finds itself elicited in projects in the form of *cognition extra ordinem* by the project or program manager or by an executive manager. The *cognition extra ordinem* was a procedural model established by Roman law used to settle public and private disputes, where the proceedings were conducted in front of a single state official who had wide powers to ascertain the facts and also the ability to judge in absentia. In the reality of a project, this concept is applied in an aberrant form by project or program managers and executives, who manifest the term *cognition extra ordinem* as an undisputable decision-making power instead of resolving the controversy through mediation, arbitration, conciliation, or negotiation. The range of being judgmental is from the arbitrary, as demonstrated from the foregoing example. to the smaller judgments one makes during a meeting about the way someone presented or the slides that were used. So when one speaks about mindfulness being non-judgmental, it does not mean that there will not be a series of judgments. What it does mean is that one will be more aware of how judgmental one's mental processes actually are on a regular basis.

That means one cultivates the capacity to see what is actually unfolding in one's brain, recognizing one's biases as they occur without judging them and understanding those biases and judgments in relationship to one's experiences. When one speaks about being non-judgmental, one is talking about being discerning in the clarity of one's compassion towards others and oneself, of understanding the interconnections among items, and recognizing that one's biases create a kind of veil or a filter in front of one's eyes which inhibits one's ability see some things as they truly are. One sees them through the filters of one's ideas, opinions, and preferences. Mindfulness means paying attention to what one is thinking while observing one's thought patterns. By observing these patterns one can acknowledge them, eliminating the redundant and useless ones. The practice of maintaining a non-judgmental state of augmented awareness of one's thoughts, emotions, and feelings on a moment-to-moment basis allows one to be mindfully aware of the unconscious drivers, beliefs, and habits that influence behavior.

The ability to be non-judgmental is important because left alone the brain will turn on its automatic pilot, continuously and unconsciously judging. One's heuristic patterns are automatically colored in this manner. Mindfulness is about being aware of this automatic pilot and taking a fresh perspective and control.

Mindfulness involves an attitude of self-acceptance, curiosity, and awareness of the present moment. It also includes an authentically non-judgmental stance toward things, no matter how "good" or "bad," as the mind would automatically label them. When mindfully aware, one sees more of the unconscious drivers, beliefs, and habits that influence behavior. One can then pass from a phase of being non-judgmental to a phase of conscious judgment that does not provide space for the proverbial, unconscious monkeys to surround us.

The key is to bring awareness and intentionality to the moments of one's life. Being aware of when the brain is automatically judging a situation or a person enables one to pause and acquire some perspective. Was this judgment just an idea that popped in one's mind? Is there another way one can see situation or person? Is the checkout person in the checkout line at the store just a shopper or someone with his or her own history? Is the staff person at the conference room table just a member of the program team soon to present or someone who has a technical background and skill relevant to the program, someone who has worked on other projects or has relevant operations experience, or someone who has worked with one of the subcontractors and understands what the subcontractor can contribute?

When one is running on automatic pilot, most of what one encounters is filtered through one's likes and dislikes. One categorizes experiences along a continuum of good to bad, pleasant to unpleasant, desirable to undesirable. One can find oneself judging the tendency to judge. Cultivating a non-judgmental attitude requires a willingness to become aware of this habit or state of judging, rather than attempting to stop the judging. One can learn to become aware of judging as one engages in the act, so one can make space to respond more skillfully. Over time and with consistent practice, one should begin to notice the judging mind recede into the background, while a clearer awareness comes to the forefront. One should notice a willingness to look beyond one's initial judgments to tolerate ambiguity and discomfort, so one is open to things one may have never noticed.

When one perceives people and situations more accurately, one should have the information needed to respond more appropriately, as is required in the environment of a complex project or program. Being non-judgmental will not mean that one will not make errors in perception or that individual perceptions will not collide on projects or programs. What this should mean is that the project or program manager will be able to listen and see more clearly what is transpiring and to understand the varying perceptions from stakeholders as to what is occurring without judgment.

"When your brain is running, it becomes extremely difficult to decide which thoughts are true or false and which actions are good or bad. This is

because your sense of self and who you are has been fused, to some extent, with the assertions of your deceptive brain messages."* What can one do to enhance the brain's activities such that one begins to refute the deceptive brain messages of the intended actions?

Acceptance

> Acceptance means seeing things as they actually are in the present. Acceptance does not mean that you have to like everything or that you have to take a passive attitude toward everything and abandon your principles and values.†

> **(Kabat Zinn)**

Acceptance does not mean accepting actions that takes place within a project or program, remaining as a passive spectator, but rather it means accepting what happens by having the awareness that what has happened belongs to the reality of the moment. Acceptance also means not necessarily approaching reality with a critical spirit of judgment, but with a judgment that can lead to a spirit of profit or gain. With the acceptance of what is, arises the possibility of cognitive growth for oneself and for the project or program team. The more esteem and positive attitude within teams, the more trust in leadership or the project and program manager grows.

Acceptance does not mean, as a project or program manager, one approves everything that comes before one as a change control. Acceptance of others' human behavior does not mean an abandoning of one's beliefs and values in favor of the beliefs and values of others. Rather, acceptance is a determination to understand and positively handle most situations. Within acceptance, it is enough to remind oneself to be receptive and open to the needs of others.

Being aware of what is happening at a specific moment in a project or program means being fully present, observing and listening to what the team members and other stakeholders say, as well as also sensing what they are hesitant about or refuse to say. For instance, one needs to be able

---

* Rebecca Gladding, M.D., is co-author of You Are Not Your Brain, a clinical instructor and attending psychiatrist at UCLA: https://www.psychologytoday.com/intl/blog/use-your-mind-change-your-brain/201106/mindfulness-is-judgmental
† Full Catastrophe Living, by Jon Kabat-Zinn, PhD, pages 33–40.

to recognize when tensions have been created among the participants in a meeting, even though those tensions may not have been explicitly expressed.

Letting Go

> Often our minds get us caught in very much the same way in spite of all our intelligence. For this reason, cultivating the attitude of letting go, or non-attachment, is fundamental to the practice of mindfulness. When we start paying attention to our inner experience, we rapidly discover that there are certain thoughts and feelings and situations that the mind seems to want to hold on to.*
>
> **(Kabat Zinn)**

How do project and program managers let go? How do they let go of their own thoughts? There are thoughts that continue to keep one awake at night; one does not know how to stop processing these thoughts. In addition, after a day of work, new thoughts are added for cross-processing. After a sleepless night and a previous full day of work, one has to sit in the middle of a private room and simply observe all the "monkeys," the issues, problems, concerns, and other items, that keep one awake, without judgment. In Zen it is said to look, hold, and then leave the three bamboos of thoughts, emotions, and sensations—without judgment.

When the project or program manager has attained the pillar of mindfulness and the ability of letting go, the project or program manager achieves a higher level of self-esteem and assurance in his or her ability to conduct the project or program with less energy expenditure. The ability to transform the distress into eustress should also be experienced. This aspect of mindfulness tends to help to avoid the burnout syndrome of the project and program manager or the executive.

Non-Striving

> Almost everything we do we do for a purpose, to get something or somewhere. But in meditation this attitude can be a real obstacle.

---

* Full Catastrophe Living, by Jon Kabat-Zinn, PhD, pages 33–40.

That is because meditation is different from all other human activities. Although it takes a lot of work and energy of a certain kind, ultimately meditation is a non-doing. It has no goal other than for you to be yourself. The irony is that you already are.*

(Kabat Zinn)

With the words of Kabat Zinn, one understands that the emphasis is on the need to decrease as much as possible the rational and analytical mental pathways or those generated by the left hemisphere in order to reactivate the right hemisphere, the seat of the more immediate elaborations. Paying attention to whatever is happening is what is demanded by mindfulness. One does not strive to judge what others are thinking or doing. One is engaged and interactive; in other words, one is present in the moment. As a project or program manager, one does not need to strive to judge the inputs from the stakeholders, but one should listen, capture, and analyze the inputs from the stakeholders in relationship to the relevant project or program information.

Trust

Developing a basic trust in yourself and your feelings is an integral part of meditation training. It is far better to trust in your intuition and your own authority, even if you make some "mistakes" along the way, than always to look outside of yourself for guidance. If at any time something doesn't feel right to you, why not honor your feelings?†

(Kabat Zinn)

Being more and more aware of one's strengths and above all one's weaknesses is fundamental not only for oneself but also for one's project or program team. To have trust in oneself does not mean to believe and to show that one believes that whatever one does or thinks is necessarily always correct. The search for trust happens externally. Therefore, the team will seek to know that they are trusted and trusted as a team unit. When

---

* Full Catastrophe Living, by Jon Kabat-Zinn, PhD, pages 33–40.
† Full Catastrophe Living, by Jon Kabat-Zinn, PhD, pages 33–40.

one's project or program team detects a trusting attitude, the team remains positive and trusting and in turn this creates more trust toward the project or program manager. What fuels this positive drive is an intrinsic motivation that has been chosen by each team member. Each project or program team member knows that they belong to a team of which they are proud to be a part. This trust relationship enables the project or program manager and the team members to act to the maximum of their abilities by becoming responsive, resilient, and creative.

There is a duel effect to this effect of mindfulness. When one acts in this to create trust from one's very first interactions with the project or program team, one will start to notice oneself becoming more and more compassionate. One becomes a leader who inspires trust and loyalty, not only within the team, but also among other stakeholders. Team members and other stakeholders will see that the project or program manager cares about their welfare and they in turn will care about the project or program manager.

Beginner's Mind

> Too often we let our thinking and our beliefs about what we "know" prevent us from seeing things as they really are. We tend to take the ordinary for granted and fail to grasp the extraordinariness of the ordinary. To see the richness of the present moment, we need to cultivate what has been called "beginner's mind," a mind that is willing to see everything as if for the first time.*

> **(Kabat Zinn)**

Seeing people, their behavior, and the resulting actions and issues through the eyes of a child or through the beginner's mind sounds intriguing, but what does this mean? The reality is it does not mean that one should not abandon the experiences one has gained over many years. What it does mean is that one should question whether one is focused enough to filter one's biases, which each person has. Viewing each experience with a beginner's eye also means setting aside one's initial expectations or perceptions of how another person should behave or react or how a meeting

---

* Full Catastrophe Living, by Jon Kabat-Zinn, PhD, pages 33–40.

should resolve. It means approaching the experience with curiosity. Walking into the next interaction with a group of outside project stakeholders on a construction project, one should enter without a preconception of how they will react to material presented or to the specifications of the design and site issues. Instead, one should enter the meeting with openness and a sense of curiosity about them as stakeholders and listen to what they are stating and why they are stating it before analyzing that information and attempting to determine the impact on the project of what was stated.

Mindfulness Can Create Significant Competencies for a Project Manager

Mindful Listening

Mindful listening is an enhancement of the soft skill of listening gained through the competence of mindfulness. When one is able to achieve mindful listening, one is able to provide the person with whom one is communicating one's full attention or the project or program team members one's full attention as the project or program manager.

When one listens with mindfulness, one is able to focus into the speaker, and regardless of the random thoughts that arise in one's mind, one is able to come back to the present-time experience of listening just to the message of the speaker. The quality of mindful listening is that one is listening with one's full awareness and compassion. One is taking one's energy to place oneself as close to the place of the speaker as one can, by reaching a place of empathetic listening by attempting to understand their motivations and drivers. This quality of mindful listening is beneficial to the project and program manager when listening to team members and other stakeholders, especially in complex projects and programs. If one fails to understand the motivations and drivers of the speaker, one often substitutes one's own motivations and drivers. One receives the wrong messages or distorted messages instead of the intended messages. This miscommunication can not only be risky for the project or program, but it can damage relationships in the long-term.

By focusing one's attention on the message of the speaker, the mindful listener should eventually develop a skill that enhances his or her ability to recall the conversation in greater clarity than that conversations prior to the development of this skill. The reason for this greater clarity is not only the more focused listening, but also the lack of interference of biases or past experiences. This lack of interference allows one to better classify the speaker's message in mental groupings that often exist prior but have become clouded over time by those interfering biases or past experiences. The ability to recall a past interaction or talk not only provides one the ability to have facts and figures at hand quicker, but enhances relationships by saying to speakers that one valued the interaction and the person.

While the project or program manager is silencing their own "inner noise," they are also becoming more self-aware. The project or program manager, by silencing the "inner noise," is becoming aware of the biases and past experiences and how they interfere in the understanding of messages. It also highlights for them how much clearer they must make their own messages so they do not become entangled in someone else's "inner noise."

In guiding a steady course through the uncertainties and unpredictability of a complex project or program, mindful listening is one of the first competencies that a project or program manager should attempt to develop to listen and listen with purpose to key stakeholders, whether those key stakeholders are part of the project or program team or are stakeholders. The project manager should spend the first part of the project or program components in what is referred to as the "incubation phase" in a previous article* applying the advanced listening skills of mindful listening. This application will allow the project or program component managers to highlight the concerns and opinions of the stakeholders by identifying the strengths and weaknesses, possible threats and opportunities to avoid scope creep, and other adverse occurrences. These statements are backed up by recent research.

Faulty listening has been the cause in the past of numerous failures of major projects, as reported in the report "Mindful Listening,"† where the authors reported a list of projects that failed because of poor communication. Since 2013, many discoveries have been made in the field of neuroscience and some of them have been applied to project management through mindfulness, and Goldstein's article is clearly one of them. In that

---

* "The Six Phase Comprehensive Project Life cycle Model" published in December 2012 (co-authored with Russell Archibald and Daniele Di Filippo) PM World Journal. https://pmworldjournal. net/?article=the-six-phase-comprehensive-project-life-cycle-model-including-the-project-incubationfeasibility-phase-and-the-post-project-evaluation-phase-2

† Goldstein, M. 2013. Mindful listening. Paper presented at PMI® Global Congress 2013—North America, New Orleans, LA. Newtown Square, PA: Project Management Institute: https://www.pmi. org/learning/library/important-project-manager-mindful-listening-5901

article, the author notes that "the listener also can have personality barriers involving strong feelings toward the topic or speaker." However, great strides have been made to explain human feelings governed by biases as described in Chapter 4 of this book. The authors also describe barriers to mindful listening as, "judging the speaker" or "focusing on what you are going to say—may result in tuning out...."

The efforts by the Project Management Institute and the International Project Management Association have not been sufficiently elaborated with research, journal articles, or published articles based upon applied knowledge of practitioners. The area requires further information for the body of practitioners to be able access the knowledge in order to begin to apply the knowledge in their own projects and programs.

Mindfulness and Situation Awareness

Inner awareness and outer awareness were discussed previously and the efficacy of being empathetic and compassionate. To complete the framework of mindfulness, the next focus relies on an outer awareness, awareness of one's external environment and to the situations that are part the complex of that external environment at a given moment. Situations in a complex project can arise suddenly without any notice and may not even be foreseeable at the time of drafting the project charter, the business plan, or when one is drafting the risk management plan initially.

Situation awareness has been recognized as a critical, yet often elusive, foundation for successful decision-making across a broad range of complex and dynamic systems, including project management, general business functions, health care, and military functions. Mica Endsley defines situation awareness informally and intuitively as, "knowing what's going on" and, more formally, as, "the perception of the elements in the environment within a volume of time and space, the comprehension of their meaning and the projection of their status in the near future."* She is president of Situational Awareness (SA) technologies and its website notes, "At its essence, Situation Awareness...is about having the information you need about the environment and the system you operate to make effective decisions."† In

---

* Situation Awareness: Review of Mica Endsley's 1995 Articles on Situation Awareness Theory and Measurement: Christopher D. Wickens, University of Illinois, Champaign, Illinois: https://pdfs.semanticscholar.org/2d07/f1eb2f7bd5081274225041db75a63c4487df.pdf
† http://satechnologies.com/about/

other words, situational awareness is having the information about what is happening in the environment around one or in which one is working or living. It is about understanding the significance of that information to one in connection to that environment.

Another interesting piece of research is the one by John Darwin and Alex Melling of Sheffield Hallam University. In the research report "Mindfulness and Situation Awareness,"* Sheffield and Melling highlighted the connection between the two concepts of mindfulness and situation awareness. Within the research paper, the authors state, *"This paper argues that mindfulness training can develop the situational awareness of the individual actor beyond a mind focused on 'what' we want to achieve, into a mind constantly engaged in updating 'how' to achieve it, given the evolving situation—a state of mind we term Mindful Competence."* Their research seems to confirm that mindfulness is an inner approach to the achievement of an advanced cognition. Situational awareness that comes from mindfulness results from the ability that the practice of mindfulness brings to the practitioner of being more aware and focused in the present in a non-judgmental way. Mindfulness, along with one's emotional intelligence, allows one to recognize and acknowledge the feelings and emotions of others, such as project and program team members and stakeholders, as they relate to the changing realities of the environment in which they are performing or engaging in project or program activities.

In the context of situation awareness, the project or program manager may make sudden decisions in situations not foreseeable or predictable. The action of the mindful project or program manager, as explained in Chapter 5 of this book, should take the form of a responsive reaction, instead of a reactive reaction. Sheffield and Melling carried out a similar research in order to enhance the probability that military commanders would use "wise decisions," instead of just reacting to unexpected situations.

Mindfulness leading to wisdom has been a much-debated topic in several conferences held in different parts of the globe. This research is in line with the thinking that mindfulness will eventually lead to a maturing or a learning that is known as wisdom. "Mindfulness-Wisdom is a harmony of changing conditions. Mindfulness-Wisdom is in harmony with changing conditions. It knows the pain of holding on and it remembers that the whole show of human emotions, thoughts, and experiences are not a personal

---

* https://www.researchgate.net/publication/235091729_Mindfulness_and_Situation_Awareness

problem or failing, but rather universal patterns of shared experience."* The author of this quote has also stated that mindful wisdom becomes the new lens or filter through which one views the interactions, environments, and experiences one has. Mindful wisdom is a new and debated area of the mindful competence and will require study and exploration.

Darwin and Melling speak of how "conscious competence" becoming "unconscious competence" over time. Managers learn how to do a task competently, and then fall into automatic pilot. Mindfulness allows project and program managers to move from conscious competence into what Darwin and Melling term "mindful competence" without falling back on heuristics or biases. The reason one does not fall back on heuristics or biases is that one remains focused and conscious of one's heuristics and biases, even when one is not in the active mode of checking for them as one is when learning to be mindful.

Mindfulness and Flow

Advances in flow research have been undertaken in the field of project management.

Under the umbrella of studying of competencies, the term flow represents the ability to enter into an "optimal mental state" where one's skills can be expressed in their entirety through maximum performance. Flow can be seen as a mental state where project and program managers, as well as team members, perform their activities immersed in a maximum concentration in a feeling of energized focus, full participation, and enjoyment in what they have been being doing. To date, increasingly within a project or program components, flow has been seen not only at the individual level but also at the team level as a collective experience.

One of the main questions researchers have been posing is whether it is enough for a team member to reach flow in a project. Mihaly Csíkszentmihályi, a Hungarian-American psychologist, first recognized and named the psychological concept of flow as follows: "flow denotes the holistic sensation present when we act with total involvement. We experience it as a unified flowing from one moment to the next, in which we feel in control of our actions, and in which there is little distinction

---

* Heather Sundberg - Garrison Institute - https://www.garrisoninstitute.org/blog/mindfulness-matures-wisdom/

between self and environment; between stimulus and response; or between past, present, and future."* Csíkszentmihályi outlined his theory that people are happiest when they are in a state of flow—a state of high concentration or complete absorption with the activity and the situation at hand. His idea of flow is identical to the feeling of being in the moment. The flow state is an optimal state of intrinsic motivation, where the individual is fully immersed in what he or she is doing.

Moreover, it is not always good for a project manager to be himself or to have his team members in a state of flow at a particular moment. While flowing or being in the cognitive zone, the individual or the team losses part or all of his, her, or their inner and outer awareness. In such a situation, the individual or group members tend to focus on the sense of perceived self-efficacy that produces more pleasure than viewing or experiencing what is occurring in the moment to move the objectives of the project forward.

If one cannot master the flow state, one might not be able to react to other contemporaneously emerging situations, be able to change one's focus from one task to another, or to manage them simultaneously. There's a need to be aware of the importance of the flow state, as well as being able to actively guide this state of mind.

Awareness of the flow state and the active guidance of the state of mind are greatly aided by mindfulness, which prepares the mind for this increased level of control. This control can transform a flow into a dynamic and controlled flow, where the individual maintains control while dealing with his or her task.

From Mindfulness to Cognitive Readiness to Reach Flow

Flow becomes an element controlled by the elements of cognitive readiness: emotional, social, and cognitive intelligences. In this new perspective, cognitive readiness not only allows a high degree of adaptability in a dynamic, unpredictable environment, but also provides the ability to move rapidly, without effort, with awareness, from one task to another, remaining in optimal flow, thus maintaining one's own perceived self-efficacy in actively and concretely influencing the progress of the project or program components. This is precisely the definition used by Morrison and Fletcher's "Cognitive readiness is the mental preparation (including skills,

---

* Mihaly Csíkszentmihályi - Flow and the Foundations of Positive Psychology.

knowledge, abilities, motivations, and personal dispositions) an individual needs to establish and sustain competent performance in the complex and unpredictable environment of modern military operations"* in which the authors noted that mental preparation comes to be "the ability to switch between one optimal mind state and another" and keep the motivation for the whole project while satisfying the need to maintain perceived self-efficacy.

Summarization of Mindfulness

Mindfulness, the "simple" practice of being aware of one's breathe, thoughts, emotions, and sensations can become the foundation for a new competence. Mindfulness is about becoming aware of how the diverse internal and external stimuli from other people and the environment can provoke automatic, immediate, unthinking responses in project and program managers.

Mindfulness allows one to connect with oneself, so one can identify and expand beyond one's personal limitations to better connect with others. There's a shift needed, which allows one to start seeing, hearing, and internalizing things from a new and interesting perspective. From this new perspective, one continues with this mind-shift to a clearer state of mind.

---

* Teaching and Measuring Cognitive Readiness Editors: O'Neil, Harold F., Perez, Ray S., Baker, Eva L. (Eds.) - Chapter 2 The Evolving Definition of Cognitive Readiness for Military Operations J. D. Fletcher and Alexander P. Wind. https://www.springer.com/cda/content/document/cda_downloaddocument/9781461475781-c1.pdf?SGWID=0-0-45-1414356-p175138187. Accessed on November 18, 2018. Cognitive Readiness Preparing for the unexpected - J.D. Fletcher - September 2004. https://www.researchgate.net/profile/J_D_Fletcher/publication/235026215_Cognitive_Readiness_Preparing_for_the_Unexpected/links/565db2ab08aefe619b2686ae/Cognitive-Readiness-Preparing-for-the-Unexpected.pdf. Accessed on November 18, 2018. Cognitive Readiness - John E. Morrison, J. D. Fletcher - October 2002. http://www.dtic.mil/dtic/tr/fulltext/u2/a417618.pdf

Chapter 7

Emotional and Social Intelligence Competencies and the Intentional Change Process

Richard Eleftherios Boyatzis, Daniel Goleman, Fabrizio Gerli, Sara Bonesso, and Laura Cortellazzo

Contents

Emotional and Social Intelligence Competencies: the Pillars of Cognitive Readiness

In earlier chapters, emotional and social intelligence competencies have been defined as one of the pillars of cognitive readiness for project managers (Archibald et al., 2013). Indeed, emotional and social intelligence competencies are frequently involved in enhancing the cognitive readiness of teams. They are extremely useful for reducing tension and increasing cooperation among team members by identifying and assessing their feelings, anticipating their actions, acknowledging their concerns, and following up on their issues (PMI, 2013). They also help acquiring flexibility in order to react promptly to challenges and threats. Emotional and social intelligence competencies are related to the understanding and management of the self and of interpersonal relationships. In this chapter, the definitions and classifications of these competencies, as well as how they can be developed in an effective and sustainable way will be explored.

Research on emotional and social competencies started in the 1970s with the seminal work of Richard Boyatzis and, subsequently, with the work of David McClelland, who provocatively argued that it would be better to hire people for competence rather than intelligence (McClelland, 1973). The underlying idea was that people who perform best in their job are not the ones who have a higher Intelligence Quotient score. A systematic comparison of best and average performers showed that distinguishing competencies are mainly the ones related to emotional and social behaviors.

Many workshops, training activities, and courses for the development of emotional and social competencies are available currently; however, these courses mainly provide some hints and knowledge about the competency, without other types of interventions such as follow-on training, coaching, and other sustainable reinforcements that support long-lasting personal change. Scientific research has demonstrated that in order to achieve effective and sustainable change, an experiential learning path must be followed. The Intentional Change Theory (ICT) presents its neurological, emotional, and behavioral implications (Goleman et al. 2002; Boyatzis, 2008a).

In this chapter, first, the importance of emotional and social competencies will be analyzed by providing a classification of different behaviors correlated with effectiveness. Second, the ICT will be presented by describing its neurological underpinning and examining in depth each of the phases of this process.

Why Emotional and Social Intelligence Competencies Matter

The concept of competency has shifted from being a novelty to being widespread in organizations since McClelland (1973) presented it as a critical factor in understanding performance differences (Boyatzis, 2008b). The "competency movement" was driven by dissatisfaction with the capacity of traditional intelligence measures, such as the Intelligence Quotient, to explain significant variances in performance. Cherniss (2000) reported the results of some studies attesting that Intelligence Quotient could explain just 4%–25% of the variance in performance. In a large variety of organizations (Goleman, 1995), it was shown that more than 80% of the competencies that differentiate leaders who excel in their role were of emotional and social types. Emotional and social intelligence competencies have been associated especially with effectiveness as measured by designated metrics in responsibility roles and leadership positions (Boyatizis, 1982; Goleman, 1995; Goleman et al., 2002; Emmerling and Goleman, 2005; Rosete and Ciarrochi, 2005; Abraham, 2006) due to their impact on the ability to manage personal relationships (Cherniss and Goleman, 2001), understand and develop teams, influence and cope with external demands and pressures, and successfully identify and manage conflicts (Abraham, 2006).

A set of different studies has demonstrated the impact of emotional and social competencies at the organizational level. These studies show the impact of emotional and social competencies for predicting subordinates' job satisfaction (Miao et al., 2006), increasing employability (Azevedo et al., 2012), decreasing stress level, and better organizational climate conditions. For people leading a team, as project managers do, emotional and social competencies can be extremely beneficial for increasing interpersonal understanding and managing positively the emotions of group members. The emotional and social competencies of the leader have an impact on operational excellence, customer loyalty, financial performance, and attracting and retaining talent. The effect of emotional and social intelligence competencies on performance has been tested in a variety of contexts ranging from financial advisors (Boyatzis, 2006) to school principals (Williams, 2008), from physician leaders (Hopkins et al., 2015) to Catholic priests (Boyatzis et al., 2010a), showing consistent results on the importance of these competencies in achieving higher levels of performance in the role.

Boyatzis (2009: 750) defines competencies as "a set of related but different sets of behavior organized around an underlying construct, which we call the 'intent'." These competencies are alternative behaviors that are manifestations of the same underlying construct. For instance,

> listening to someone and asking him or her questions are several behaviors. A person can demonstrate these behaviors for multiple reasons or to various intended ends. A person can ask questions and listen to someone to ingratiate him or herself or to appear interested, thereby gaining standing in the other person's view. Or a person can ask questions and listen to someone because he or she is interested in understanding this other person, his or her priorities, or thoughts in a situation. The latter we would call a demonstration of empathy. The underlying intent is to understand the person. Meanwhile, the former underlying reason for the questions is to gain standing or impact in the person's view, elements of what we may call demonstration of influence (Boyatzis, 2009:750).

These abilities that make people outstanding in the workplace have been classified into three main clusters that will be presented in detail in the following paragraph: the ability to recognize, understand, and manage one's own emotions or emotional intelligence competencies; the ability to recognize, understand, and manage others' emotions or social intelligence competencies; and the ability to analyze information and situations or cognitive competencies.

What are Emotional and Social Intelligence Competencies?

Emotional and social intelligence competencies are classified in three main groups (Boyatzis, 2009).

Emotional intelligence competencies are crucial for leading and managing ourselves. This cluster refers to the ability to recognize one's own feelings, preferences, and resources, and the ability to manage one's own moods, impulses, and emotions in a way that facilitates rather than interferes with the task to be performed. It includes *emotional self-awareness*, which is defined as the ability to understand what one feels in a given moment and to use these preferences to guide the decision-making process and also comprehend the capacity to have a realistic assessment of one's skills.

Moreover, it encompasses *self-management competencies*, namely emotional self-control, which is crucial in highly stressful working environments; positive outlook, which is the ability to see the positive side of things; drive to achieve, which concerns the ability to set personal challenging standards and continuously find a way to improve; and adaptability, which is useful in volatile and unstable environments because it helps to quickly metabolize change. In the organizational context, but also in everyday personal life, self-management competencies matter a lot because the person's mental state and moods end up influencing the mood of others through an emotional contagion (Goleman, 2006).

Social intelligence competencies involve understanding others and managing relationships with other people. On one side, *social awareness competencies* help to understand what people experience, to be able to see their point of view, and to cultivate relationships in tune with a large number of different people. Competencies of this type are empathy and organizational awareness. Empathy concerns the ability to get in tune with others by understanding and perceiving their emotions. This requires being able to listen carefully and understand their point of view, which may be different due to background or cultural differences. Organizational awareness consists of the ability to identify social and power networks as well as the underlying values that drive the functioning of groups. On the other side, *relationship management competencies* are more related to managing emotions in interpersonal relationships and interacting with others. This group includes all competencies used to persuade and guide, negotiate, resolve conflicts, and achieve collaboration, such as influence, coach and mentor, inspirational leadership, teamwork, and conflict management. Influence is the ability to have a positive impact on others. It involves persuading or convincing others to get them to support one's ideas, whereas coach and mentor is the ability to foster the long-term learning or development of others. Inspirational leadership refers to the ability to guide others by involving them and triggering emotional resonance phenomena, which means instilling a sense of pride as part of the group and inspiring people through a compelling vision, bringing out their best. Teamwork is one of the most important competencies in organizational life and entails being respectful and collaborative toward the group, encouraging other members to actively and enthusiastically engage in the common cause, strengthening the team spirit, and encouraging the participation of all. Conflict management is the ability to handle difficult individuals, groups of people, or tense situations with diplomacy and tact.

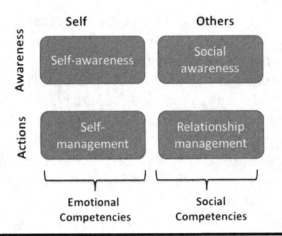

Figure 7.1   The emotional and social intelligence competency model.

The aforementioned two clusters cover four distinct areas of abilities, as depicted in Figure 7.1.

The third cluster concerns cognitive competencies, which refer to abilities related to understanding the reasons for complex events and recognizing patterns in situations or events. Two main competencies compose this group: system thinking and pattern recognition. The first is the ability to explain complex situations and understand the role of different factors and how they influence each other; the cause–effect relationships implied in a certain situation; and the results they bring. The second consists of the capacity to recognize underlying schemas or models among information or situations that seem causally related, identify similarities, and use analogies to describe concepts.

The Development of Emotional and Social Competencies: The Neurophysiological Base

Despite the importance of emotional and social competencies in and outside of the workplace, common belief often questions how these competencies can be developed, or if they can be developed at all. Indeed, decades of research in different fields, such as psychotherapy, training programs, and education, have shown that people can actually change their behavior (Cherniss and Goleman, 2001; Boyatzis, 2008b). However, it appears clear that emotional and social competencies are more complex and difficult to develop than technical hard skills. The reason appears to be that acquiring or improving emotional and social competencies ultimately requires a change in our neural connections and, consequently, in our common behavior. Neural connections are created over time and form a structure that routinizes our automatic response to stimuli. The more a repertoire of thoughts, feelings, and actions is used, the stronger the neural connections become, thus creating a dominant pathway for nerve impulses that represents the brain's default answer and leads the person to deploy a certain behavior automatically and spontaneously when facing a certain situation. As opposed to connections that are not used which become weak, leading to progressive disuse of the related behaviors. The change of well-established and rooted behaviors requires re-programming neural circuits, involving both the rational part of our brain (the neocortex) and the emotional one (the limbic system). While the neocortex is used to gain knowledge and acquire ideas, such as learning the concepts of revenues and costs, the limbic system requires practice, repetition, active involvement, and feedback to learn. This separation of function clearly explains why it is not possible to learn the competency of empathy just by reading an article on the topic, and the functioning of the limbic system also shows that learning or improving a behavioral competency takes time. Previous studies have highlighted the need for engaging in experiential activities and being involved in a process of reflection, feeling, and practice to affect a real behavioral change. The Intentional Change Process, which is presented in the next section, relies specifically on these concepts.

The Process of Developing Emotional and Social Competencies: The Intentional Change Theory

Drawing on decades of research in the field, the Intentional Change Process (Boyatzis and McKee, 2005) has evolved to be a theoretical framework that takes into account the essential components of desirable, sustainable change in people's behavior, thoughts, feelings, and perceptions (Boyatzis, 2008a) and constitutes a way to engage successfully in personal transformation. The process entails working on five stages or discoveries aimed at nurturing motivation and awareness, creating a structure for the learning process, practicing new behaviors, and receiving feedback. This process should lead to sustainable changes in habits, perceptions, and behaviors, as well as a greater ability to achieve results in life through a deeper understanding

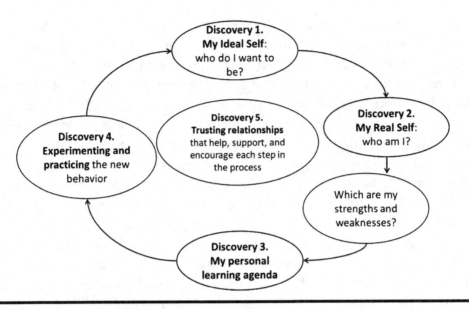

Figure 7.2   Intentional change process. (Adapted from Boyatzis, R.E. 2008a. *Consulting Psychology Journal*, 60 (4), 298–313.)

of one's own and others' emotions. The five discoveries of the Intentional Change Process are described as follows (Figure 7.2).

The ideal self: In this phase, the person asks himself who he wants to be in the future and what kind of person he wants to become. This step helps a person understand his or her own aspirations and deep personal desires concerning both private and professional life. This awareness finally leads to the creation of a personal vision, as a manifestation of the ideal self to be a driver to change.

The real self: This phase entails the need to understand the actual behaviors and personal characteristics of the person. This understanding may be done by taking into account a self-evaluation, and the evaluation by other people of the person's behavior. This phase enhances personal awareness, but also requires openness to feedback. The comparison of the ideal- and real-self enables a person to identify his or her own strengths and weaknesses. Congruent areas between the two selves represent strengths: competencies that are demonstrated and are in line with the achievement of the personal vision. Non-congruent areas are considered weaknesses, as they refer to personal characteristics that the person does not demonstrate but are important for the achievement of his or her future objectives and personal efficacy.

The learning agenda: In order to exploit the strengths and work on the weaknesses, it is necessary to develop a learning plan to guide a person through the activities he/she needs to carry out to fill the gap between the real and the ideal self. To be effective, the plan needs to take into account expectations, learning styles, planning preferences, and time needed to accomplish results.

Experimenting and practicing new behaviors: As explained before, the way to make a solid change lasting over time is to rethink, try, and practice new behaviors until such behaviors become automatic. At the beginning of this stage, it is often useful to experience and practice new behaviors in a protected environment.

Developing trusting relationships: The fifth phase concerns the identification of people who can help a person go through the process of change, such as friends, colleagues, a partner, or a coach. This phase transversely affects all others, primarily because the process of change is long and complex, and the help of other people may be indispensable in supporting transformation, and secondarily because relationships are a fundamental part of our lives and environment, and emotional intelligence emerges above all through relationships (Goleman, 1995).

Three main connected elements characterize this process:

The process is intentional and self-directed: One of the main reasons for failure in a personal change process is a lack of motivation. Indeed, adults tend to change only if they want to change. Since developing emotional and social competencies is a complex and long process in terms of time, strong motivation is needed. The ideal-self phase is accomplished by giving the opportunity to reflect on and visualize the best version of the future the person could achieve. The personal vision, which carries dreams, aspirations, personal values, and hope, represents an important driver to approach the desired end state. Once the ideal-self is activated, it monitors and guides actions and decisions toward the emergence of a new state of being or the maintenance of the current one with increased awareness and mindfulness (Boyatzis and Akrivou, 2006).

Moreover, this process relies on the self-determination of learning objectives according to the comparison between the ideal and the real self (Boyatzis et al., 2002; Boyatzis and Saatcioglu, 2008). This self-determination is crucial in making the process effective, because people tend to learn what they want and need to learn. Autonomy and self-determination are important elements for pursuing an effective personal transformation. Usually, ideas and behaviors in which the individual is not directly interested are acquired only temporarily. Even in situations in which the person is asked to change behavior under coercion, the behavior is often extinguished after the force condition is removed. One of the biggest strengths of the

Intentional Change Process is to make people aware of their main desires for the future and the competencies they need and involving them in a development activity in which they care about the learning objectives.

It is sustainable: The Intentional Change Process is composed by steps that make the change sustainable in time. First, it is based on strong personal motivation derived by the articulation of the personal ideal-self, which reduces the risk of process abandonment. Second, it fosters a high degree of awareness of one's own personal characteristics, not just looking at the individual's perspective, but also engaging the person in an external, 360-degree assessment that gives that person the opportunity to see how others see him or her. Awareness of what is possible and what is needed to achieve the ideal final state is a driver for conscientious developmental engagement. Once the person understands the importance of changing, he or she is much more persistent in getting through the entire process. Lastly, a mechanism of reinforcement of motivation is included in the fifth phase related to the development of trustful relationships, key factors in sustaining the individual in all phases of the process.

It includes feedback: The development and use of positive social relationships is relevant in this process. Social relationships are inevitably part of our daily life and constitute the base of interaction to experience and improve our emotional and social competencies. Exploiting connections with trusted people is a key element in every step of the process. Honest dialogues with others can open people's minds to new possibilities and paths by making them reflect on their true desires. External feedback is especially useful in enhancing awareness of manifested behavior by giving honest comments about how the person is perceived from the outside. Moreover, other people may help indicate whether the person is progressing during the practicing phase of the process and help better direct his or her efforts toward change.

In the following section of this chapter, the five phases of the Intentional Change Process will be analyzed and described in detail.

Ideal Self: Crafting a Compelling Vision

The first phase of the Intentional Change Process concerns the discovery of an individual's ideal-self. The term *discovery* is used to underline the fact that even though people know the importance of reflecting on their deep desires and considering a positive image of themselves in the future, they rarely take time and make an effort to do so. Instead, people favor a more limited and static conception of their future life. This perception is particularly true when a person is bonded to daily routines and working stress and is not alert to any need of change. The ideal-self phase fosters a newly acquired awareness of people's desires, which may result in an epiphany.

The ideal-self is the ideal image of the person one wants to be in the future, considering his or her personal life, family life, professional life, identity, and purpose. It is *"a psychological component of the self, partially conscious and partially unconscious, varying from individual to individual. It is both privately conceptualized and socially influenced"* (Boyatzis and Akrivou, 2006: 625). Being ideal, it functions as an instrument of regulation and motivation that allows you to orient, direct, and organize the will to the desired change. Three main components converge in the articulation of the ideal self: the image of a desired future, the core identity, and hope.

The image of a desired future is the articulation of the person's dreams, aspirations, and fantasies. It is of a cognitive nature and the result of a combination of passions, dreams, and values. Passions should be part of one's ideal-self, as they constitute something one likes, considers important, and invests with time. Passions convey energy and pursuing them implies higher motivation and well-being. Values are durable convictions or the organization of beliefs concerning preferable modes of conduct or end-states (Rokeach, 1973). These values are key factors to take into account when articulating the ideal-self, because values guide, sometimes unconsciously, the selection and evaluation of behaviors and situations. Associating the individual's desired future with a set of deep and important values increases motivation toward the realization of the desired future and favors its achievement (Carton et al., 2014).

Another component of the ideal self is the person's core identity. The core identity is a relatively stable set of enduring individual characteristics, constituted mainly by motives, traits, and roles adopted consistently in social settings. Traits are primarily unconscious and drive toward a certain behavior, while motives represent the reason for one's behavior. The core identity is the personal context that shapes the articulation of the ideal-self by creating coherence with the historical elements that have always characterized and distinguished the individual.

Hope is the affective driver of the ideal-self, conceived as an emotional state (Aspinwall and Leaf, 2002). When a person feels a sense of hope he or she feels excited about the future and considers it achievable. This achievability raises the spirit and moves the energy to the use of the personal resources to achieve one's goal. According to the perspective given by social sciences, hope combines the articulation of goals with the conviction that these goals can be achieved, outlining a course of action and generating a sense of well-being, as a result of the process of achieving the goal (Boyatzis and McKee, 2005). The thought of being able to somehow control and be the creator of one's own destiny and the euphoria of believing the goal is achievable make hope the spark that illuminates and guides the change. Hope is composed of two main elements: optimism and self-efficacy. On the one hand, the degree of people's optimism has an effect on the conviction of being able to succeed in their intentions and realizing their dreams. On the other hand, self-efficacy determines the perception of a person's possibilities by measuring what he or she can really do, thus creating a degree of realism necessary to avoid falling into utopian and unrealizable hopes. According to Armor and Taylor (1998), people's predictions are not indiscriminately optimistic, but tend to obey the constraints of reality and therefore to be more or less realistic according to the needs of the situation and the psychological state of the individual. By combining optimism and self-efficacy, people seem to be able to simultaneously satisfy their need to extract meaningful information from their environment, even when it is negative or threatening. They are also able to maintain a positive outlook on themselves and the future. An optimistic vision can adapt the present behavior toward achieving a future goal (Sharot et al., 2007) by increasing motivation, commitment, and perseverance, even in the face of obstacles that might otherwise compromise performance (Armor and Taylor, 1998).

At the individual level, the ideal-self is often compromised and suppressed by one or multiple "ought-selves" (Boyatzis and Akrivou, 2006, p. 627). In contrast to the ideal-self, the ought-self is someone else's desire or interpretation of what a person's ideal-self should be (Boyatzis and Akrivou, 2006). It explains an image of the desired future imposed by others that the individual may accept and follow in order to please them. It is reasonable that reference groups or social identity groups may influence the individual's perception of the self, and, to the extent this perception becomes intentionally integrated into a person's ideal-self, no conflicts emerge. However, pursuing an ought-self not coherent with one's own real desires will generate frustration and anger, once the person realizes he or she followed dreams and expectations for which he or she has never been passionate.

The manifestation of the ideal-self is a personal vision, the most important representation of the person's dreams and aspirations, filled with hope and strong personal meaning, which can provide a sense of mission toward the change, more than goals. A personal vision needs to inspire individuals to act to make a constructive change toward the desired future. In organizational settings, shared vision has been proven to lead to more effective group interactions, followers' motivation (Sosik et al., 1999), and greater satisfaction with both the group and the leader (Dumdum et al., 2002).

In this phase it is important that the project manager becomes aware of his or her core identity and creates an image of his or her desired future filled with hope. This vision will work as motivation for undertaking and persist in the individual change process and will move the individual toward action in trying to achieve his or her desired future.

The Real-Self: Understanding Who a Person Is

The second phase of the Intentional Change Process concerns the awareness of who a person is in the present moment. Understanding the real-self is important to set the starting point of the change process and to better plan the activities to achieve the ideal-self. The real-self allows you to grasp the elements of the self and the context to achieve personal goals, creating a clear and realistic view of the path to be taken. The real-self also acts as a tool for controlling the progress and advancement to the ideal (Taylor, 2006).

In order to understand the real-self, a first step is to analyze how a person has become what he or she is. Everyone is influenced by his or her experiences. An eye to the past allows you to explore life deeply by highlighting the most significant changes, such as lessons learned and how a person grew to become what he or she is in the present (McKee et al., 2008). This concept returns to the experiential learning approach, which argues that by analyzing an experience, through reflection, evaluation, and reconstruction, it is possible to give it a meaning that translates into knowledge.

The real-self phase presupposes a fundamental component of awareness, self-knowledge, and acceptance of vulnerability (Boyatzis and McKee, 2005). Awareness is a key element of the Intentional Change Process because it allows us to understand our emotions, thoughts, physical sensations, and reactions at different times. Consequently, this awareness allows one to recognize the need for change and to understand one's real desires, which are often set aside because energies are spent meeting the desires of others.

The conscious experience of people's emotions and the ability to appreciate and comprehend their complexity is influenced by their level of emotional knowledge related to how they experienced emotions in the past. The awareness of a person's own emotions can significantly affect his or her behavior and social interaction. For example, Gregory Balestrero (2012), when talking about the introduction of Emotional Intelligence assessments when he was CEO of PMI, underlined great results in terms of awareness creation and improvement of relationships. Creating awareness of their emotions and actual behaviors helped creating a baseline for identifying opportunities for better interaction and decision-making.

To build awareness, Boyatzis and McKee (2005) suggest a combination of personal, practical reflection, and the use of personal support relationships that help to understand the surrounding world.

Taking into account the elements presented, a person can examine himself or herself more fully and be able to define a true image of his or her real-self. However, a full awareness through self-evaluating methodologies is difficult to obtain and requires exercise and commitment, because people tend to have psychic self-defense mechanisms that protect the image they have of themselves from external information that is not coherent with that image. Given the tendency to perceive oneself in a self-improved way, it is difficult for a person to self-evaluate properly. In many cases, a multitude of aspects related to one's own idea of oneself do not match with the perception of others, creating distortions (Taylor, 2010).

External observations are therefore needed to obtain a more complete assessment. Collecting information from others and integrating them with one's own thinking is obtained through a 360-degree assessment or multi-source feedback (Taylor, 2006), which will be described in detail in Chapter 8. The underlying idea is to give the person the possibility to receive honest and constructive feedback from external parties able to assess his or her behavior in order to obtain a comprehensive image from the perspective of others and compare it with the self-image.

If the feedback received from others is not in line with his or her expectations, the drawback is the possibility that the person feels betrayed or demoralized or that he or she assumes a cynical and detached attitude (Wimer and Nowack, 1998). This drawback is because internal elements can inhibit the search for one's real-self. For example, self-defense mechanisms, such as projection, isolation, and negation, can lead to the avoidance or distortion of received feedback. If the person is seeking the real-self when ignoring the ideal-self, another problem may occur, thus losing the necessary cognitive and emotional energy (Taylor, 2006). In order to avoid falling into a demoralizing phase, two elements are indispensable: being aware of one's vulnerability, which makes the person able to accept the challenge of a self-improvement objective (Boyatzis and McKee, 2005), and avoiding focusing efforts solely on resolving weaknesses, instead of giving room for strengths and utilizing them as a way to change (Nowack, 2005). Moreover, within the Intentional Change Process, people who contribute to the evaluation of the individual are chosen among those considered reliable, with enough knowledge and maturity to be able to judge, who have the will and the involvement needed to help the person in his or her transformation. This selection allows for genuine, truthful, and duly argued feedback, as well as a secure context in which the individual does not feel threatened or does not need to seek approval.

Next, the individual is led to analyze the differences between the self-evaluation and the external evaluation and to compare the real-self with the ideal-self in order to identify competencies he or she demonstrates and can use to achieve the vision and competencies he or she needs and which are not part of his or her portfolio. Discrepancies or congruences between the actual-self and the person's ideal-self result in unique emotional and behavioral consequences (Boldero and Francis, 1999). Important information is extracted from the assessment to better define a development plan that should include the most relevant competencies to develop.

Learning Agenda: Define the Path

The learning agenda phase consists of organizing learning objectives, setting deadlines and providing sets of activities to complete. In order to be effective and durable, the plan needs to be created according to the characteristics and needs of the person; it must be realistic and consistent with continuous progress toward the goal. To pursue real and sustainable change, it is necessary to start from the acquired awareness, and turn one's own desires into action. The learning agenda phase is the step that allows a person to go from wanting to doing. The reason a person needs a plan is that even if he or she has the intention and energy for change, it is easy to be distracted by the wrong things during the path. Thus, after having developed a personal vision and good awareness of the real-self, and having traced and identified resources and weaknesses, it is necessary to create a useful, effective, and meaningful plan to achieve the desired outcome.

The basic assumption of theories on goal setting asserts that objectives are immediate regulators of human action (Locke et al., 1981) and act as mediators between behavior and extrinsic incentive factors. Goals affect performance because they direct attention and action, accentuate the effort, and increase motivation and persistence to maintain a direction in time. Goals also indirectly influence action by activating the skills, knowledge, and strategies relevant to that task (Locke and Latham, 2002). However, the result also depends on the level of the individual's involvement in relation to the goal. The involvement is high when a person is setting goals through careful analysis of his or her desires. Goals that do not create emotional involvement can completely lose their motivational effect. According to Creed et al. (2011), once goals have been established, individuals use a number of self-regulatory processes to reduce the discrepancy between their current situation and their ideal situation; however, depending on the context and personal characteristics, individuals may have a predilection for different types of goals.

A main distinction can be made between learning goal orientation and performance goal orientation. The first focuses on the development of competencies to achieve high standards; tends to compare personal competencies with an absolute standard; considers commitment crucial to achieve the result; and accepts feedback as a motivation and comparison element to increase effort or revise goals. The second focuses on demonstrating competencies in order to gain positive feedback and evaluations; tends to compare personal competencies with those of others; and sets goals with a good probability of success. Adopting a performance goal orientation determines a defensive attitude and the need to test oneself with the possibility of disappointing others or oneself. Adopting a learning goal orientation opens up new possibilities and experiences by concentrating energies on something considered really important for the person.

In the Intentional Change Process, the person needs to be convinced that he or she may be able to change, develop and, therefore, adopt a learning approach. To properly structure a development process, it is necessary to adapt the development process to the person's learning style. Experiential learning theory (Boyatzis and Kolb, 1995) provides a model that considers the learning process as a whole, a product of four different phases: concrete experience, reflective observation, abstract conceptualization, and active experimentation. According to this model, the best way to learn is to undertake a path that comprehends all four phases of learning; however, the four phases actually represent two pairs of opposite poles between which the individual tends to choose (Kolb and Boyatzis, 2000). The first pole concerns how the individual acquires information from the outside world, and it can occur through direct experience or through reconstruction of experiences. The other pole refers to the transformation of knowledge that can occur through active testing of ideas and experiences in the real world or through reflecting internally on the different attributes of experiences and ideas. Each person typically develops a preference in choosing between opposing poles, which is defined as his or her learning style. It is important to take this style into account when constructing a learning plan. If the plan drives people to engage in activities that are not consistent with their preferred learning style, the activities will be difficult to adopt and demotivating, which often leads the person to give up. Different activities to develop emotional and social competencies can be undertaken according to the prevalent style, such as the use of diaries, fieldwork, discussions, and brainstorming.

To create a learning agenda, three main phases must be followed: (i) identify the main outcomes of the individual and external competency assessment; (ii) articulate the main strengths and weaknesses according to the comparison between the ideal- and the real-self, prioritizing the most helpful ones for the achievement of the personal vision; and, (iii) outline more clearly the goals in terms of competency development, which must be in line with desires, be ambitious but achievable, and describe concrete actions or behaviors coherent with the individual learning style. The real change occurs when the learning agenda is implemented by the continuous practice of new behaviors in different contexts and situations.

Experimenting with New Behaviors

After the definition of the learning plan, the most active and delicate phase of the process concerns the experimentation with new behaviors. This stage entails the use of real life contexts as learning laboratories. Through the previous discoveries, the person has developed awareness of the different behaviors to be improved or acquired and defined concrete actions in order to perform the change. In this phase, concrete actions are undertaken and put into practice in everyday life. At the beginning, a level of vigilance is needed to identify situations in which older patterns of behavior might occur and newer patterns need to be performed. As explained prior, repetition will help strengthen the behavior until the behavior becomes the automatic response to external stimuli. This phase requires a period of experimentation with new behaviors, and relative outcomes are compared. It is common to start this process in a safe context, such as among family and friends, and later applying it to work environments. However, it is very important to apply it to different life contexts in order to make the behavior persistent and durable over time.

Exploiting Trustful Relationships

Changing is a difficult process and making it a part of one's busy life is even more complicated, so it is better not to deal with the process alone but to have the support of others in difficult moments. Individuals, small groups, or coaches can help support motivation and hope (Singh, 2006), help the person reflect on his or her future and present, and facilitate the success of the change process. The underlying idea is to identify people with whom a person has a trustful relationship who can give emotional support, provide sincere feedback, and believe in growth potential. These individuals may be a partner, close friends, or professional coach whose aim is to sensitize, encourage, and facilitate change. The coach does not teach the individual with his or her life experiences but makes the individual examine his or her own experiences to reach meaningful conclusions. In this sense, this refers to what is called coaching with compassion (Boyatzis et al., 2006), which means coaching for the development of others to help them achieve their dreams or aspirations, rather than coaching just to pursue the organization's benefits. Accordingly, in this case coaching does not consist of training the individual to become capable of doing something, but entails providing help to another person for the purpose of the person's own desire to develop. Coaching with compassion requires three main components: understanding the feelings of the person, caring about him or her, and willingness to act in response to his or her feelings (Boyatzis et al., 2006).

Exemplar Cases of Application of ICT

Extensive empirical evidence has demonstrated that the Intentional Change Process has been successfully applied to the development of emotional and social competencies in different contexts (Boyatzis et al., 2002; Boyatzis and Saatcioglu, 2008; Boyatzis et al., 2010a,b). At the Weatherhead School of Management, the Leadership Assessment and Development course was designed on the basis of the Intentional Change Process and applied to the Masters of Business Administration curriculum. Since 1990, data have been collected showing a strong increase of emotional and social competencies among candidates attending the course (Boyatzis et al., 2010a,b). Findings reported in 2002 showed that full-time MBA students strongly increased their goal setting, action, initiative, leadership, helping, sense-making, information gathering, and relationship skills compared to other groups that did not attend the course (Boyatzis et al., 2002). Similar evidence taken from other longitudinal studies on the same school and described in the study of Boyatzis and Saatcioglu (2008) confirmed these results, showing an increase in candidates' accurate self-assessment, initiative, adaptability, emotional self-control, achievement orientation, optimism, empathy, cultural awareness, communications, conflict management, influence, bond building, systems thinking, and pattern recognition.

A similar program has been adopted in other higher educational institutions, such as the ESADE Business School in Barcelona and Ca' Foscari University in Venice. The Leadership Education and Development program of the ESADE Business School and other several business schools provide a variety of tools, including personal reflection exercises, coaching sessions, and evaluations to help young professionals evaluate their strengths and weaknesses and understand what their goals are to activate a positive attitude toward their achievement; be aware of their own characteristics and those of others to effectively exploit diversity; and develop a personalized learning plan for the individual and the group (Canboy et al., 2016). Following these experiences, in 2012 the Ca' Foscari University of Venice gave birth to the Ca' Foscari Competency Centre (CFCC), a research center whose purpose is to carry out research to improve the performance of people through the development of emotional and social competencies. The ICT has been used as a methodological approach for a series of interventions related to students', managers' and professionals' development (Bonesso et al., 2017).

Summary

This chapter described what emotional and social intelligence competencies are and why they are important in enhancing cognitive readiness and ultimately performance. Moreover, we provided evidence on how the Intentional Change Process can help people with different backgrounds and experiences undertake a personal development path and improve or acquire their emotional and social competencies. It is important to recall that learning objectives can vary from individual to individual according to the person's ideal-self and his or her own strengths and weaknesses. The learning objective must be relevant for the present and future of the person, which will make the efforts meaningful and the motivation persistent. According to the specific professional roles, different emotional and social competencies can emerge as distinctive in affecting effective performance. In the next chapter, we will address the issue of what are the emotional and social intelligence competencies that characterize outstanding project managers.

References

Abraham, A. 2006. The need for the integration of emotional intelligence skills in business education. *The Business Renaissance Quarterly*, 1 (3), 65–80.

Archibald, R.D., Di Filippo, I., Di Filippo, D., and Archibald, S.C. 2013. Unlocking a project team's high-performance potential using cognitive readiness: A research study report and call to action. *PM World Journal*, 2 (11), 1–46.

Armor, D.A., and Taylor, S.E. 1998. Situated optimism: Specific outcome expectancies and self-regulation, in Zanna, M.P. (ed.). *Advances in Experimental Social Psychology*: 30 (Academic Press), pp. 309–379.

Aspinwall, L.G., and Leaf, S.L. 2002. In search of the unique aspects of hope: Pinning our hopes on positive emotions, future-oriented thinking, hard times, and other people. *Psychological Inquiry*, 13 (4), 276–288.

Azevedo, A., Apfelthaler, G., and Hurst, D. 2012. Competency development in business graduates: An industry-driven approach for examining the alignment of undergraduate business education with industry requirements. *The International Journal of Management Education*, 10, 12–28.

Balestrero, G. 2012. An Awakening to a Higher Purpose. http://www.allpm.com/index.php/component/k2/ item/476-an-awakening-to-a-higher-purpose-by-gregory-balestrero

Boldero, J., and Francis, J. 1999. Ideals, oughts, and self-regulation: Are there qualitatively distinct self-guides? *Asian Journal of Social Psychology*, 2 (3), 343–355.

Bonesso, S., Gerli, F., and Cortellazzo, L. 2017. Promoting emotional and social competencies in higher education: A case study in the italian context. *Atlanta: Academy Of Management Annual Meeting*, Atlanta 2017.

Boyatzis, R.E. 1982. *The Competent Manager: A Model for Effective Performance*. (John Wiley & Sons, New York).

Boyatzis, R.E. 2006. Using tipping points of emotional intelligence and cognitive competencies to predict financial performance of leaders. *Psicothema*, 18, 124–131.

Boyatzis, R.E. 2008a. Leadership development from a complexity perspective. *Consulting Psychology Journal*, 60 (4), 298–313.

Boyatzis, R.E. 2008b. Competencies in the 21st century. *Journal of Management Development*, 27 (1), 5–12.

Boyatzis, R.E. 2009. Competencies as a behavioral approach to emotional intelligence. *Journal of Management Development*, 28 (9), 749–770.

Boyatzis, R.E., and Akrivou, K. 2006. The ideal self as the driver of intentional change. *Journal of Management Development*, 25 (7), 624–642.

Boyatzis, R.E., Briz, T., and Godwin, L. 2010a. The effect of religious leaders' emotional and social competencies on improving parish vibrancy. *Journal of Leadership & Organizational Studies*, 18 (2), 192–206.

Boyatzis, R.E., and Kolb, D.A. 1995. From learning styles to learning skills: the executive skills profile. *Journal of Managerial Psychology*, 10 (5), 3–17.

Boyatzis, R.E., Lingham, T., and Passarelli, A. 2010b. Inspiring the development of emotional, social and cognitive intelligence competencies in managers, in Rothstein, M., Burke, R.J. (eds.). *Self-Management and Leadership Development*. (Edward Elgar, Cheltenham, UK; Northampton, MA).

Boyatzis, R.E., and Mckee, A. 2005. *Resonant Leadership*. (Harvard Business School Press, Boston).

Boyatzis, R.E., and Saatcioglu, A. 2008. A 20-year view of trying to develop emotional, social and cognitive intelligence competencies in graduate management education. *Journal of Management Development*, 27, 92–108.

Boyatzis, R.E., Smith, M.L., and Blaize, N. 2006. Developing sustainable leaders through coaching and compassion. *Academy of Management Learning & Education*, 5 (1), 8–24.

Boyatzis, R.E., Stubbs, E.C., and Taylor, S.N. 2002. Learning cognitive and emotional intelligence competencies through graduate management education. *Academy of Management Learning and Education*, 1, 150–162.

Canboy, B., Montalvo, A., Buganza, M.C., and Emmerling, R.J. 2016. Module 9: A new course to help students develop interdisciplinary project using the framework of experiential learning theory. *Innovations in Education and Teaching International*, 53 (4), 1–13.

Carton, A.M., Murphy, C., and Clark, J.R. 2014. A (blurry) vision of the future: How leader rhetoric about ultimate goals influences performance. *Academy of Management Journal*, 57 (6), 1544–1570.

Cherniss, C. 2000. Emotional intelligence: What it is and why it matters. *New Orleans: Annual Meeting of the Society for Industrial and Organizational Psychology*.

Cherniss, C., and Goleman, D. 2001. *The Emotionally Intelligent Workplace*. (Jossey – Bass, San Francisco).

Creed, P.A., Tibury, C., Buys, N., and Crawford, M. 2011. Cross-lagged relationships between goal orientation and career aspirations in early adolescents. *Journal of Vocational Behavior*, 78 (1), 92–99.

Dumdum, U.R., Lowe, K.R., and Avolio, B.J. 2002. A meta-analysis of transformational and transactional correlates of effectiveness and satisfaction: An update and extension, in Avolio, B.J. and Yammarino, F.J. (eds.). *Transformational and Transactional Leadership: The Road Ahead.* (Elsevier, Oxford, England), pp. 35–66.

Emmerling, R.J., and Goleman, D. 2005. Leading with emotion. *Leadership Excellence*, 22 (7), 9–10.

Goleman, D. 1995. *Working with Emotional Intelligence.* (Bantam, New York).

Goleman, D. 2006. *Social Intelligence: The New Science of Human Relationships.* (Bantam, New York).

Goleman, D., Boyatzis, R.E., and Mckee, A. 2002. *Primal Leadership: Realizing the Power of Emotional Intelligence.* (Harvard Business School Press, Boston).

Hopkins, M.M., O'Neil, D.A., and Stoller, J.K. 2015. Distinguishing competencies of effective physician leaders. *Journal of Management Development*, 34 (5), 566–584.

Kolb, D.A., and Boyatzis, R. 2000. Experiential learning theory: Previous research and new directions, in Sternberg, R.J. and Zhang, L.F. (eds.). *Perspectives on Cognitive, Learning, and Thinking Styles.* (Lawrence Erlbaum, NJ).

Locke, E.A., and Latham, G.P. 2002. building a practically useful theory of goal setting and task motivation: A 35-year odyssey. *American Psychologist*, 57 (9), 705–717.

Locke, E.A., Shaw, K.N., Saari, L.M., and Latham, G.P. 1981. Goal setting and task performance: 1969–1980. *Psychological Bulletin*, 90 (1), 125–152.

McClelland, D.C. 1973. Testing for competence rather than intelligence. *American Psychologist*, 28, 1–14.

Mckee, A., Boyatzis, R., and Johnston, F. 2008. *Becoming a Resonant Leader.* (Harvard Business Press, Boston).

Miao, C., Humphrey, R.H., and Quian, S. 2006. Leader emotional intelligence and subordinate job satisfaction: A meta-analysis of main, mediator, and moderator effects. *Personality and Individual Differences*, 102, 13–24.

Nowack, K.M. 2005. Longitudinal evaluation of a 360 feedback program: Implications for best practices. *20th Annual Conference of the Society for Industrial and Organizational Psychology*, Los Angeles, CA.

PMI (Project Management Institute). 2013. *Guide to the Project Management Body of Knowledge/PMBOK*, 5th ed.

Rokeach, M. 1973. *The Nature of Human Values.* (Free Press, New York).

Rosete, D., and Ciarrochi, J. 2005. Emotional intelligence and its relationship to workplace performance outcomes of leadership effectiveness. *Leadership & Organization Development Journal*, 26 (5–6), 388–399.

Sharot, T., Riccardi, A.M., Candace, M.R., and Phelps, E.A. 2007. Neural mechanisms mediating optimism bias. *Nature*, 450 (7166), 102–105.

Singh, D. 2006. *Emotional Intelligence at Work: A Professional Guide*, 3rd ed. (Response Books, London).

Sosik, J.J., Kahai, S.S., and Avolio, B.J. 1999. Leadership style, anonymity, and creative behavioral group decision making support systems: The mediating role of optimal flow. *Journal of Creative Behavior*, 33, 227–256.

Taylor, S.N. 2006. Why the real self is fundamental to intentional change. *Journal of Management Development*, 25 (7), 643–656.

Taylor, S.N. 2010. Redefining leader self-awareness by integrating the second component of self-awareness. *Journal of Leadership Studies*, 3 (4), 57–68.

Williams, H.W. 2008. Characteristics that distinguish outstanding urban principals: Emotional intelligence, social intelligence and environmental adaptation. *Journal of Management Development*, 27 (1), 36–54.

Wimer, S., and Nowack, K.M. 1998. 13 Common mistakes using 360-degree feedback. *Training & Development*, 52 (5), 69–78.

Chapter 8

Emotional and Social Intelligence Competencies for Project Management

Richard Eleftherios Boyatzis, Daniel Goleman,
Fabrizio Gerli, and Sara Bonesso

Contents

The Reasons behind an Individual's Success

Eiji Nakatsu was in charge of the Technical Development Department of the Shinkansen train, otherwise known as the Japanese high-speed bullet train. One day he was asked to reduce the amount of noise produced by the pantograph when the train was travelling at high speeds, and to reduce the loud bang that the train produced, when it entered a tunnel, which was caused by changes in the air pressure, as it annoyed the people living near the tunnel. The solution was difficult to find. But one day he listened to a speech by an ornithologist and discovered that the owl is capable of flying completely silently to avoid being detected by its victim. Another bird, the kingfisher, seamlessly goes from air to water to catch fish. The kingfisher performs the most efficient transition from a low-pressure environment, the air, to a high-pressure environment, the water, in the animal world. Nakatsu took one owl and one kingfisher and studied them with his team and reshaped the pantograph and the nose of the train accordingly.

Harry Beck lived many years before the high-speed trains. He worked for the Signals Office of the London Tube in the 1930s. The map of the tube was initially difficult for travelers to understand and perhaps this difficulty in understanding was the reason tube usage did not increase as expected. The first maps were based on the map of the above ground town, and consequently they did not include some peripheral stations, and were not clear about stations that were in close proximity to each other. Beck adopted a completely different view and focused on the information that was most important for the travelers: the sequence of the stations and the connections between and among them. To do this, he used only horizontal, vertical, or 45° lines and zoomed in and distorted the central part of the map. At first, the publicity department rejected the design, but he persisted. Beck asked for 500 trial copies that were immediately taken by customers, who found them to be extremely beneficial.

Jenny Baer-Riedhart, on the other hand, was the project manager in charge of a futuristic project by the National Aeronautics Space Agency: the Pathfinder project at the Dryden Flight Research Center (Laufer, 2012). The Pathfinder was a solar-powered airplane and was considered to be a minor project for the National Aeronautics Space Agency, even if it was very complex and involved many external partnerships. Baer-Riedhart needed the approval for the budget from the National Aeronautics Space Agency's headquarters. At first, she had a meeting that was unsuccessful because she tried to sell the project by emphasizing its characteristics without being attuned to the personalities in the room and their requirements. She was perceived as an enemy who wanted to suck up the resources the other project managers needed for their projects. But she was lucky; she had a second chance. On this occasion, she put herself in her colleagues' places; she gathered information from the National Aeronautics Space Agency's own reports, met people and figured out what mattered most to them and, finally, reached her goal.

What can one learn from these three stories? These people, of course, were technically prepared, but it was not their technical expertise that made them successful. They reached their goals thanks to a set of emotional, social, and cognitive competencies. In the first example, the competencies were the capability to question how to improve things, to observe different contexts and environments to gain knowledge, to follow a trial and error process, to identify similarities in different contexts, and to have initiative. In the second example, the competencies were the capability to follow the customers' needs, to adopt a different perspective, and to be persistent and persuasive. In the third example, the competencies were the capability to persist, to understand other people's needs, to change one's own approach, and to develop a message consistent with other people's expectations.

A recent study conducted with 150 project managers demonstrated that currently a project manager's key challenge is coping with frequent unexpected events (Laufer et al., 2015). Consequently, the traditional approach to project management based on long-term planning, controlling, and managing risk needs to be progressively integrated with a nimbler methodology, which asserts that project success requires flexibility throughout its life cycle. This practice requires project managers who are able to demonstrate cognitive readiness, namely the mental preparation, including skills, knowledge, abilities, motivations, and personal dispositions, needed to establish and sustain outstanding individual and team performance in the complex and rapidly changing environment of project, program, and portfolio management. A person who is cognitively ready demonstrates not only the ability to effectively adapt to unexpected events, but also shows proactivity in the management of assigned tasks, empathy for team members, a positive attitude in the face of failure and the threat of failure, as well as a strong orientation toward the attainment of goals (Archibald et al., 2013). The aforementioned personal characteristics are elements of the emotional and social competencies framework. In other words, emotional and social competencies can be considered pillars or crucial components of a project managers' cognitive readiness.

The fact that behavioral competencies are an essential part of the skills required to be a project manager is not a recent hypothesis in the project management field. Indeed, during the 1980s and 1990s, empirical investigations were conducted to identify the set of personal characteristics needed to make "above average" project managers (Posner, 1987; Thamhain, 1991; Strohmeier, 1992; Birkhead et al., 2000, Edum-Fotwe and McCaffer, 2000; El-Sabaa, 2001) (see Table 8.1). The seminal research conducted by Posner in 1987 on a sample of 287 project managers showed that communication, organization, team building, leadership, and coping skills were assessed by project managers as more relevant than technical competencies, challenging the commonplace belief that project managers need to primarily be "technical experts." Similarly, Thamhain (1991), through a field investigation of 220 project managers, pointed out that in addition to technical knowledge, such as managing technology and understanding markets and product applications, and administrative skills, such as planning, staffing, budgeting, scheduling, performance evaluations, and control techniques, project managers require leadership and people management skills. These skills are namely the ability to motivate, communicate, resolve conflicts, build teams, and facilitate group decision-making. Birkhead et al. (2000) found that planning and controlling are the organizational skills that received the highest ranking in terms of project managers' core competencies in the construction, engineering, and information technology fields. The authors also showed that the competency profile of project managers has become more complex than in the past, since the competency profile encompasses other types of behavioral skills. By asking 126 project managers to indicate which skills they associate with successful performance and careers, El-Sabaa (2001) demonstrated that human skills were the most essential competencies, ranking higher than organizational and technical skills. These studies arrived at the same conclusion and recommended that project managers should integrate their consolidated technical and organizational skills with more people-oriented behavioral competencies.

Over the last decade, emotional and social competencies have become even more essential for the role of project manager. As suggested by Mersino, "(Project managers) PMs who master emotional intelligence will set themselves apart from other PMs. They will be able to achieve more with the same team. They will excel in their careers. And they will feel more satisfied with themselves and their relationships with others" (2007: 6). In contrast with the past, PMs face new challenges that force them to frequently deploy specific emotional and social behaviors to successfully

Table 8.1 The Most Important Skills for Project Managers According to the Literature in the 1980s, 1990s and in the Early 2000s

Posner (1987) PM skills	Thamhain (1991) Leadership skills components for PM	Strohmeier (1992) Competencies to face PM's challenges
• Communication (listening and persuading) • Organizational skills (planning, goal-setting, analyzing) • Team building (empathy, motivation, esprit de corps) • Leadership (sets example, energetic, vision, delegates, positive) • Coping skills (flexibility, creativity, patience, persistence) • Technological skills (experience, project knowledge)	• Manage unstructured work environments • Organizational awareness • Motivating people • Conflict management • Communication • Problem solving • Team building • Credibility • Influence • Initiative	• Influence and motivation • Managing conflicts • Communication • Teamwork and cooperation
Birkhead et al. (2000) Core competencies required for project managers	**Edum-Fotwe and McCaffer (2000)** Most important skill elements for PM	**El-Sabaa (2001)** The skills and career path of an effective project manager
• Planning and controlling • Personal influence • Goal focus • Problem solving • Team leadership • Project team development • Project context	• Leadership and delegation • Planning and scheduling • Chairing meetings • Negotiation • Communication	I. Human skills: Mobilizing • Communication • Coping with situations • Political sensitivity • High self-esteem • Enthusiasm II. Conceptual and organizational skills: Planning • Organizing • Strong goal orientation • Ability to see the project as a whole • Ability to visualize the relationship of the project to the industry and the community • Strong problem orientation III. Technical skills: • Special knowledge in the use of tools and techniques • Project knowledge • Understanding methods, processes, and procedures • Technology required Skills in the use of computer

deliver their projects. First, the number of project-based organizations is increasing in different sectors and across different types of firms. Companies are progressively adopting projects to manage organizational changes and non-incremental innovations, since "projects are perceived as particularly adequate to conduct new activities, which require experimentation and new combinations of expertise" (Alioua and Simon, 2017: 1427). Exploratory projects are characterized by a higher level of uncertainty that calls for a project management approach based on continuous adaptation. Furthermore, exploratory projects involve combining the knowledge of team members from different backgrounds, as well as external actors who contribute to the different stages of the development of the project according to the open innovation paradigm (Grönlund et al., 2010), which implies "the use of purposive inflows and outflows of knowledge to accelerate internal innovation, and expand the markets for external use of innovation, respectively" (Chesbrough et al., 2006: 1). Therefore, leading projects requires the ability to be flexible and be able to quickly redesign the external network of partners with complementary capabilities for the product development process, along with building commitment toward the project goals among stakeholders with different perspectives (Bonesso et al., 2014). Moreover, as suggested by Clarke (2010: 6) the temporary and multidisciplinary nature of projects asks PMs to quickly build trust and commitment as well as support knowledge exchange through interpersonal interaction.

This chapter aims to shed new light on the repertoire of emotional and social competencies that PMs should mobilize to deliver an outstanding performance in the competitive environment. In the next section, the emotional and social competencies model discussed in Chapter 7 will be analyzed considering the specificity of the PM role, taking into consideration the changes that have occurred in PMs' skill requirements in the last decade. The aim of this section is also to reconcile the fragmented perspectives on PMs' emotional and social competencies in a more comprehensive framework. Two empirical studies will then be presented. The first study discusses how a PM's competency profile can be measured in the organizational setting, adopting different techniques for assessing emotional and social competencies. The second study, contrary to the majority of research based on ranking provided by PMs, identifies the emerging emotional and social competencies most frequently exhibited by PMs when they successfully perform their job. Finally, implications in terms of PMs' competency portfolio assessment and development will be discussed.

PMs' Competency Profile: The Different Dimensions of Emotional and Social Intelligence Competencies

Research in the field of project management acknowledges that behavioral competencies contribute to reducing the rate of project failures (Gillard and Price, 2005), since the "hard" technical skills were not enough to ensure positive results (Stevenson and Starkweather, 2010). Studies in the realm of emotional and social competencies claim that these competencies play a crucial role in predicting project outcomes across different sectors, both in terms of superior performance and career advancements (Mersino, 2007; Obradovic et al., 2013). However, as highlighted above, the skillsets required for project managers have changed dramatically in the past few years. If the agile methodology to project management focuses on people and action, in contrast to the traditional method that was focused on planning and control, which emotional and social competencies should be part of the competency portfolio of high-performing project managers?

Reviewing the recent empirical studies in the project management field, this section aims to provide a comprehensive picture of the behavioral competencies that are relevant for achieving a successful project performance. In doing so, we analyzed the literature through the lens of the emotional and social competencies model presented in Chapter 7 (Figure 8.1).

Table 8.2 reports the competencies identified in the last decade of research in the project management field as relevant for project managers' success for each of the four clusters: self-awareness, self-management, social awareness, and relationship management. In contrast to the seminal

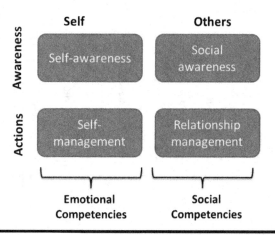

Figure 8.1 The emotional and social intelligence competency model.

Table 8.2 The Emotional and Social Competencies for Successful PMs: A Literature Review of the Last Decade

	Yasin et al. (2009)	Skulmoski and Hartman (2009)	Zhang and Fan (2013)	Keil et al. (2013)	Brière et al. (2014)	Medina and Francis (2015)
Self awareness	Confidence • Has high self-esteem • Accepts flaws of others		• Emotional self-awareness			• Presence and confidence in the role
Self management	Management Skills • Goal setter • Manages priorities • Strategic thinker • High levels of personal motivation • Effective resources allocator • Broad organizational knowledge Desire for Achievement • Driven by values • Objectives-focused Managerial Style • Intuitive • Risk taker	• Decisiveness • Objectivity • Ownership of Tasks	• Emotional self-control • Adaptability • Positive outlook	• Project planning • Scope management	• Adaptability • Working Capacity • Coping with Stress • Humility • Patience • Thoroughness • Intuition • Engagement	• Structuring and organizing the work • Calm Behavior • Flexibility and Openness to Change • Taking Active Responsibility
Social awareness		• Listening skills • Political awareness/ agility/tact	• Empathy • Organizational awareness • Cultural understanding	• Listening	• Understanding One's Environment	• Handling and understanding people

(Continued)

Table 8.2 (Continued) The Emotional and Social Competencies for Successful PMs: A Literature Review of the Last Decade

	Yasin et al. (2009)	Skulmoski and Hartman (2009)	Zhang and Fan (2013)	Keil et al. (2013)	Brière et al. (2014)	Medina and Francis (2015)
Relationship management	Attitude Toward Others • Loyalty to the organization • Loyalty to subordinates • Honest in all dealings • Effective organizational politician • Demonstration of trust • Accept responsibility Effective Team Player • Consensus builder • Open to new ideas and innovative practices • Interdisciplinary teams builder Managerial Style • Empowers subordinates Visionary • Effective delegator Social Skills • Utilizes a network of contacts • Has charismatic personality Vision • Long-term orientation	• Effective questioning • Generating feedback • Verbal skills • Open communication • Collaborate • Writing skills • Presentation skills • Create an effective environment • Motivate self and others • Share—information and credit • Protect the team • Persuasiveness • Consensus building • Negotiation/facilitation skills • Conflict/dispute resolution • Compromise • Mediation/"umpire" skills • Vision-oriented/articulate the business problem	• Communication • Inspirational leadership • Conflict management	• Leadership • Verbal communication	• Communication • Leadership • Dispute Resolution • Team Work • Negotiate • Establishing a Sense of Trust	• Communication and information handling • Allowing participation and collaborating • Handling external demands and internal/external communication • Feedback and appreciation • Availability/visibility • Positive and constructive leadership • Conflict handling • Follow Up

works discussed in the previous section, the most recent research on the competency profile of a project manager demonstrates that organizational and technical skills are ranked lower than emotional and social competencies. This evidence suggests that project managers should focus primarily on management activities, while they need a basic understanding of the specific techniques and methodologies to deliver the project, since they can rely on a team of technical experts.

Maqbool et al. (2017) confirmed the positive impact of the emotional and social competency clusters on project success, which were measured through the following criteria: being on time, being on budget, quality, and stakeholders' satisfaction. However, the literature review in Table 8.1 revealed that some clusters are perceived to be more relevant for achieving a higher project performance. Among the four emotional and social competency clusters, the competencies included into the relationship management cluster, specifically leadership, persuasive communication, and teamwork, turned out to be the most frequently mentioned skills.

Self-Awareness

This cluster represents the building block of the emotional and social intelligence competency framework and consists of the ability to recognize our emotions and the effects on us and on others (emotional self-awareness), to be aware of our strengths and weaknesses (accurate self-assessment), and a strong sense of our self-worth and capabilities (self-confidence).

Zhang and Fan (2013) included emotional self-awareness among the competencies found in outstanding project managers. Project managers face challenges during the project life cycle, such as stakeholders with conflicting perspectives or risks as threats which pose the probability of consequences to the accomplishment of the project's objectives. All these challenges cause emotion arousal that can be expressed through blame, rant, withdrawal, or rigidity. Self-aware project managers ponder their emotions and deeply understand their effects on project performance. Furthermore, a high level of self-confidence and an accurate assessment of personal resources allow project managers to face challenging events and react positively to them.

Self-Management

Self-management competencies enable individuals to regulate their own emotions, to identify and prevent emotional triggers, as well as thoughts that can lead to emotional breakdowns (Mersino, 2007). Why can projects benefit from project managers who exhibit self-management skills? The job of the project manager is demanding, complex, and varied. Several factors, such as schedule and budget constraints place pressure on the project manager, who should demonstrate the ability to restrain negative actions and stay poised and positive. Moreover, project managers continually deal with uncertainties and changing events that modify their planning, therefore the ability to be flexible and work effectively within a variety of changing situations and with different individuals and teams is paramount for project managers. They should also demonstrate self-initiative and be focused on achieving challenging goals, along with a constant need for improvement. Indeed, project managers act as change agents (Turner et al., 1996; Crawford and Hahmias, 2010), since innovation is an integral part of their project objective and often project deliverable.

Social Awareness

This cluster of competencies allows people to accurately read situations and empathize with the emotions of others. Active listening enables project managers to identify and understand the project status and risks, as well as stakeholders' expectations (Keil et al., 2013). Besides being empathic, project managers should be capable of recognizing and satisfying team members' and clients' needs. They also need organizational and political awareness, which is especially critical at the beginning of the project: a project manager has to know to whom to talk and how to talk to get approval and support to proceed (Skulmoski and Hartman, 2009).

Relationship Management

Project management is widely acknowledged to be the art and business of getting work done through others (Mersino, 2007). As suggested by Yasin et al. (2009: 51), the project manager "must be an effective organizational politician, but at the same time demonstrate trust to the project team members." In their empirical study, Yasin et al. (2009) discussed a wide range of competencies that can be ascribed to the relationship management cluster. Skulmoski and Hartman (2009) and Keil et al. (2013) confirm that leadership continues to be the most essential competency for project managers. Broadcasting their vision for shared project objectives allows project managers to attract, inspire, and motivate the project team and different stakeholders to work together toward a common goal. Moreover, project managers establish a direction by developing a vision of the future and identify strategies to produce the necessary changes. Skulmoski and Hartman (2009) also highlighted that, especially during the initiation phase of the project, the most important competency is persuasion, since project managers should be able to sell the project to the stakeholders, followed by consensus building on project specifications. As the project enters the implementation phase, conflict management and facilitation skills assume an increasing relevance. When conflicts arise, project managers are asked to settle disputes through consensus in order to avoid compromising the project. Empirical studies agree on the relevance of team building, since it favors a positive work environment and high team morale. Networking has also emerged as an important skill in the study conducted by Yasin et al. (2009), since "the manager must know whom to contact for information and who will provide the most accurate and up-to-date project data" (2009: 51).

The aforementioned evidence presents a common limitation: these studies are primarily based on the perception of their participants. Indeed, the aforementioned lists of competencies have been obtained thought the administration of interviews, Delphi or ranking-style questionnaires in which project managers and experts in the field were asked to express their opinion on competencies they believed were most critical for project success.

Competencies Observed in Outstanding Project Managers

Identifying the Distinctive Competencies through Multiple Perspectives

When the first competency-based studies started to spread in the 1970s, the first critical issue concerned how to measure these constructs. As discussed previously, competencies are capabilities that require a set of related but different behaviors organized around an intent. This requires measurement methods to assess both the intent and the patterns of action. There are two recognized methods to measure emotional and social competencies; the first is based on an inductive approach and the use of interviews, the second is based on multi-source feedback assessments.

The two methods are described below, illustrating a study conducted at a major research and development laboratory department in a United States government agency (Boyatzis et al., 2009).

The first method adopted in this study used the Behavioral Event Interview technique. This technique—built upon the Critical Incident Interview (Flanagan, 1954)—is an inductive method, which allows the discovery of relevant competencies in a job setting or role. This technique focuses on gathering detailed information on specific effective and ineffective events the interviewee recently experienced. A typical question he or she is asked in order to recall the event is: "Tell me about a recent event in which you felt effective in your job." Once the episode is elicited, the interviewer facilitates the narration of the interviewee with questions aimed at describing the context and the people involved, what he or she thought, felt, said, and actually did, the problems encountered, and the solutions and outcomes (Dainty et al., 2005). This interview, by deepening thoughts, decisions, and actions of the respondent, allows the disclosure of the behaviors deployed by the interviewee in actual job-related situations. Usually this interview lasts from 60 to 120 minutes, during which the interviewee is asked to describe between two and three effective episodes and between two and three ineffective episodes.

Interviews are recorded and transcribed verbatim to allow the analysis of the narrated episodes. Two or three coders independently assess the presence of behaviors that are considered a manifestation of a competency. This action is usually done with the support of existing codebooks (e.g., Boyatzis, 1982; Spencer and Spencer, 1993; Boyatzis, 2009) in which well-known emotional and social competencies are described in terms of alternative behaviors by which they are manifested. In order to identify the presence of other types of competencies not included in codebooks, the interview can also be analyzed using the Thematic Analysis technique, aimed at identifying additional patterns of behavior.

To identify competencies related to more effective behavior, Boyatzis et al. (2009) analyzed a sample composed of a group of superior project managers and a group of average project managers. To obtain a distinction in terms of performance, a nomination technique was used (Boyatzis, 1982; Luthans et al., 1988; Boyatzis, 2008). Middle-level managers and their bosses were asked to fill in a form and list the names of the project managers they considered to be highly effective in their role. A superior performer was identified when he or she was nominated by one boss, two peers, and two subordinates. Both groups went through Behavioral Event Interviews, and, according to the results of the coding, the competencies that superior performers displayed more frequently were analyzed.

This method enables a rich analysis of the recurrent behavioral characteristics of the subject, and in previous studies showed a high predictive validity (Boyatzis, 2009; Ryan et al., 2009). It is useful when exploring a new context or job role; however, it is time-consuming and requires the involvement of professional interviewers and coders.

A second method adopted in this study used the multi-source feedback, or 360-degree assessment, which incorporates systematic and anonymous observations of an individual's behavior provided by people who work with him or her. This method has been found to be the best predictor of a leader's effectiveness, actual business performance, engagement, job, and life satisfaction (Goleman and Boyatzis, 2017). The assessment tool is based on a questionnaire, the aim of which is to evaluate the frequency that a subject performs specific behaviors related to a competency. The questionnaire includes a number of behavioral indicators corresponding to a set of emotional and social competencies. The rater is asked to assess the frequency with which he or she commonly sees each behavior in the evaluated subject. The final competency score is the mean of the frequencies of the behavioral indicators.

The main attribute of this method is the possibility to assess competencies through multiple perspectives. Indeed, the questionnaire includes both a self-assessment and external assessments. In the study conducted by Boyatzis et al. (2009), the boss, as well as a group of peers and subordinates, were asked to complete the same type of questionnaire for the project managers under evaluation. Differences in competency scores were then analyzed, comparing the group of superior and average performing project managers distinguished with the use of the nomination technique. Besides nomination, performance differences may be measured by considering indexes on project performance, such as project budget performance, schedule, and quality.

The use of a 360-degree perspective is useful because it allows the integration of different observations and the definition of a more comprehensive assessment. Moreover, it overcomes the bias related to self-evaluations and collection of data from independent respondents. Due to unconscious self-defense mechanisms and many personal factors that influence one's ability to perceive oneself accurately (Yammarino and Atwater, 1993), external evaluation is considered to be more reliable than self-assessment.

Table 8.3   Summary of Competencies Which Distinguish Outstanding from Average PMs

Emotional Intelligence Competencies		
Competencies	*360-degree Assessment*	*In Critical Incidents from Work*
Planning	From all 3 sources	X
Self-Confidence	From 1 source (subordinates)	X
Efficiency Orientation	From all 3 sources	
Attention to Detail	From 1 source (peers)	
Self-control	From 1 source (subordinates)	
Social Intelligence Competencies		
Group Management	From all 3 sources	X
Empathy	From 2 sources (peers and subordinates)	X
Persuasiveness	From 2 sources (peers and subordinates)	X
Developing Others	From 1 source (peers)	X
Negotiating	From 1 source (peers)	
Cognitive Intelligence Competencies		
Systems Thinking	From 2 sources (peers and subordinates)	
Pattern Recognition	From 2 sources (peers and subordinates)	X

Source: Boyatzis, R.E. 2009. *Journal of Management Development*, 28 (9), 749–770.

For each assessment technique presented above, Table 8.3 reports the distinctive emotional, social, and cognitive competencies that were identified in the sample of project managers analyzed by Boyatzis et al. (2009) to be superior performers. The second column shows those emotional and social competencies that characterize superior project managers by means of 360-degree assessment, by supervisors, subordinates, and peers, whereas the third column reports competencies detected through the Behavioral Event Interviews, therefore competencies activated by outstanding project managers in concrete events at work. The findings confirm that superior performers manifest a complex repertoire of emotional and social competencies that (a) can vary according to the different actors with whom the PM interacts, and (b) need to be activated specifically when the project manager faces critical incidents at work.

Emerging Emotional and Social Competencies for Successful PMs

The project managers involved in a study from some Italian information technology service companies worked for a wide range of clients like banks, insurance companies, manufacturing companies, and public administrations, offering projects such as consulting, software integration, and application services.* Data was collected in 2016 through the Behavioral Event Interview technique. Each project manager was asked to recall some critical situations that had occurred during the previous year in which she or he felt effective for a total of 180 critical events. The interview, by deepening the thoughts, reactions, decisions and actions of the respondents, made it possible to identify the behaviors and competencies displayed by the project managers. The interviews were recorded and transcribed verbatim for the subsequent coding.

The coding process started drawing on the competency codebooks already adopted in other research (Boyatzis, 1982; Spencer and Spencer, 1993), and enriching them through the analysis of the emerging competencies identified in the project management literature. Moreover, additional emerging themes have been codified through thematic analysis. A total of 1,284 behaviors related to emotional, social, and cognitive competencies emerged from the on-field analysis. A competency was scored every time one of its corresponding behaviors emerged at least once per episode. The frequency for each competency was then computed, as the recurrence with which one specific competency was expressed as normalized by the number of events described during the interview. In other words, in contrast to the lists of skills perceived to be important for project managers, the frequency measures how often project managers actually activate a certain competency. Therefore, this measure does not provide an insight to the relevance of specific skills but describes the composition of the overall competency portfolio that project managers need to mobilize in their job to successfully deal with non-routine situations.

Table 8.4 reports the frequency distribution of the competencies that emerged in the situations, pointing out the wide array of behaviors manifested by project managers. Considering the most frequently manifested competencies when critical situations in managing projects arise, project managers conduct an accurate examination of the situation describing the nature of the problem in order to solve it, which is expressed by the

---

* The empirical research described in this section has been carried out by Fabrizio Gerli and Sara Bonesso at the Ca' Foscari Competency Centre.

Table 8.4 Emotional and Social Competencies Manifested by PMs in Critical Events and Corresponding Frequency Distribution

Emotional, Social and Cognitive Competencies	Definition	Frequency (% Episodes)
Diagnostic thinking	The capacity to conduct an accurate examination of the situation, describing the nature of the problem.	62.8
Achievement orientation	The capacity to uphold the standard of excellence, not discouraged by obstacles in the pursuit of a goal.	49.8
Empathy	The capacity to understand people, to listen carefully, interpret and respond to the wishes of others.	47.0
Emotional self-awareness	The capacity to know your inner moods, your resources, insights, and skills.	44.7
Accuracy	The capacity to seek order and predictability by reducing uncertainty.	41.0
Efficiency orientation	The capacity to perceive the relationship between input and output and increase efficiency.	39.8
Persuasion	The capacity to convince one or more people of the value of your point of view.	38.1
Planning	The capacity to identify and organize the future and organize the activities necessary to achieve a goal.	38.0
Organizational awareness	The capacity to understand the relationships and the culture of an organization.	35.9
Initiative	The capacity to take action to achieve a result, even if it is not required or imposed by the situation	32.4
Inspirational leadership	The capacity to take leadership of a group or inspire and drag others.	31.3
Customer orientation	The capacity to focus your efforts in the research and meeting of the needs of others.	29.7
Teamwork	The capacity to stimulate the members of a group to work together effectively.	29.1

(Continued)

Table 8.4 (*Continued*)   Emotional and Social Competencies Manifested by PMs in Critical Events and Corresponding Frequency Distribution

Emotional, Social and Cognitive Competencies	Definition	Frequency (% Episodes)
Risk management	The capacity to control uncertain activities and contain losses and/or negative impacts.	28.5
Developing others	The capacity to stimulate someone to develop his/her skills or improve his/her performance.	28.2
Pattern recognition	The capacity to recognize an underlying structure in a complex set of unorganized information.	25.3
Experimenting	The capacity to explore the world and experience new things constantly.	21.2
Observing	The capacity to observe the world around you with the aim of finding new ideas.	18.9
Opportunity recognition	The capacity to perceive the opportunities emerging from the environment.	14.4
Systems thinking	The capacity to understand and explain multiple causal events and to interpret a situation from a systems perspective.	13.9
Adaptability	The capacity to adapt to changing circumstances or to change the behavior consistently.	11.2
Analogical thinking	The capacity to access a known domain of knowledge to solve a problem.	7.9
Strategic thinking	The capacity to understand the strategic and competitive environment of the company.	7.8
Organizational learning orientation	The capacity to develop the knowledge base of the company through learning processes.	7.8
Self-control	The capacity to retain control of your emotions in stressful or emotional situations.	7.2
Engaging others	The capacity to engage individuals to achieve the identified objectives.	7.2
Conflict management	The capacity to stimulate groups or individuals to solve their conflicts.	6.1

(Continued)

Table 8.4 (*Continued*)   Emotional and Social Competencies Manifested by PMs in Critical Events and Corresponding Frequency Distribution

Emotional, Social and Cognitive Competencies	Definition	Frequency (% Episodes)
Questioning	The capacity to formulate questions to understand the nature of the problems and change the status quo.	5.6
Change orientation	The capacity to recognize the need for change, remove barriers, and find solutions.	5.0
Associative thinking	The capacity to create logical connections between issues, disciplines, and ideas which are seemingly unrelated.	3.3
Lateral thinking	The capacity to try new ways of looking at problems, adopting different perspectives.	2.3
Networking	The capacity to build and use relationships, including personal ones, in achieving objectives.	2.2
Resilience	The capacity to see opportunities rather than threats, trusting that the future will be better than the past.	1.7
Risk taking	The capacity to take a risk or to carry out an activity with uncertain outcome.	1.1
Quantitative analysis	The capacity to use quantitative methods for diagnosis and operation in various fields.	0.6

cognitive competency diagnostic thinking. Other cognitive competencies that emerged in the episodes narrated are the capacity to interpret a situation from a systems perspective—system thinking—to recognize an underlying structure in a complex set of unorganized information—pattern recognition—to access a known domain of knowledge to solve a problem—analogical thinking—to create logical connections between issues, disciplines and ideas which are seemingly unrelated—associational thinking—and to try new ways of looking at problems by adopting different perspectives—lateral thinking. These competencies unravel the complexity of the problem-solving process activated by project managers demonstrating the creative side of their professional role. The orientation toward innovation is also expressed by a further set of competencies that emerged from the interviews: the ability to formulate questions to understand the nature of the problems and change the status quo—questioning—to spend time observing the world around them with the aim of finding new ideas—observing—and to experience new ideas with a hypothesis-testing mindset—experimenting (Dyer et al. 2008).

The results also show frequent behaviors related to the "awareness" competencies: self-awareness, empathy, and organizational awareness. Confirming that in order to react to critical events, project managers need to interpret their own emotions and have confidence in their personal resources, but also to understand others and the relationships that permeate the team they lead, the values and culture of their organization and the organizations, such as clients or external partners, with whom they interact during the life cycle of the project.

The emotional competencies are activated by project managers to work toward a standard of excellence by setting measurable goals and attaining them notwithstanding the presence of obstacles—achievement orientation—to organize the activities needed to achieve a goal—planning—to seek order and predictability by reducing uncertainty—accuracy—to contain losses or negative impacts—risk management—as well as to demonstrate the concern for increasing efficiency—efficiency orientation. Moreover, project managers demonstrate the capability to take action—initiative—and seek out new opportunities of business for their companies.

An in-depth empirical analysis of the data shows that project managers activated simultaneously more than one competency in specific situations. Therefore, the findings provide evidence that different emotional, social, and cognitive skills interact with each other in combinations or bundles to allow project managers to pursue positive outcomes. Some quotes from the interviews are provided to exemplify how project managers activate different behavioral competencies simultaneously:

> …In that case I transferred to the client the passion for my work. For me two things really matter in my job: to work in a team—which gives me satisfaction—and to successfully finalize the project without problems (**self-awareness**). Through several tests (**experimenting**) I solved quickly the specific problem that was raised during the project and I worked very hard to attain the goals (**achievement orientation**). I continually kept the client involved in order to reassure him and to meet the expected requirements (**customer orientation**)….

...In that situation, I faced a problem of technical nature and another one related to the team. Concerning the technical problem, I understood that I had to change the infrastructure that allowed me to attain the speed required by the project goals (**diagnostic thinking**). I had three options to undertake in order to solve this problem, but I chose to change the infrastructure because the new technologies would have given an advantage (**opportunity recognition**). I started to read up about the new infrastructure (**observing**) and I realized that its adoption would have allowed me to take away large parts of the code (**efficiency orientation**)....

...Two strong actors were involved in this project (**organizational awareness**) and I mediated between them writing emails, organizing meetings, asking information to the external stakeholders, anticipating their requests and answers. During a meeting, I understood that the different parties faced the specific problem as a conflict since they started to speak louder (**empathy**). We got stuck and I intervened suggesting to devote two or three days to think and study more in-depth the problem, reflecting separately on the possible alternatives to follow (**conflict management**)....

Considering the competency profile of the samples of project manager quotes that emerged from the on-field analysis, the main findings of this research suggest the following:

- Contrary to those studies that rank the most important skills that a project manager should demonstrate to attain project success, research provides evidence for a wider set of actual behaviors manifested by project managers to successfully handle critical events during the project life cycle. Even though some competencies present a lower frequency of manifestation in comparison to others, it does not mean that their impact on the project success is less relevant. In order to achieve positive outcomes, project managers are required to activate the aforementioned skills coherently with the characteristics of the situation faced.
- Aside from the social competencies such as leadership, teamwork, and persuasion, and emotional skills such as achievement and efficiency orientation, planning, and risk management that are recurrent in the project management field, this study emphasizes that project managers should exhibit a broad portfolio of emotional, social, and cognitive competencies. Specifically, cognitive

competencies are increasingly required when finding solutions to problems, issues, and risks, promoting and developing innovation, in line with the recent trend that asks project managers to lead exploratory projects into new areas. Moreover, the self and organizational awareness competencies turned out to be critical in order to better understand the different stakeholders and to be confident in their own skills and competencies.

■ Emotional, social, and cognitive competencies complement each other, since they are jointly activated in combinations that contribute to the performance of a project manager. A promising area of investigation is to comprehensively analyze a larger sample of project managers, where large numbers of competencies are required to handle the different stages of the project.

Summary

Project managers are and will be asked to redesign their job profile with a set of emotional and social intelligence competencies that are proven to be relevant for project success and their professional career. They should be aware of their level of manifestation of these competencies on the job in order to coherently orient their efforts toward their acquisition. On the other hand, organizational procedures for human resource practices for project managers in terms of recruitment and selection criteria, training programs, performance management, and career advancements should be consistent with the set of emotional and social competencies necessary to achieve superior performance at work. Finally, higher education institutions, in order to equip graduates and undergraduates with the necessary competencies to enhance the future competency portfolio of project managers should customize educational programs around the most salient skills together with the methodological insights provided by the Intentional Change Theory, which provided some exemplar cases of the application of the experiential learning approach to competency development.

References

Alioua, H., and Simon, F. 2017. Managing time pacing in organizations transitioning to a project based mode – 3 cases studies of two multinational companies. *International Journal of Project Management*, 35 (8), 1427–1443.

Archibald, R.D., Di Filippo, I., Di Filippo, D., and Archibald, S.C. 2013. Unlocking a project team's high-performance potential using cognitive readiness: A research study report and call to action. *PM World Journal*, 2 (11), 1–46.

Birkhead, M., Sutherland, M., and Maxwell, T. 2000. Core competencies required of project managers. *South African Journal of Business Management*, 31 (3), 99–105.

Bonesso, S., Comacchio, A., and Pizzi, C. 2014. *Project-Based Knowledge in Organizing Open Innovation*. (Springer-Verlag, Berlin Heidelberg).

Boyatzis, R.E. 1982. *The Competent Manager: A Model for Effective Performance*. (Wiley Interscience, New York, NY).

Boyatzis, R.E. 2008. Competencies in the 21st century. *Journal of Management Development*, 27 (1), 5–12.

Boyatzis, R.E. 2009. Competencies as a behavioural approach to emotional intelligence. *Journal of Management Development*, 28 (9), 749–770.

Boyatzis, R.E., Fambrough, M., Leonard, D., and Rhee, K. 2009. Emotional and social intelligence competencies of effective project managers, in Clelland, D., and Bidanda, B. (eds.). *Project Management Circa 2025*, pp. 273–288.

Brière, S., Proulx, D., Navaro, F. O., and Laporte, M. 2014. Competencies of project managers in international NGOs: Perceptions of practitioners. *International Journal of Project Management*, 33 (1), 116–125.

Chesbrough, H., Vanhaverbeke, W., and West, J. 2006. *Open Innovation: Researching a New Paradigm*. (Oxford University Press, UK).

Clarke, N. 2010. Emotional intelligence and its relationship to transformational leadership and key project manager competences. *Project Management Journal*, 41 (2), 5–20.

Crawford, L., and Hahmias, A.H. 2010. Competencies for managing change. *International Journal of Project Management*, 28 (4), 405–412.

Dainty, A., Cheng, M., and Moore, D. 2005. A comparison of the behavioural competencies of client-focused and production-focused project managers in the construction sector. *Project Management Journal*, 36 (1), 39–48.

Dyer, J.H., Gregersen, H.B., and Christensen, C. 2008. Entrepreneur behaviours, opportunity recognition, and the origins of innovative ventures. *Strategic Entrepreneurship Journal*, 2, 317–338.

Edum-Fotwe, F.T., and McCaffer, R. 2000. Developing project management competency: Perspectives from the construction industry. *International Journal of Project Management*, 18 (2), 111–124.

El-Sabaa, S. 2001. The skills and career path of an effective project manager. *International Journal of Project Management*, 9 (1), 1–7.

Flanagan, J.C. 1954. The critical incident technique. *Psychological Bulletin*, 51 (4), 327–359.

Gillard, S., and Price, J. 2005. The competencies of effective project managers: A conceptual analysis. *International Journal of Management*, 22 (1), 48–53.

Goleman, D., and Boyatzis, R.E. 2017. Emotional intelligence has 12 elements. Which do you need to work on? *Harvard Business Review*, February.

Grönlund, J., Sjödin, D.R., and Frishammar, J. 2010. Open innovation and the stage-gate process: A revised model for new product development. *California Management Review*, 52 (3), 106–131.

Keil, M., Lee, H.K., and Deng, T. 2013. Understanding the most critical skills for managing IT projects: A Delphi study of IT project managers. *Information & Management*, 50 (7), 398–414.

Laufer, A. 2012. *Mastering the Leadership Role in Project Management*. (FT Press, Upper Saddle River, New Jersey).

Laufer, A., Hoffman, E.J., Russell, J.S., and Cameron, W.S. 2015. What successful project managers do. *MIT Sloan Management Review*, 56 (3), 43–51.

Luthans, F., Hodgetts, R.M., and Rosenkrantz, S.A. 1988. *Real Managers*. (Ballinger Press, Cambridge, MA).

Maqbool, R., Sudong, Y., Manzoor, N., and Rashid, Y. 2017. The impact of emotional intelligence, project managers' competencies, and transformational leadership on project success: An empirical perspective. *Project Management Journal*, 48 (3), 58–75.

Medina, A., and Francis, A. J. 2015. What are the characteristics that software development project team members associate with a good project manager? *Project Management Journal*, 46 (5), 81–93.

Mersino, A.C. 2007. *Emotional Intelligence for Project managers: The People Skills You Need to Achieve Outstanding Results*. (Amacom Books, American Management Association, New York, NY).

Obradovic, V., Jovanovic, P., Petrovica, D., Mihic, M., and Mitrovic, Z. 2013. Project managers' emotional intelligence - A ticket to success. *26th IPMA World Congress*, Crete, Greece, 2012 Procedia - Social and Behavioral Sciences 74, 274–284.

Posner B.Z. 1987. What it takes to be a good project manager. *Project Management Journal*, 18 (1), 51–54.

Ryan, G., Emmerling, R.J., and Spencer, L.M. 2009. Distinguishing high performing European executives: The role of emotional, social and cognitive competencies. *Journal of Management Development*, 28 (9), 859–875.

Skulmoski, G.J., and Hartman, F.T. 2009. Information systems project manager soft competencies: A project-phase investigation. *Project Management Journal*, 41 (1), 61–80.

Spencer, L.M., and Spencer, S.M. 1993. *Competence at Work: Models for Superior Performance*. (Wiley, New York, NY).

Stevenson, D.H., and Starkweather, J.A. 2010. PM critical competency index: IT execs prefer soft skills. *International Journal of Project Management*, 28 (7), 663–671.

Strohmeier, S. 1992. Development of interpersonal skills for senior project managers. *International Journal of Project Management*, 10 (1), 45–48.

Thamhain, H.J. 1991. Developing project management skills. *Project Management Journal*, 22 (3), 39–44.

Turner, J.R., Grude, K.V., and Thurloway, L. 1996. *The Project Manager as Change Agent: Leadership Influence and Negotiation*. (McGraw-Hill, London).

Yammarino, F.J., and Atwater, L.E. 1993. Understanding self-perception accuracy: Implication for human resource management. *Human Resource Management,* 32 (2&3), 231–247.

Yasin, M.M., Gomes, C.F., and Miller, P.E. 2009. Characteristics of Portuguese public-sector project managers. *Project Management Journal,* 40 (3), 47–55.

Zhang, L., and Fan, W. 2013. Improving performance of construction projects. A project manager's emotional intelligence approach. *Engineering, Construction and Architectural Management,* 20 (2), 195–207.

Chapter 9

Training, Cognitive Readiness Competence Development, and Implementation

Dave Gunner

Contents

Introduction

Now that the theory and good practice have been covered, in other words, effectively the "what," it is now time to look at how it may be put into practice. The project or program manager is usually the one who gets the finger pointed at them if activities within the project, program components, or overall program do not go according to plan. In many cases, it is not solely the project or program managers' fault, but they can indeed improve their chances of success if they ensure what they intend to do is aligned with and supports the needs of the organization and the projects or program components that they are managing. However, changing behavior positively and taking on new learning is not necessarily easy, and in this chapter we will look at what can be done to help and then take a look at how implementation can be optimized.

Traditional Training

Many organizations view training as the solution to the problem, whatever the problem is or even whatever the problem is perceived to be; if projects are not deemed to be a success, the usual knee-jerk reaction is to send the responsible project or program manager to a training course, which may not be the complete solution or the needed solution. This approach is often done without considering what the issues are that face the project or program manager and how best to address them. While training can be appropriate, it need to be the right training, at the right time, for the right issue or problem set. It is now recognized that knowledge retention after being in a passive training environment is at most 30 percent.* There are other forms of knowledge transfer, or more specifically learning, that have a much higher rate of success and retention.

Whereas so-called traditional training does have its place, it may not be the most effective way of ensuring that the project and program management communities are equipped with the skills and competencies that they need to perform their job and to progress in their careers.

Organizations that base some or all of their organization around managing projects and programs do, in many cases, encourage and promote certifications. This step is usually done for two reasons: (1) it is a consistent standard recognized across various industries; and (2) when recruiting, it provides the company with reassurance that the individual being hired at least has the basic knowledge of principles, disciplines, and good practices surrounding project and program management. For companies that deliver projects and programs to and for clients, the fact that their project and program managers are certified establishes their credibility. Whereas both of these reasons are perfectly valid in the area of organizational competition, having a certification does not automatically mean that the individual

---

* Accessed at the following URL on August 28, 2018: https://siteresources.worldbank.org/
  DEVMARKETPLACE/Resources/Handout_TheLearningPyramid.pdf

can actually apply the knowledge that the certification represents or that the individual possesses the cognitive readiness to deliver the project or program in a complex environment. This is why one needs to look elsewhere.

Assessing What Is Important to the Organization and Establishing a Baseline

Initially, organizations need to understand what is important to them as a business, both strategically and from an operational business model, and how and what projects and programs they should and will manage. This latter concept is more than the traditional triangle of time, cost, and quality or scope. The governance board or strategic leader of an organization needs to first understand what the priorities of the organization are; in other words, are those priorities in an industry where quality and low defects are paramount, such as an engine manufacturer? This priority determination is not about compromising on some aspects of the business model in order to meet deadlines, as the negative consequences would simply be too great in terms of the impact on human life as well as the impact on the future of the organization itself. It also does not mean that the organization should disregard dates and budget completely. What it does mean is that the organization should ensure that the projects and programs are optimized by focusing on the right aspects of the product or project for the business model selected. These "right things" will vary from one organization to another. Understanding this process is an important part of the decision process of governance, allowing the organization to acquire both buy-into for the idea of the importance of continuous competence development and the active sponsorship and monitoring of the same toward organizational, program, and project progress.

The following is a list of six main factors that executive leadership and management should assess with regard to what is important for their organization, plus one other placeholder entry for another factor that may be specific to the business or industry, although there could be more for an individual organization. The assessment will influence the approach the organization may take with regard to the competence development and training needed in order to optimize the organization's project and program management capability.

This list is not intended to be definitive, but it offers some factors that should be considered when looking at both prioritization and approach.

- *Speed*: How quickly a project or program can or needs to be deployed is a key consideration into the project or program management approach to be selected. Whereas most sponsors may want a project or the program components as soon as possible, it is not always the most important consideration when compared with other factors. This time consideration may become obvious once the other factors have been assessed.
- *Reliability*: In some organizations and with emphasis on some industry sectors, the ultimate reliability, the consistency or repeatability, of a product or service may not be as important a factor as, for example, getting the product to market quickly or keeping the cost to market low to keep the costs to be borne by the consumer lower. Whereas for other organizations, reliability is paramount and could adversely and irrecoverably damage the organization, if it was not given the highest priority.
- *Cost*: In most business case analyses, cost will be a constraint at some level; however, it may not always be the number one consideration for a project or program, especially one that has a high associated risk, whether the risk is held by the organization or the client.
- *Quality*: Quality and reliability are closely linked and are in many cases affected by the constraints of speed and cost. If quality in performance standards is a key factor then the governance and review structure that the organization adopts will be a major consideration.
- *Flexibility*: For some organizations and their projects and programs, the scope, requirements, and other factors are unstable, subject to change, and remain in a state of continuous flux. In some cases, this state of change may be unavoidable and the methodology, as well as the selection of project or program manager needs to account for this state. For example, the organization may need to prove that it has the appropriate human resource recruitment process in place that allows the organization to bring on board new human resources to the project or program on short notice or human resources that have experience with complex projects or program that involve enormous degrees of change management. Further, the requirements for the project or program manager would need to have a complement of intelligences in order to handle a project or program management team that will

need to accommodate the changing management needs as the project or program progresses. For example, a project manager who possesses a high-degree of social intelligence and who will understand the team dynamics of introducing new human resources with differing skills and the impacts this flux will have over time on the team will be required in a project environment rich in change.

■ *Relationships*: Ideally, stakeholders, including customers, should be in agreement with regard to the general objectives and outcomes of the project or program. This for most organizations is often not the case. For most organizations, at least at the onset of a project or program, the gaps among various stakeholders and stakeholder groups may appear to be quite large. While in some organizations, consensus and agreement are really important, and this factor is considered to be of the highest priority, other organizations will accept the fact that stakeholders will be separated and appear not to be possessed of consensus.

■ *Others*: This category is for any factors, one or more, that may be specific to the organization or industry sector and are not considered core or relevant to other organizations.

The diagram below could be used to help with assessing the relative importance of these factors in the current projects of an organization (Figure 9.1).

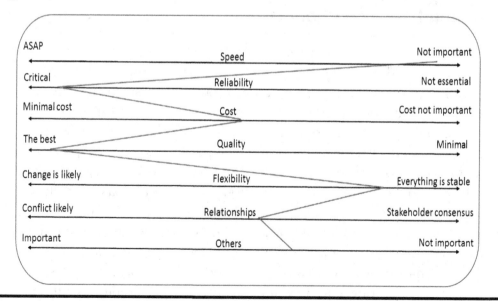

Figure 9.1   Prioritization assessment.

In this particular example, speed is not that critical; however, reliability is paramount, as is quality. If one considers a scenario of an airline engine manufacturer, this example could well be their assessment profile. In such a situation, reliability and quality could be essential assessment criteria for the organization, whereas speed and flexibility may not be. This profile tells one that the main focus from a cognitive readiness or competence and training perspective should be around enabling projects to be delivered with minimal defects, with quality, and with repeatable processes.

Once the organization agrees as to what is important and what their priority is with regards to managing its projects and programs, the next step is to assess the overall current situation. How well are the projects, programs, and program components currently being managed? For example, if speed and cost are assessed to be the priorities, one would determine whether the projects, programs, and program components are being delivered on time and within budget. The organization will also find that it will be essential to establish this baseline before proceeding with any training or the development and reinforcement of the set of necessary competencies the teams will require to achieve cognitive readiness. This information will then also form part of the organization's business case for funding and on-going sponsorship.

Assessing the Project Management Community of Practitioners

After the priorities of the organization have been agreed on, those priorities should be established firmly within the organization through various communication means. The organization should then establish a means of collecting data, collating the data, and assessing the data as to how the projects and programs are being managed. The next assessment to be done is one to be conducted on the practitioners; in other words, the project and program managers, the management teams, as well as the supporting teams need to be assessed. This assessment should not be only based on degrees, certifications, and other formal qualifications, but also, and perhaps most importantly, on how well this knowledge and competence has translated to practice. This area of practice includes not only the hard skills that require the information from the degrees and certifications, but the soft skills that are often developed from other interactions, mentoring, and some development training that is followed by mentoring and qualified input.

Once evaluation is understood, and only once it is fully understood, can the appropriate development plans be put in place to meet the development needs that exist as identified.

Another important benefit of this process is the identification of the experts in specific areas or competencies. These experts can provide important input into the development process through mentoring other less experienced personnel. The assessment process should consider more than the hard skills that may need mentoring. The reason for this statement is that mentoring is a skill that requires a threshold of emotional and social intelligence from the mentor to be effective. Aligned with skills that are found in emotional and social intelligence that facilitate such mentoring, one should look for skills that are often enhanced by mindfulness, such as listening and situation awareness. The identification of experts and mentoring helps the organization enable that the mentored individuals become optimized in terms which maximize the probability that those human resources are assigned to the most appropriate projects and programs. The benefit increases with complex or highly sensitive projects or programs. The other benefits to the human resources and the organization are that the human resources continue to grow and develop to assist with future projects and programs.

The next stage is to pull together a set of questions that can be used to capture how well the community of project and program management practitioners is applying its knowledge, skills, and experience. The key term in the previous statement is "applying." Many project and program managers have the knowledge and certifications, but they are neither able to simply apply them nor do they have the requisite intelligence, such as social intelligence, to apply the knowledge. For example, interactions with stakeholders require the project or program manager to develop rapport with them both individually and as a group, often at the same time, while conveying and listening to information. The ability to sense what others are feeling, as well as listening to what they are saying, and communicating the necessary information for the project or program is not something conveyed in most degree or certification programs.

To be of value, the input and answers to the questions developed in the next stage also needs to be obtained from the appropriate people. In the majority of cases, these people are not peers or team members but are those individuals in the organization who are ultimately responsible for the delivery of the respective projects or programs. These individuals could be the customer, the sponsor, or an internal leader or executive manager.

Ideally, this process needs to be in addition and supplemental to the existing performance management process, many of which gather feedback from peers and team members. Therefore, the questions need to be written such that the questions (a) assess how well the person is performing a particular competence; and, (b) have managers provide accurate and constructive feedback.

With regard to item "a" for example, when assessing someone's scheduling capability, the questions should not only relate to knowledge of critical chain and other important methods, but, more importantly, need to be focused on the application of the capability rather than just the knowledge of the application elements. Are milestones met and are the projects planned effectively and in accordance with the internal processes and standards? It may be the case that the managers who are best placed to provide the feedback do not have a project management background, and as such it is important that the questions in the survey should not be technical questions within the field of project management, but rather should be based on outputs and stated business results. These should reflect specific business results that the respective project or program managers have contributed.

Continual performance development should be part of the assessment process from the individual's perspective. However, most people think that they know what they are performing well and where they need to make improvements. While this may well be the case, in reality what they do not always know is how well they are able to apply their knowledge and skills. In other words, one may have test scores to validate the knowing of the knowledge or basic skills, but seldom does one have tests scores demonstrating application in a work environment of those same sets of knowledge and skills. This feedback is key, if one is to maximize one's potential. Even the most self-aware individuals are seldom aware, especially early in their careers, of how well they are applying the knowledge and skills they possess.

Personal development needs to be part of the culture. Project and program management practitioners need to be receptive to feedback on their development needs. Cognitive readiness of project and program management consists of more than the knowledge and skills of the discipline. One of the motivations of cognitive readiness for project and program management that should exist is openness to continue to grow through feedback.

There has been various research done on how best to retain information, from memory skills to mnemonic devices, and as we have previously mentioned, the general consensus is that if one reads and or listen to training, such as attending a lecture, after two weeks the knowledge retained is in the region of 20 percent or less. Whereas listening to a computer-based-training module may well be perceived by the organization as making progress, in reality this action is simply a "tick-in-the-box" exercise. Also, if some or all of the knowledge is retained, there needs to be evidence to show the knowledge is being correctly applied. The application of this knowledge is where the competence assessment comes back into play. Once the original assessment of how the individual applies their knowledge is conducted, the individual should undertake some form of developmental action. Following the developmental action, it is vital that further feedback is obtained to determine whether or not there has been a noticeable and positive improvement in the application of the knowledge or skill.

Listed below are some of the activities that can be undertaken to help develop and grow knowledge; the percentages shown are indicative of the knowledge level retained based upon an assessment deemed appropriate to the knowledge being transferred after a period of two weeks.*

Two-Week Retention (%)	Activity
5	Attend Lecture
10	Reading
20	Audio Visual
30	See a demonstration
50	Participate in a discussion group
75	Practice by doing and record the outcome or progress
90	Teach or present to others

This list is not intended to be a definitive list, and other effective activities could be included. One may enhance the success rate or retention by one or more of methods described:

Mentoring: The mentor is usually someone who is a recognized expert or at least possesses a high-level of expertise within the organization in a particular field or knowledge area and is not usually the individual's

---

* Accessed at the following URL on August 28, 2018: https://siteresources.worldbank.org/DEVMARKETPLACE/Resources/Handout_TheLearningPyramid.pdf

line manager. The mentor will be able to provide both general advice and guidance, as well as helping out with specific challenges and issues that the project or program manager may be encountering.

Shadowing: The project or program manager shadows one more experienced who is performing a specific task or set of specific tasks. For example, in this context, if a project or program manager is not comfortable interacting in meetings with a client or customer, watching a more experienced performer is a productive way of passing on not just knowledge but good practices. These experiences can be excellent ways through which to learn techniques and approaches that are sometimes called tacit knowledge. Tacit knowledge is hard to explain and pass on to someone else, such as a doctor's explaining end of life issues to a patient and the patient's family. Many of the skills and knowledge elements that are transferred in this manner are soft skills and must be observed several times and then practiced with a mentor, thus requiring a combination of methods.

On-The-Job-Training: Sometimes nothing is better than doing the job. On-the-job-training involves putting into practice specific knowledge and skills in a way that allows one to absorb the knowledge deeper while applying it. It is important that the individual reflects on what they have done by documenting their progress, either on their own or with a mentor. Again, a combination of methods furthers the retention of the learning.

Role-Playing: Practicing skill techniques and new learning through role-playing allows one to embed the knowledge for retention and start to develop it as a newly acquired skill. The organization needs to buy into role-playing and understand the importance and investment of such an initiative. Role-playing requires elements of realism and of the job to be performed. It requires engagement of experts in the knowledge and skill areas to be applied to assist those individuals who will be role-playing.

Gamification: Although this method is very similar to role-playing, it involves the use of technology in creating scenarios whereby a safe environment is created in which the individual can make decisions, view the results those decisions would provide, and then adjust their approach accordingly. The value to the individual from this type of activity is optimized when the results are reviewed with the individual's line manager or mentor and feedback is provided immediately.

Peer-To-Peer: Project and program managers can actually learn from their fellow project and program managers. It is possibly one of the most informal and common modes of learning and is quite effective. With so many different types of projects and programs in different industries with different organizational approaches, project and program managers gain insight by listening to fellow project and program managers, who may have different experiences, which can be an invaluable source of knowledge.

Again, it is essential that there is a documented plan for performance improvement, with agreed upon actions, outlining the learning techniques that should be adopted. This plan should include milestones and details of who and how the particular knowledge transfer will be undertaken and assessed.

Reflection and Career Journals

Clearly documenting what the organization intended as a performance plan for an individual and then signing up to the plan is important. For individuals, it is also important to document the steps they have taken toward the performance plan, and then reflect on the results they have achieved. This individual documentation and reflection can be achieved in the form of a reflective or career journal. A reflective or career journal can take many forms; however, it is important that some or most of the following be captured in some manner:

1. What is the issue, problem, or challenge?
2. What techniques have been applied?
3. How were they applied?
4. What were the results?
5. What worked and what could be improved upon?
6. What has been learned?
7. What will one do differently next time?

These notes in the journal should then be reviewed on a regular basis with the individual's mentor or line manager. It is essential that this is an ongoing, continuous exercise. Notes from these reviews should also be captured; and the individual should set aside time to reflect on the information originally captured as well as the review notes to assist them to improve. In many cases, it will require the project or program manager to set aside his or her heuristics or biases to accept the input.

There are numerous other types of learning which could be considered "informal." However, these types of learning or training can also offer high value and should form part of the ongoing, continuous learning culture that the project and program managers need to adopt in their quest to achieve cognitive readiness. Some of these activities are:

- Conference attendance
- Web-Online conferences
- Books and Journals
- Blogs and discussion forums
- Joining communities
- Any other networking means

What Has Actually Worked?

A process is necessary to assess and measure cognitive readiness and to monitor the effectiveness of the learning in terms of business results. As part of this process, the individuals who have undertaken the learning within whatever learning setting and with whatever learning mode is selected also need to know that their progress will be monitored. If individuals believe that their actions will not be reviewed and feedback obtained, then it is less likely that individuals will follow through with their development activities and then apply them. This finding is underpinned by the author's personal experience in his many years of organizational project and program management training and competency development. Moreover, it is important that individuals view this monitoring and feedback in a positive light; in other words, it is to assist them in advancing their competence, as opposed to punishing them for non-compliance or failure to apply the knowledge or skill completely.

The Organizational Perspective

For the organization to continue sponsorship, the senior leadership needs to know that their investment is delivering results. The best way to accomplish the measurement of result delivery is through having a set of key performance indicators. Traditionally, having key performance indicators for training and specifically project and program management has been viewed as very difficult, especially as it has been challenging to prove that any improvements can be attributed to an individual's personal development or some other factor, such as process or organizational change. Therefore, an agreed-upon set of key performance indicators that can be linked back to identifiable organizational results is important. While it is easy to arrive at key performance indicators around how many courses have been attended or training modules completed, the issue is that these key performance indicators do not measure the application of knowledge or skills acquired by the individual. In other words, these key performance indicators do not pass the "so what?" test. The fact that a course has been attended is not an indicator that anything has improved at all; it certainly does not demonstrate that the cognitive readiness of the individual has improved.

One well-known example among training professionals of how counting courses can skew this perception is that the student's attention in computer-based training modules is frequently undertaken in a half-hearted manner, while multi-tasking or doing another job. However, if the number of project management certifications is measured, this number does show that the individual actually acquired some knowledge and was able to demonstrate that they understood how knowledge was to be transferred for the purposes of the certification examination in simple, limited state application use cases. Whereas this metric can certainly be seen as a positive measure, it still does not provide data on improvement in terms of the organization. Therefore, it is recommended that there is a key performance indicator based on improvement that is organizationally relevant as to cognitive readiness in regard to the application of knowledge and skills. One way to do this is to go back to the managers who provided the feedback on which the development activities are based and ask them if there is any noticeable improvement in an individual's performance in his or her role. It is still, admittedly, a mainly subjective measure, and should be done after a certain, agreed-upon period of time, allowing the individual sufficient time to both undertake developmental activities, and then be measured on the application of what they have learned. Ultimately, it would be ideal to create a set of key performance indicators around projects and programs delivered on time and within budget, other project and program relevant areas, or based on factors important to the organization.

Careful consideration should be given before proceeding to conduct the performance reviews, as there are many internal and external factors that can influence these outcomes, many of which are outside the control of the project or program manager. Although over time, if the developmental activities have been effective, there should be signs of a positive trend. Below are examples of three such key performance indicators that might be used. It is, however, important to emphasize that the key performance indicators must be measurable.

KPI Number	KPI Description	Target
1	Number of project managers officially certified.	80% of total PM work force.
2	Feedback from managers on noticed improvement in an individual's performance, in relation to specific business outcomes. To be referenced back to previous development needs identified.	75% of feedback received after 2–3 months shows that there has been a positive improvement.
3	Number of projects delivered on time and within budget and in accordance with the original scope.	80% projects delivered within time, budget, and scope.

Key performance indicators should be reviewed on a regular basis along with the targets. If the results are not in accordance with what was expected, an in-depth analysis to ascertain why the results do not align should be done and adjustments should be made. This analysis could find that the results are influenced by a number of factors, such as the individual not doing the developmental work that they had been assigned or not doing it effectively. Some of these factors may include the following:

Misunderstanding of what the developmental need was: This issue is quite common, especially when the manager providing feedback does not have a project management background. An example of this issue being realized is if a project manager is constantly missing deadlines, then they are sent on a scheduling course. The actual situation, however, may have been caused by an inability to manage scope or negotiate with the customer effectively, rather than a deficiency in scheduling.

The lack of a mentor: The project or program manager may have done the appropriate, targeted training, but may not have had anyone to discuss and review the outputs to allow them to be more effective.

External factors affecting outcome: Organizational changes can have a major impact on project or program outcomes. If team members are swapped or removed and less experienced team members assigned, or if organizational processes are revised, then these changes are likely to have an adverse impact on the project.

Please note that, in some cases, it may be that the key performance indicator may be inappropriate or irrelevant and as such it needs to be regularly evaluated in accordance with the needs of the business and future business strategy.

Summary

Once an organization has established a training, cognitive readiness competence development initiative, it is important that the initiative be maintained. Individual project and program managers need to also understand how they are able progress their own careers through the initiative. One way to communicate this is to provide that the competencies, knowledge, and skills are aligned to job roles. When a project or program management professional understands that once they obtain certain skills and competencies and are able to effectively demonstrate them, then they will know how they can progress within the organization with regard to their career.

An individual's development can only achieve a certain level of performance and outcomes when it is also underpinned by an appreciation of the project and program management maturity of the organization. If the organization has a low level of process maturity, then the training and development of its project and program management work force can only be taken so far. An organization needs to evaluate its maturity and match its training program to its maturity level to provide more satisfaction among its project and program management staff as they strive to attain a level of cognitive readiness necessary to meet the organization's needs.

Afterword

The question becomes now, where does the study of cognitive readiness and mindfulness go from here and what does it encompass in the world of project and program management. Further, the question becomes, as it impacts the world of project and program management, what is the direct impact on project and program managers.

Some answers to these questions may seem obvious on their face. This text did not provide tools for measuring the impacts of cognitive readiness or mindfulness for the practicing project or program manager. Instead, the text provided only an introduction to the areas of study and provided only hints at application in various specific areas of practice. What was provided in the text were the processes and general approaches used in the field, but no tools that have been applied directly to project and program managers in their fields of practice. Project and program managers practice in numerous fields, from construction to information technologies, and from biotechnologies to pharmacology and numerous unmentioned fields. They also practice under various conditions, from office situations that vary from traditional hard walls to completely open settings, and from laboratory settings to field settings, including construction sites to ecological sites that can vary from oceans to deserts.

Questions will also need to be explored as to when in the life cycle of the project or program, the project and program manager, as well as the teams, should apply such tools and techniques. These questions should also include when a project is initiated, what constitutes initiation, and the extent, if any at all, to which the project manager is involved at the point where initiation is determined.

The text introduced for the purposes of the discussion the construct of complexity. It noted that one researcher, Melanie Mitchell, suggests that each profession should define complexity for its own purposes. However, given the breadth and depth of project and program management, there may be a need to explore whether a greater understanding is required of the application of complexity as well as, perhaps, the need for more parsing of the definition in the varying fields in which project and program management are practiced. Such a text would require research into how project and program managers in the varying fields with projects and programs of varying sizes, staffing, scope issues, and risks, among other variables, view the application of complexity in their field. The application of cognitive readiness and its involvement in the reduction of the view of complexity would also need to be researched. One of the issues is that when organizations view a project or program as complex, an experienced project or program manager is generally assigned as a result of their cognitive readiness, as well as technical expertise and their ability to reduce some of the complexities that would be faced by a less experienced project or program manager, to handle the complexity. The general stated hiring statement is that the person was hired for their technical capability or degree; however, the person is often hired for their success rate in meeting the objectives of the project or program within the stated variances of the schedule and budget. In order to achieve such successes the person requires many, if not all of, the ten components of cognitive readiness stated in Chapter 2, as well as their own technical capacity.

As with complexity, the issue of cognitive readiness may require more definition for the professions of project and program management and perhaps some further refinement for the fields in which one practices project and program management. The definition supplied in Chapter 2, as noted, came from the United States Department of Defense and has been accepted for now as a high-level definition, but one should question whether each of the parts of the definition apply equally and if not, to what degree do they apply given the job one is performing or is there any difference? This review or debate needs to be explored and researched, especially as the human being and machine interface becomes more critical to the performance of the job and the issue of artificial intelligence looms on the horizon in the performance of simple tasks to the future of complex tasks.

Within these research parameters are issues of biases and the systems in which the project and program managers function. The discussion of biases and systems were an introduction to the topics. What is required is the discussion of the research into the function of biases in teams and specifically in project and program management teams and the impact on the systems in which they function. Some of the research is still required to be accomplished, especially in the area of the impact of the team's biases upon the systems in which the project or program teams function in an organization or across organizations.

On the topic of mindfulness, the literature is still being written on its effectiveness and when it should be incorporated in the workday. Some organizations have developed complete programs to incorporate it into their workdays for their employees; others have developed times for employees interested in engaging in mindfulness programs at varying times during the day, from prior to the workday to during the workday to the end of the workday. Yet there are still others that mention such activities in their wellness programs, but it is up to the individual employee to find the time to incorporate it in his or her day. Finally, there are still organizations that do not believe there are benefits to such activities as mindfulness and do not mention such activities or discourage involvement during work time. The reason for this breadth of mixed views is that the research is still being done and the findings seem to vary across individuals and organizations. The consensus seems to indicate that more research needs to be done.

Part of the research that is ongoing is in the neuro-sciences, and it is continuing. Understanding the short- and long-term effects of mindfulness in the workplace and in individuals' private lives appears to be continuing. The reason is that mindfulness is not a new activity and has been practiced in many areas of the world for hundreds of years, but it has not been studied. It has been an accepted practice and the positive results were spoken and documented by individuals that were not mainstream researchers. Therefore, research by accepted academicians is required to provide the documentation required by many communities of practice.

This afterward is not meant to encompass the full range of topics left to the authors, but it does indicate that the topics presented in this book will provide the foundation for future texts. This book is solely an introduction to a variety of topics, which currently are impacting today's project and program managers and are meant to be helpful for them, but which are presented to them without much information to enable them to be used to their fullest extent and impact for the project or program manager and for the organization.

Rebecca Winston

Index

Note: Page numbers followed by "*fn*" indicate footnotes.

Printed in the United States
by Baker & Taylor Publisher Services